NARRATIVES OF GUILT AND INNOCENCE

Narratives of Guilt and Innocence

The Power of Storytelling in Wrongful Conviction Cases

Ralph Grunewald

NEW YORK UNIVERSITY PRESS

New York

NEW YORK UNIVERSITY PRESS
New York
www.nyupress.org

Please contact the Library of Congress for Cataloging-in-Publication data.
ISBN: 9781479818198 (hardback)
ISBN: 9781479818235 (library ebook)
ISBN: 9781479818204 (consumer ebook)

This book is printed on acid-free paper, and its binding materials are chosen for strength and durability. We strive to use environmentally responsible suppliers and materials to the greatest extent possible in publishing our books.

Manufactured in the United States of America

10 9 8 7 6 5 4 3 2 1

Also available as an ebook

Für Clairchen—seeker of justice

CONTENTS

I first heard of the problem of wrongful convictions in the United States at the end of my academic training in Germany. What surprised me the most was not so much the fact that a criminal justice system fails in its pursuit to only convict the guilty; rather, I did not understand why remedying such injustices even in the light of new evidence was so difficult. I decided to study how differently "truth" is conceptualized in the American and German criminal process and joined the University of Wisconsin–Madison to work with the Wisconsin Innocence Project. That experience was eye-opening in many ways because I saw that, despite similar goals and procedural protections, differences in the legal cultures and procedures have a great impact on how truth and finality are balanced. But there was more. While close-reading many trial transcripts and case files, I realized that wrongful convictions cannot be explained by isolated "factors" alone and that truth is not the sum of all available pieces of evidence. Many of the cases I studied were shaped by processes of narrativization and the particular way in which "facts" were represented and woven into a larger narrative fabric. This realization became a turning point in my career. I saw narratological patterns become apparent that were not sufficiently exposed in the literature. This book is the result of merging insights from two disciplines in my scholarship. My intention here is not purely intellectual—that is, providing an alternative (narrative) view on the reconstruction of legal reality in wrongful convictions; it is also to make visible the processes that every legal practitioner consciously or unconsciously employs—processes that in the end are responsible for what we define as "guilt" or "innocence."

I have the very good fortune to be a faculty member in UW–Madison's Department of English, which values interdisciplinary and comparative studies and has fully embraced my contributions as a legal scholar. I especially thank David Zimmerman, Christa Olson, and Karen Britland for their mentorship and feedback on my text. I am grateful to Marvin

Zalman (Wayne State University) for many hours of lively discussion and his encouragement to keep going down the narrative rabbit hole. I also thank the two anonymous reviewers who read the manuscript with so much care and shared their thoughtful feedback and insights.

I am very thankful for the financial support I received for this research. It was provided by the University of Wisconsin–Madison, Office of the Vice Chancellor for Research and Graduate Education with funding from the Wisconsin Alumni Research Foundation, the Department of English, and the Center for Law, Society, and Justice.

The following institutions supported this book by providing access to restricted resources and criminal case documentation: the Innocence Project in New York City and Winston & Strawn, the Kriminologische Zentralstelle (Center for Criminology) in Wiesbaden (Germany), Jenner & Block in Chicago, and the Staatsanwaltschaft Landshut (District Attorney's Office in Landshut, Germany).

And: Anja, without you, I would not be here and would not have written this.

A word of caution: this is a book about the function of narrative in the legal discourse. As analytical as this topic might appear—and it is—I also write about individual suffering on the side of the wrongfully convicted and those who became victims of often gruesome, violent crimes. I tried to be sensitive when I depicted these crimes, but the visual details and contexts of these crimes are all part of the narratives I analyze. Readers should be aware that the text occasionally includes graphic description of acts of violence, including homicides and sexual assaults, which can be disturbing. These crimes often trigger strong emotional responses, even a desire for vindictive justice in those charged with investigating and prosecuting them. This sense of justice could be the reason why truth and integrity are often lost when the desire to win and convict takes over. In this book, I argue that this urge must not under any circumstances prevail and drive the criminal process, because there is no justice without truth.

Ralph Grunewald
Madison, Wisconsin, January 2023

Introduction

Realms of Truth and Justice

I am thus led to the proposition that there is no fiction or
non-fiction as we commonly understand the distinction:
there is only narrative.[1]
—E. L. Doctorow

On August 17, 1992, 11-year-old Holly Staker was raped and stabbed to
death while babysitting at a home in Waukegan in Lake County, Illinois.
When the parent returned, she found her two-year-old daughter on a
bed in the children's bedroom and Holly's dead body on the floor. Ten
weeks later, investigation led police to interview Juan Rivera, who was
incarcerated at that time for an unrelated crime. Rivera, who had an IQ
of 79, allegedly made statements about the murder to another prisoner
and was then questioned over four days. At the end, after the interrogation became accusatory, Rivera broke down crying and purportedly
nodded when asked if he had raped and killed Holly Staker. Later, it was
confirmed he was suffering from a psychotic episode that night. Police
prepared a written confession for him to sign, which he did. Based on
that confession, Rivera was indicted, convicted, and sentenced to life in
prison for Holly's murder. He was innocent.

In 1996, the Illinois Appellate Court reversed the conviction based
on procedural issues; two years later Rivera was tried, convicted, and
sentenced to life in prison again. That conviction was vacated after the
Center on Wrongful Convictions in Chicago obtained DNA evidence
that eliminated Rivera as the source of seminal fluids. Although Rivera
was excluded as the source, the state retried him in 2009, explaining
that DNA evidence from the victim might have been contaminated and
that the victim could have had sex with someone else earlier. On May 8,
2009, the jury found Rivera guilty, and he was sentenced to life in prison

for the third time. The appellate motion pointed out the many issues that riddled the case. This time, the appellate court ruled in favor of Rivera, arguing that the prosecutor distorted reality "to an absurd degree" and that the prosecution's story was "highly improbable." The state's attorney (the prosecutor) finally abandoned the case, and Rivera was released.[2]

In January 2000, Delwin Foxworth, who like Holly Staker lived in Lake County, was beaten to death with a piece of wood. Blood found on the wood carried the same DNA as the semen found in Holly Staker. It is likely that the man who committed the rape and murder of an 11-year-old girl in 1992 went on to commit another murder eight years later. The perpetrator has not yet been found.[3]

For the 20 years Rivera served in prison, he received $213,600 in state compensation; after filing a wrongful conviction lawsuit against Lake County law enforcement officials, he settled for $20 million in 2015.

All the currently 3,351 wrongful convictions listed by the National Registry of Exonerations trigger strong emotional responses. The force of these cases lies in their clarity, because the underlying stories are vivid, and the injustices in their simplicity are easy to understand and feel on an emotional level. Especially when "coupled with the authoritative ring of DNA evidence, the stories have tremendous power."[4] Such cases have been known to all criminal justice systems for a long time. In the 1990s a movement began that was dedicated to exonerating those who were innocently convicted and uncovering the factors that lead to such miscarriages of justice. The Innocence Project, founded in 1992 by Peter Neufeld and Barry Scheck at the Benjamin N. Cardozo School of Law in New York City, was not the first entity dedicated to exonerating the wrongfully convicted, but it became almost synonymous with the innocence movement itself, partly because it used DNA fingerprinting as a method to provide "stone-cold proof"[5] of the wrongfulness of a verdict and the failure of the justice system. Beginning in the late 1980s, scholars isolated factors that contribute to these miscarriages of justice. Among these canonical factors are false eyewitness identifications, coercive interrogation methods, official misconduct, ineffective assistance of counsel, faulty forensic science, false confessions, and incentivized witness testimony (i.e., from "snitches"). Most wrongful convictions present a combination of these factors. Juan Rivera was falsely identified and incriminated by another inmate, he was subjected to coercive interrogations that went over hours and days, there was official misconduct, and there was also false or misleading forensic evidence.

But as Rivera's case demonstrates, the existence of DNA is not a panacea. Not only is DNA unavailable in most crimes; it is also used only in a fraction of exonerations.[6] As any piece of evidence, it is subject to contextualization, interpretation, and narrativization. We cannot trust that advances in forensic sciences will solve the problem of wrongful convictions. In Rivera's case, prosecutors developed a theory why the DNA was irrelevant: Holly must have had consensual sex with someone else, that is, there was what is sometimes called an "unindicted co-ejaculator." Such a proposal sounds objectionable or outright tasteless but can be introduced into a legal narrative for as long as it serves the parties' purpose and their case. In court, as a witness for the prosecution, Holly's twin sister helped explaining away the DNA:

> [W]hen she and the victim were eight years of age, a friend's brother molested them by forcing them to perform oral sex. Staker also testified regarding an incident in which she and the victim once showed each other how they masturbated.[7]

This "sickening" episode, as the defense noted, presents Holly as sexually experienced or at least interested, as someone who could potentially have had a partner. The state explained that "as unlikely as it seems, this young girl apparently had sex with someone else."[8] No proof for that was provided, but in this moment the exculpatory DNA evidence lost at least some of its force. There were two narratives now, each portraying the victim differently. In one, Holly does what girls do—dancing, having sleepovers, sitting out in the yard, and participating in gymnastics or bike-riding with a friend.[9] In the other, Holly is sexually mature and has an unknown sexual partner with whom she had intercourse the morning of the crime. DNA can either help supporting the first story or become part of "powerful mischief."[10] As in most criminal cases, there rarely are only two identifiable narratives. There are the larger framing narratives that characterize the case broadly—a young man abused and killed a little girl, a homicide out of passion or jealousy, and so on—but within those larger narratives exist many smaller narratives, sometimes even micro-narratives, that build each side's case. Often a few words are sufficient to evoke a story. For instance, calling an expert the "$36,000 man"[11] (the sum he charged for his analysis) is a brief characterization (and not a narrative in the sense understood here) that represents the expert's testimony and work as being motivated by monetary compensation but not truth.

The prosecutor probably saw the issue with the DNA but was convinced of Rivera's guilt. That created "cognitive dissonance," which he refuted by appealing to an audience (like the victim's sister) that shared the contradicted beliefs.[12] Building a factual scenario that diminishes the evidentiary value of DNA required the prosecutor to show "how wrong experts can be":

> [I]t shows you that experts take the stand, swear under oath, tell you that the three-four allele excludes the defendant and then, you know, maybe it's mine. You can purchase an opinion for the right price, and I contend to you, ladies and gentlemen, they should have gotten better opinions for how much they paid in this case.[13]

> And then this ridiculous stuff about an absence of epithelial cells relative to the ratio of the sperm shows it was recent. Was he contending that Holly Staker stopped secreting her own epithelial cells, they stopped and then the sperm was just large in the sample? No, it's just silly. But once again, you pay $40,000 for an opinion, they'll shade it for you.[14]

By calling the expert's opinion "just silly" or "ridiculous," the prosecutor directly addresses the scientific validity of the evidence when he had not received adequate training to do so. In fact, in a prior exchange where the prosecutor offered suggestions as to why some sperm cells were missing parts of their tails, the expert characterized the prosecutor's idea as "being ridiculous."[15] There is no other discourse in which a layperson can easily and effectively contradict a trained specialist. Throughout the trial, the prosecutor pursued a narrative of sloppy lab work in a "DNA cesspool"[16] that resulted in contamination by an incompetent expert whose opinion is for sale. In closing, the state did not bring up the DNA again, but the defense did. The defense counsel suggested that the person who left the DNA—"Unknown Male Number One"—was responsible.

Once a jury is convinced of a story and then convicts the defendant, the case's story line solidifies and is hardly reviewable in later stages of the appeal. Appellate courts in the United States fear that entertaining claims of factual innocence at appeal can have a "disruptive effect" on the system. Exonerations are not the result of routine appeals; they require intensive, yearslong litigation, often by teams of attorneys from law firms and law schools. Such so-called post-conviction appeals are not designed to challenge facts—they typically require proof of constitutional violations, and only through the backdoor of procedural errors can cases be retried and new evidence introduced. The appellate court in Rivera later found that the state's "theories distort to an absurd degree" the notion that someone other than Rivera must have been the source of the sperm and that "a reasonable fact finder could not credit them beyond a reasonable doubt."[17] So what did that make the jury in Rivera's case? *Un*reasonable?

The processes through which the master narrative of a case develops are complex, and common approaches (legal, psychological, sociological) to explaining wrongful convictions offer only a partial image of the problem, since wrongful convictions did not stop once the factors had been identified. In the time between the beginning of 2021 and June 2022, there were 296 exonerations, 226 of which had convictions that were issued after 2000.[18] Even decades into the innocence movement, the criminal process still fails to filter out the innocent, which calls into question the role and relevance of factual truth and how criminal law values and protects it. A fuller picture of wrongful convictions cannot be complete without considering their broader context, including elements, like narrative, that escape the legal filter. This more comprehensive image must also consider whether wrongful convictions are a predominantly American problem. How do other, nonadversarial (and less contest-oriented) criminal justice systems develop their case narratives? And what role does factual truth play?

Existing wrongful conviction scholarship has not provided an answer to a very simple question: How is it possible that prosecutors can convince juries and themselves of the guilt of an innocent defendant despite the introduction of strong exculpatory evidence in court? The underlying thesis of this book is likewise simple: *It is the power of narrative that influences how police, prosecutors, juries, and judges construct suspicion,*

legal reality, and the evidence for legal reality, even when that reality is
objectively inaccurate. Narrative analysis enhances our view on wrongful
convictions because even the most technically advanced procedures have
strong narrative undercurrents and are prone to losing sight of truth
and questions of reasonable doubt. Although lawyers use narrative very
consciously in presenting their cases—"lawyers tell stories"—neither
juries nor lawyers approach case stories through the lens of narrative
theory. One cannot base an appeal on a biased framing narrative, after
all. In this book I expose processes of the narrativization of guilt and
innocence that can drive wrongful conviction cases and contend that
narrative—its imagination, construction, and presentation—has a force
so strong that it goes beyond legal reasoning and scientific evidence. The
arguments I offer in this book apply to all criminal cases because of the
inherent narrative nature of investigation and adjudication. Wrongful
convictions are exemplary (i.e., archetypal events that carry evaluative
meaning) that they help to show the impact of such narratives.

Approaching Wrongful Conviction Narratives: Realms of Truth and Law

Although we constantly observe forms of criminal injustice rooted in
race, resources (or lack thereof), personal appearances, and the like,
wrongful convictions are striking examples because the criminal case
that was allegedly proven beyond a reasonable doubt against a defendant
was in fact simply imagined. The law (writ large) provides a centuries-
old promise to separate the realm of facts and the realm of law. The facts
of a case should be neat, condensed, and objective, and what counts as
fact should be a matter of reasonable determination and logic, undis-
turbed by narrative desires or personal convictions. Out of these neat
stories, guilt and the proper sentence should emerge logically so that
another fact finder or judge would come to the same conclusion. This
concept is as old as Roman Law—*da mihi factum, dabo tibi ius* ("give me
the facts, I will give you the law").[19] Wrongful conviction narratives call
into question the paradigm that story and argument are two separate
modes of cognitive functioning that are "irreducible to one another."[20]
This kind of thinking must be considered obsolete from a practical and
psychological point of view. Law provides a narrative groove before an

officer even arrives at the crime scene. It steers fact finders through the construction of a case, and without it there are no legally relevant facts.

Criminal cases are typically constructed upside down, beginning with an imagined, legally prescribed crime narrative that serves as a mold that is filled with the available facts, utilizing a logic that is driven by the need to explain and narrate. The development of a crime story follows a certain narrative blueprint that is primarily provided by the law (the separate elements that need to be proven to convict and the way in which that is done), but the assembling of elements is subjected to the narrative demands and agendas of the parties. The criminally relevant acts, states of mind, and evidence to prove them are not objectively given; they are constructed and malleable, and they receive their relevance through an interpreter and narrator. Even the most trivial objects—like a few words scribbled on a scrap of paper found under a murder victim, or perhaps a discarded plastic bottle discovered at the crime scene—can be turned into evidentiary proof that is stronger than exculpatory DNA evidence. Narration also comes with an implicit explanation that affects our understanding of causation.[21] In that, a crime narrative does not need to be true to be convincing; it only needs to plausible, but plausibility is a matter that lies outside of the realm of falsifiability. This is true for all criminal cases, not just wrongful convictions. And while the arguments I make throughout this book are based on wrongful convictions, they point at universal issues.

In this book I contextualize wrongful convictions in three overlapping ways—the *legal*, the *narratological*, and the *comparative*—to create a new image of wrongful convictions and shed light on the role truth plays in the American (and other) criminal justice system. Although fields like rhetoric or linguistics have always been intertwined with the law, narrative as a way to look at law (and not only a tool in its application) has only recently gained a strong scholarly and focused interest. As Peter Brooks asserts, legal narratology "demands analytic consideration in its own right."[22] It not only amplifies "the lived experience of marginalized groups or individuals in a way that traditional legal reasoning doesn't";[23] it also provides the critical awareness necessary to understand the storied nature of legal thinking. If we consider criminal proceedings as a system of communication among actors, as the sociologist Niklas Luhmann argued, then narratology has the capacity to look at the various ways in which events are communicated and represented on the level of the individual actor as well as the whole system.[24]

The common trope that law and storytelling are connected somehow disguises what little is known about the intricate role storytelling plays in legal proceedings. This is surprising given how much law and legal procedures regulate elements like discovery, admissibility, and other processes and rules that can become part of the official (court) narrative. Yet law does not recognize them as elements of a narrative structure that comes with its own dynamics, thereby creating its own relevance. "Narrative" more than represents truth or events (the "story"); it creates them regardless of their veracity.[25] The sphere of the story and the sphere of representation are separate, even if such an understanding contradicts the more colloquial meaning of "story" (an account of imaginary or real events often told for entertainment). Translated into more precise terms, when someone says "I read a good story," they mean "I read a (good) narrative of a (good) story."[26] Applied to wrongful convictions, the actual story (the events as they objectively occurred) is not represented accurately in the verdict (whether it is written or formed in the minds of the fact finder), with the result that the law is applied to an inaccurate factual basis. How such narratives come about, and develop a force that is strong enough to sway judges and juries, is the main subject of this book. It addresses the question of how criminal narratives form, who their narrators and narratees are, and how storytelling affects the truth and outcome of a case. While not at the center of the analysis, there is a second narrative subgenre that requires attention: *exoneration narratives*—the narratives of how the wrongful conviction was overcome, stressing advocacy and perseverance. Such narratives also include multiple perspectives and are dependent on the narrative blueprints of a given system.

Because of the complexity of legal narration, no single theory of or approach to narrative can sufficiently cover all facets of the many discourses at play in a trial or within the criminal process in general. Since I describe wrongful convictions as suffering from a representation error—a discord between events (a crime) and their representation in a specific discourse (the police, court, jury narrative)—a functionalist approach will be the basic starting point. And since many parts are open to analyses beyond the concept of *fabula* and *syuzhet*, I do not claim to comprehensively apply narrative theory, rather it serves as a beginning, to view criminal proceedings using tools from that theory.[27]

The adversarial contest between prosecutor and defense has long been considered an effective means to arrive at the truth. Yet this contest, which permeates not only the trial but also all stages of a case, often takes over so that the search for truth succumbs to the dynamics of the contest. In light of this uncomfortable relationship between narrative and truth, a question must be raised as to whether there exists an entity that is purely interested in finding the truth or, conversely, if the commonly accepted notion of the truth-serving function of adversarialism is a mere myth. That leads to the question of whether other systems not based on the adversarial model produce truer narratives and as a result are more successful in preventing wrongful convictions. In *inquisitorial justice systems*—systems that charge judges to establish the objective truth through trials that are designed as a continuing investigation—narratives appear in different ways but play just as important a role in the construction of legal reality as they do in adversarial systems. In the German system, the legal system of comparison I use throughout this book, the idea of a narrative contest as a means to find the truth is absent; instead, a strong emphasis is placed on a legal discourse that follows logic and is driven by an impartial and independent investigation into the truth of a case. Factual truth is a value of constitutional magnitude. Even the concept of finality is interpreted in light of factual truth and finds its limits when a new, more accurate historical truth can be proven. However, the ideal of a legal logic and an objective investigation into the facts of a case by judges (and not laypeople) as fact finders must be contrasted with the reality of wrongful convictions. The interpretation of the law, like its application, is not an objective process in Germany either: it is influenced by narrative, only in a different way. In recent years, wrongful convictions have come to light that question the ideal of law and proceedings as being of almost scientific precision and accuracy.

Argument and Overview

I contend that legal guilt is a narrative construct, influenced by the narrative dynamics present in criminal proceedings. The approach I follow is qualitative, not quantitative. I do not, for example, count how often certain narrative tropes are used and if a certain number makes a wrongful conviction more likely. I attempt to demonstrate how law and storytelling interact in the American adversarial system (based on common law) and the German inquisitorial system (rooted in the civil law tradition) by looking at wrongful convictions as exemplary narratives. That sometimes requires the generalization of features and processes of the criminal justice system, since it is not feasible to explore and tie in every procedural facet that exists on the state and federal levels in the United States and Germany—neither would it advance the arguments of the book. One of the main threads I develop is that narrative is an undercurrent in all systems and that it deserves attention in its own right. Legal narratology is an effective tool to analyze cases, and multiple representative wrongful conviction cases will be closely read with the purpose of exposing narrative at work—whether these are the larger framing narratives or, alternatively, micro-narratives that happen within a few minutes.

The cases that I discuss throughout the book were selected with exemplarity in mind. They include wrongful convictions in which strong exculpatory evidence (like DNA) existed at the time of the trial or earlier, because if there was strong exculpatory evidence that prosecutors and jurors knew of, there must have been powerful narrativization to explain it away. The case of the Central Park Five is among the best-known examples for this type of case.[28] I also look at cases that represent the canonical factors known to be leading to wrongful convictions and apply a narratological filter. False confession cases, for instance, are studied from legal and psychological vantage points, but they also provide insights into the role of narrative agency and authorship, not only in a particular case but also in how the criminal justice system treats these aspects in general. Out of the many potentially appropriate cases, those that were selected had sufficient documentation and complete records. Michael Morton's case is one of them. Here, I could access the documents that represented the wrongful conviction narrative (transcripts, court files, news articles) and the exoneration narrative (innocence project briefs, Morton's autobiography, news articles) as sources.

Close readings reveal structures that (very likely) influenced the outcome of a case while drawing on a multitude of narrative topoi and features (like the frame of the telling, the telling, and the told; identifying types and roles of tellers and the role of the narratee; etc.). Such readings can never be complete, and cases read by different readers will yield different conclusions. This also requires consideration of the layers of legal and cultural systems and their connection to narrativization. The analysis I put forward in this book is based on the assumption that at the core of every case, when all the doctrines, rulings, laws, and procedures are peeled off, lies a story that is narrativized with an agenda in mind motivated by a "narrative desire,"[29] a desire that is often suspiciously ambivalent about the truth (i.e., the story itself).

The structure of the book follows the three themes mentioned above: law, narrative, and comparative analysis. Chapter 1 introduces wrongful convictions as a legal and literary theme. The chapter proposes that innocence stories have become a genre, and not only in literary texts. *Actual Innocence* by Scheck, Neufeld, and Dwyer is the prototypical case study that recounts how an innocent person was convicted and then exonerated; it also tells stories of perseverance and overcoming hardship. Many exonerees have written or co-authored autobiographies in which they process their experiences. These experiences have also been fictionalized in a collection of stories by prominent mystery writers, giving them new meanings. The underlying themes of this new genre are developed in the first section of that chapter. The second section provides background on the development of the innocence movement and summarizes scholarship on what we know about the causes of wrongful convictions.

Chapter 2 develops the foundation for understanding the narrative dimension of wrongful convictions. The analyses in this book are based on the formalist approach to narrative that distinguishes between the events (as they happened or are imagined) and their representation (in testimony, a verdict, etc.). This approach is particularly useful because wrongful convictions present a dissonance between factual truth and legal truth. However, this approach does not preclude, but rather invites, other narrative perspectives. And often it is useful to include broader narratives (cultural, racial, etc.) to understand certain features of representation. Given the multitude of "narratives" that exist, the arguments made here try to stay close to the functionalist paradigm.

The notion that law is narrative is commonplace, yet the narrative aspects of legal processes remain understudied. Across all media, trials are portrayed as contests of narratives through which the truth of a given case will come out. This ideal of truth-finding through contests must be questioned from an epistemological point of view because, when it comes to truth, law remains the only field that relies on adversarial truth-finding. The question of how law reconstructs reality, and how much truth law actually requires, are discussed and compared to discourses similar to law, like the historical. One of the main points chapter 2 develops is that imagination drives case narratives and that this imagination is legally unregulated. The last section discusses the concept of authorship and authorial agency, particularly pertinent in false confession cases where it is not clear who tells the defendant's story and what role authorial autonomy plays.

Chapter 3 builds on chapter 2 and first addresses the development of legal narratology; it then provides a narrative reading of the case of Michael Morton. It is prefaced by a discussion of what I call the "narrative blueprint"—a preordained mold of a legal story that every criminal justice system provides. The discussion of Morton's case further shows how much the "contest of narratives" paradigm is a myth and how wrongful convictions show that, if there was a contest, it was unbalanced and rarely on a level narrative playing field.

I then cover aspects of comparative law and narratology. There does not exist a commonly agreed upon methodology for comparative legal research,[30] and since the focus here is on wrongful convictions, a combination of a functionalist approach (the protection of truth through law in two systems) and a law-in-context method (the way law works in practice) is followed. This allows for fine-grained readings of law and case transcripts while simultaneously maintaining an openness to contextual (i.e., narrative) consideration.[31] Inquisitorial systems like in Germany pursue truth more directly and through all stages of a case by charging judges to find the true facts of a case. How the search for truth influences the inquisitorial narrative blueprint is addressed in the first part of chapter 4, in which the basic tenets of criminal procedure are laid out. Beyond the idea of inquisitorial fact-finding, the German justice system is marked by a belief in the quasi-scientific nature of positive civil law and its application. Interpreting and subsuming law, I contend, is to a great extent motivated by a narrative desire; it is a process that begins long before a prosecutor writes a statement of facts. Still, legal hermeneutics clearly distinguish between facts and law, but as will be seen, narrative thinking is implicit in the application of statutory law—in both common and civil law systems.

Chapter 5 provides an overview of current wrongful conviction research in Germany and then closely reads what is probably the best-known wrongful conviction in Germany: the case of the missing farmer. In that case, four defendants were convicted of the gruesome murder of Hans Baker whose body they allegedly dismembered and disposed. After their conviction, Baker's body turned up, proving much of the narrative to be wrong. And yet prosecutors opposed reopening the case. The argument put forward is that, despite the strong mandate truth has in the German justice system, narrative not only overrides strong exculpatory evidence; it is also an undercurrent often unaffected by law. The ideal of a rational, judge-driven, truth-oriented legal system falls apart when police, prosecutors, and judges look for a plausible (and not necessarily true) story.

The conclusion summarizes the main findings of the book and presents an outlook on how more narrative thinking could be implemented in law and thereby bring the ideal of truth and justice to a fuller realization.

1

Discourses of Guilt and Innocence

The Innocence Movement as a Narrative Movement

Now the fabric of false guilt is laid bare.[1]
—Dwyer, Neufeld, and Scheck

They watched some TV. And sometime during the late hours of the 12th, still before midnight, the Defendant on his birthday decided he wanted to have sex with his wife. . . . She wanted to go to bed, and so she said, "No," and went to bed. The Defendant left the bedroom. And he had rented a videotape, a very sexually-explicit videotape, and he viewed that sexually-explicit videotape and he got madder and madder. And he went and he got some sort of blunt object, probably a club, and he took that club, and he went into the bedroom and he took it and he beat his wife repeatedly to death. The blows are to the face. . . . And he sat in that room as his wife's body was there, beaten, and he thought. And the first thing he did was he took the sheets and the pillow and put them up over the body, and then he took the comforter and put it up over the body.[2]

On August 13, 1986, Christine Morton, was found beaten to death in her family home. Her husband, Michael Morton, became a suspect the moment police arrived at the crime scene. He was soon arrested, tried, found guilty and then sentenced to life in prison for this brutal murder—a murder he did not commit. The story the prosecutor conveyed in his opening statement—excerpted above—was false. There was a videotape, he had planned on having sex with his wife that night, and the sheets and pillow were put over Christine Morton's body. However, none of these elements were evidence of Morton's involvement in the crime, and some were not evidence for the crime at all. Morton spent 25 years in prison before the DNA analysis of a blood-stained bandana that Morton's brother-in-law had found close to the house directed police to the actual perpetrator.

Michael Morton's case is among the more than 3,300 wrongful convictions in the United States recorded by the National Registry of Exonerations. It exemplifies many of the known and well-established factors that contribute to wrongful convictions and the authority of post-conviction DNA testing. Through comparative DNA testing, innocence projects have falsified the famous claim by Judge Learned Hand that the "ghost of the innocent man convicted . . . is an unreal dream."[3]

A large body of scholarship dedicated to wrongful conviction studies produced what is now seen as a canon of factors that are typically found in wrongful convictions: Eyewitnesses misidentify suspects; forensic evidence can be fraudulent and misleading; highly motivated informants (like "jailhouse snitches") receive benefits for incriminating testimony; and officials including police officers and prosecutors develop tunnel vision and violate professional, ethical, and legal rules to achieve convictions, often in situations where a defendant is represented ineffectively.[4] That list of factors is the result of predominantly inductive reasoning. Many of the first exonerations involved eyewitness identification errors. The processes that lead to misidentifications were then studied through all possible lenses and discussed intensively. The problem-spotting approach has been useful but did not capture larger, systemic concerns. Occasionally, authors point beyond traditional factors by proposing that there exist larger, environmental circumstances that create cognitive biases and foster wrongful convictions in the first place—public pressure, an unpopular defendant, abuse of the adversarial process, and "noble cause corruption" within the criminal justice system.[5] Political and systemic responses to the findings of wrongful conviction scholarship addressed the issues at hand by, for instance, creating task forces to change eyewitness identification processes via mandating sequential (as opposed simultaneous) police lineups. Overall, however, fact-finding processes at the pretrial and trial levels have not changed much; neither has the appellate landscape, where little factual review is possible. While almost all states have enacted post-conviction DNA statutes as a response to wrongful convictions, many of these laws provide only limited support. As the Innocence Project summarizes, these laws present "insurmountable hurdles" to the person seeking remedy by effectively putting the burden of solving the crime on the petitioner. Certain laws bar access to DNA testing when the defendant pled guilty or is no longer incarcerated. Several laws do not allow to appeal a denied petition for testing.[6] Beyond DNA statutes, no law (like in Germany) exists in the United States that permits out-of-time appeals where fresh evidence (and not just DNA) of innocence emerges.[7] And any kind of review that is possible is rarely undertaken by an independent agency but woven into the adversarial fabric of the criminal justice system.[8] So, the limited extent to which wrongful conviction narratives are reviewable does not affect the larger, systemic argument I make in this book.

The existing scholarship has not addressed a comparatively simple question: How was (and is) it possible that prosecutors can convince juries and themselves of the guilt of an innocent defendant absent credible evidence in support or against strong exculpatory evidence that existed at the time of the trial? The underlying thesis of this book is likewise simple: *The power of narrative influences how police, prosecutors, juries, and judges construct reality and the evidence for it.* If this sounds too simplistic, consider that in Michael Morton's case no evidence directly tied Morton to the crime. Circumstantial evidence—the note he wrote for his wife, the sexually explicit video tape he intended to watch with her, and the way Morton and Christine communicated throughout their marriage—were read and connected in a way so that a story of murder motivated by sexual frustration could be told to the jury. In the end, prosecutors must present a legally relevant event (the crime) based on the facts they find. Whether or not these facts (the note, the tape, etc.) are "evidence" depends on how the "crime" is imagined. A frustrated husband who did not get what he thought he deserved for his birthday is one way of reading it. The other way would be to see (and at least consider) a coincidence: a murder committed by someone else and the note and everything else being evidence of disappointment, maybe frustration, or just the idiosyncrasies of a relationship—but not murder.

Storytelling is a potent method, and not just in law. It is "the everyday communicational practice that is used to organize information, to transmit understandings among participants, and to guide the judgments of jurors."[9] Lawyers and the legal profession acknowledge that stories can be enormously persuasive and "an important piece of the lawyer's toolbox."[10] However, we are only beginning to understand how storytelling functions and what its effects are. The role of narrative is even more important since fact-finding—the jury's or judge's task to establish the facts of a case—is to a large extent influenced by and legitimized through legal procedures that on the surface focus on regulating the contest of narratives (what is admissible and what is not?) as a means to arrive at the truth. However, the particular truth that a verdict (literally, the "spoken truth") incorporates is by nature a legal construct. Legal truth often does, but need not, coincide with factual truth. Therefore, a guilty verdict creates a double reality whereby all following instances are bound. First, it establishes *normative* accountability—a law has been violated, and the defendant is guilty of that violation.[11] Second, through the verdict, the underlying *case story with all its facts* is considered to be true beyond a reasonable doubt. A jury decides that a certain law was broken by the defendant through a described action (the story of the case), and that action is now the solely legally relevant reality. That reality is constructed in court by the jury, but not as a result of its own investigation; rather it is the outcome of a complex narrative process between the adversaries and the jury. The presentation of a story by narrators and how it is received and perceived by the narratee is not an objective process. As Bennett contends, at "every stage of the storytelling-interpretation process, both storytellers and interpreters make choices about how to symbolize a story element, what con[n]ections to set up among these elements, and what frames of reference to apply."[12] This process is susceptible to unintended distortions and malleable to the narrative agendas of the narrators and narratees.[13] A verdict is based more on how plausible the jury found any of the stories and how the discursive symbols are interpretated rather than the truth.[14] Even in trial systems where courts and judges are charged with finding factual truth—such as inquisitorial criminal justice systems in Europe—narrative plays an important role in the construction of legal reality; wrongful convictions can still occur, even if for different reasons.

A Concept of Narrative

Narrative—as a concept and the term itself—has become a universal method of conveying forms of knowing and describing any number of phenomena. Thus it is no surprise how it has been applied to and used in many fields, even when these in the past did not lend themselves to "narrativization,"[15] like imagery that itself is not narrative but resonates with narrative templates in our minds.[16] Even genres like portraiture now seem to invite the use of narrative language, where it connotes "that extra element," "feeling," connecting environment with the subject, and the certain approach to "what type of story" an artist wants to tell.[17] The situation in which a photo was taken is referred to as the "plot," "details" in a photograph are "told," the environment "speaks," the subjects are "the characters," and the way the story is told depends on its audience and themes the artist intends to convey. A photo of a camera pointing at a subject is considered a "reflective" narrative. Narrative portraits can "transcend the subject matter."[18] The point here is not to argue for the hegemonization of narrative—though I agree with Olson[19] that the expansive use of narrative is problematic—but to clarify that narrative means many things in many areas and that the first question we should ask when the term "narrative" is used is: What is the purpose and function of narrative in the given context? Is it used to emphasize and elevate a certain meaning or feeling? Or does it provide context within a conceptually coherent framework so it can make structures visible that otherwise would not be apparent?

Studying how events are represented in a text, play, film, or any other form, or what functional elements can be identified in narratives, has been a primarily literary endeavor mainly rooted in (apart from Plato and Aristotle) eighteenth-century French, German, Russian, and British scholarship on genres like the novel, saga, folktale, poem, short story, and other types of literary narration.[20] Prominent narrative theorists often draw on literary texts and studies, for instance Gérard Genette, whose *Narrative Discourse* focuses on Marcel Proust's *A la recherché du temps perdu* (*In Search of Lost Time*; orig. 1913)—a novel. Although narratology branches out to disciplines like anthropology, folklore, and history, it remains a domain that has its home in literary criticism.[21] This is surprising considering the "almost infinite diversity of forms" of narrative as a basic and constant form of human expression. Narrative is ever-present, "international, transhistorical, transcultural: it is simply there, like life itself."[22] While narrative is a ubiquitous and almost irresistible[23] way of creating meaning, and despite a "renaissance"[24] of narrative scholarship, a general model or method of narrative analysis does not exist so that even an overview of the highly diversified central developments would go far beyond the scope of this book.

Neither is such an overview necessary. Even within the literary domain, narrative as a term and concept is not uniformly understood and conceptualized.[25] Narratives serve different functions in different genres. The purpose of a medical narrative in a patient file differs from a statement of fact in a criminal file.[26] All scholarly and professional disciplines employ nuanced discourses in how they represent the factual world. While medical narratives seem to reason as part of a larger, therapeutic process, legal narratives primarily are aimed at recounting certain events. Understanding the differences in these narrative discourses requires an awareness of the underlying functions and purposes. Social, literary, and legal scholars will likely read the George Floyd case with a different focus, emphasizing different elements of the story. The consciousness of different ways of reading and telling is not always apparent when scholarship uses the term "narrative" without defining its conceptual meaning. And while this might be a symptom of the interdisciplinary, even within the field of literary criticism, a diverse, ununified arsenal of narrative terminology has developed over time,[27] and no consensus on any of the key issues of narrative has been achieved.

As H. Porter Abbott does in his *Introduction to Narrative*,[28] I distinguish between two major uses of the term "narrative". First, it is the loose and generally recognizable understanding referring to "longer structures that we call narratives even though they may contain much non-narrative material."[29] Genres like tragedy, comedy, epic, short story, film, drama, portraiture, and an "abundance of other genres" are qualified as narrative. The defining characteristic of such narratives is typically a form of intrinsic (but not systematic) narrative coherence.[30] Narrative as a concept is open and is often applied to "any manner of phenomena." In the legal discourse, that can mean that narrative is used to address "the history of a given legal culture, the aesthetic evocation of a story in a given text, a legal-political trend, as well as the history of a given case or legal norm as well as more specific aspects of legal storytelling."[31] The concept of narrative at work in these discussions is rarely defined and often thin.[32] This thinness makes it difficult to identify the function narrative has in that specific circumstance. As I contend throughout this book, our understanding of wrongful convictions improves when we see them as errors of representation—where the story is not accurately represented in narrative. That does not mean that wrongful convictions could not be rendered as the first, "looser" kind, as tragedies, stories of overcoming hardship, redemption, injustice, and stories of sentimentality or feeling—they could; but the focus here is on how legal systems (law and its agents) represent the underlying stories (i.e., crimes) so the moments where truth was lost can be identified. A larger perspective is important when it affects the representation of events (like, for instance, racial bias, tunnel vision, etc.) but such approaches lack conceptual uniformity and blur the line where narrative ends and an interpretative reading of a case begins.

The second approach, which will be the basis for the understanding of narrative in this book, is more compact than the first. Here, narrative is defined as the *representation of an event or a series of events*.[33] This definition is rooted in structural formalism and is more restrictive, since it primarily distinguishes between the sphere of the events ("the story") and to the sphere of representation (through "narrative discourse"). But what sounds restrictive helps to distinguish between the happenings and their representation.[34]

Without events there can be no narrative.[35] The difference between events and their representations is the difference between a story (the event or sequence of events) and narrative discourse (how the story is conveyed).[36] The concept of *event* has been broken down further and is now usually seen as a change of state.[37] Abbott follows the structuralist, formal concept of narrative. The appeal of this concept as a starting point is that wrongful convictions at the core are cases of factual misrepresentation. An accident, for instance, can be represented as a crime by attributing criminal agency to an individual so that the crime narrative does not represent the real. A story or happening can be represented in many ways, depending on what narrative discourse an author chooses. This model lends itself to a legal-narratological analysis, especially for cases of wrongful convictions, because it keeps the realms of the happening (whether in real life or as part of the imagination) and its representation analytically separate. It is a model that considers the many ways in which narratives can expand and contract, leap backward and forward, but as we take in information from the discourse we sort it out in our minds, reconstructing an order of events that we call the story. The story . . . can be true or false, historical or fictional. But insofar as it is a story, it has its own length of time and an order of events that proceeds chronologically from the earliest to the latest. The order of events and the length of time they are understood to take in the story are often quite different from the time and order of events in the narrative discourse.[38]

The trial is the most commonly discussed instance where the reordering and resequencing of events, whether true or fictional, is practiced. Narratives are often presented more fully, with more than just the mere description of a series of events. In addition to representing events, every narrative also represents "objects or characters that are the result of what we now call *description*,"[39] a description refers to the physical and spatial existence of an object, independent of any event and any temporal dimension.[40] Genette argues that description "is quite naturally *ancilla narrationis*, the ever-necessary, ever-submissive, never-emancipated slave"[41] and can hardly imagine that a "narrative would serve as an auxiliary to a description."[42]

Within the legal context, however, it is not unimaginable because descriptions of a crime scene, the physical state of a victim, a photo of the murder weapon, or the physical appearance of the suspect all add and give meaning to the larger narrative.[43] While descriptive elements are not narrative in the formal sense, they should be considered influential in the evaluation of the narrative. That means that an understanding of narrative must be left open to ideas that leave the structuralist realm and recognize many of the "other definitions as definable narrative subsets and useful in their own right."[44] An important feature of postclassical narratology is its shift of focus to the process and not merely the product of narratological inquiry. Stories are more than preexistent structures that can be found, they are properties of the object being investigated. That stresses not only the process of narrativization but also the importance of the narrator, the reader, and the function of the narratives they produce and receive. The context of knowledge that produced the object (e.g., a text) is as important for its understanding as is the reading of the object itself. Deconstruction functions through dismantling existing categorical certainties, showing that terms "can only function in relation to each other: they exist only by virtue of their complementary and supposed difference."[45] A criminal case as such is not just one text (it often entails more than text—like images, oral statements, gestures, and the like that may or may not be made part of the text at some point) with a clearly identifiable author, narrator, and so on; it is an artifact that, because of its complexity, can and must be read in many ways. Reading a case goes beyond the actual process of parsing text and interpreting laws. A crime scene is read and interpreted; "things" are read as to their potential for evidence, just like witness accounts are interpreted. This process is not pure or objective but is always dependent on what can be called scripts or in terms of legal hermeneutics as "fore-understanding."[46]

A Hindsight Caveat

The power of wrongful conviction stories hinges on knowledge that was gained in hindsight (*ex post*), that is, after the conviction is unraveled. Any evaluation of narrative processes (or any other factor having potentially influenced the verdict) must be cognizant of the fact that such clarity might not have existed or was distorted *ex ante*.

Alice Sebold's first-person account of her brutal rape and its aftermath in her memoir *Lucky* shows how a powerful and convincing narrative of victimization and overcoming trauma becomes one of false accusation and bias. Sebold was raped in May 1981 by a Black man in Syracuse's Thornden Park. One day, she sees "her rapist" on the street. "He was smiling as he approached. He recognized me. He smirked at me, remembering. . . . He was laughing because he had gotten away with it."[47] Although Sebold was not able to identify the suspect in a lineup, she is confident that she identified the right person. Her certainty helped the state in preparing the case, calling her an "excellent witness"[48] and "the best rape witness I've ever seen on the stand"[49] because she testified so confidently. There is no critical reflection on racial bias and how the accusation by a young white woman against a Black man alone might be enough to drive a narrative of guiltiness. Her doubts about having identified the correct perpetrator appear more performative than honest because, in the end, she enters the courtroom with a note to herself written on her skin: "'You will die' was inked into my legs in a dark blue ballpoint. And I didn't mean me."[50] When Anthony Broadwater was found guilty of the crime, Sebold requested the maximum sentence, which Broadwater received. He served 16 years until his conviction was overturned because a court recognized the faulty science (hair analysis) and the problematic identification process as being the cause of the conviction.[51]

Crime narratives typically start at the end of a series of events, events that resulted in a specific harm. Sebold's narrative begins with the conviction of the person she had identified. Hindsight research shows that people have a strong tendency to believe that an event was more predictable than they thought beforehand once they know the outcome.[52] This problem appears in many shapes and affects not just how investigations are narrated but also how the innocence movement itself has been narrativized. For instance, to say that it "does not seem surprising" that Barry Scheck and Peter Neufeld sparked the innocence movement given their respective backgrounds,[53] and that it would be "only natural" that Scheck and Neufeld worked on cases together,[54] loses sight of what Alan Dershowitz calls the "naturalistic fallacy," the belief that there is some kind of laid out plan.[55] It is crucial to be mindful of one's perspective and the assumed reach of an argument. Narratives frame, create new contexts, turn coincidences into causation, and can even explain away evidence that has the potential to exculpate the defendant.

Although in this book I focus on wrongful convictions, the narrative factors that potentially lead to miscarriages of justice are also present in many cases in which factual guilt existed so that the actual conviction might not be wrong. My study of cases of actual innocence that led to exonerations is evidence that strong narrative forces always exist and make otherwise hidden discourse structures visible. The point is that we underestimate the pervasiveness and the influence of narrative in the criminal process, as exemplified in wrongful convictions. Understanding narrative will make them less likely.

What Is a Wrongful Conviction?

Wrongful conviction is not a sharply defined legal concept and is often used interchangeably with "exoneration" or "innocence"[56]—neither of which are technical legal terms. A criminal conviction can be considered *wrong* for a multitude of reasons based on legal, ethical, social, or other considerations. It could be considered wrong to send a poor person to jail because they stole expensive but lifesaving medicine for a family member. Convictions can also be wrong when they are "marred by serious constitutional or other procedural or due process errors."[57] Guilt and innocence are never clear, are never mono-dimensional, and often depend on the context considered to be relevant.[58] In its effort to make cases decidable, law simplifies questions of right and wrong so they can be assessed and processed. Law prescribes what a "wrong" action is and the process that must be used to prove it. So if police and prosecutors played by the rules[59] but simply read the evidence wrong (because it could have been read that way) and charged and tried the wrong person whom the jury then convicts, that conviction is not legally wrong: it is factually wrong because it treats the blameless unjustly. When after ten years exculpatory evidence is found for the defendant who is exonerated, we would speak of a "wrongful conviction."

Wrongful conviction as understood here is primarily based on the ideal-typical and exemplary understanding that concept has developed within the innocence movement. The innocence movement has been concerned with types of cases where either (a) the wrong person is convicted of a crime that someone else committed, or (b) someone is held accountable for harm not directly caused by anyone (like a natural death or accident).[60] Wrongful convictions are typically seen as factually false convictions,[61] cases in which the factual basis—the "master narrative" as the final statement of facts—does not represent the actual facts properly.[62] Although such false convictions have been known for a long time, only recently has this type of case left the realm of the anecdotal and become a typical, systemically relevant type of case that exemplifies systemic dysfunction.[63] Other criminal justice systems have not had to deal with the vast number of wrongful convictions and continue to wrestle with definitions of "wrongful" convictions—sometimes to an extent that comes close to denying their existence. This could be attributed to the comparatively low number of known cases, suggesting that these systems might still be in the anecdotal and not exemplary realm of research on wrongful convictions, but it might also be due to more efficient and more numerous instances for factual appeal. If the criminal justice system allows for opportunities to introduce new evidence after a conviction, a following acquittal would not be noted as an "exoneration." This means that "exoneration" is a concept specific to procedural setting. Even in the American context, scholars work with varying ideas about that concept: How much evidence is required to prove "actual innocence?" How "official" must the declaration of innocence be? Is sending a case back for retrial because of newly found evidence an exoneration? What if the prosecutor then drops charges?[64] In going forward, defining "exoneration" sharply is not necessary because that term, just like "wrongful conviction," is descriptive of a certain type of process that can differ in shape. It should be understood as a "criminal conviction overturned to a large extent on the grounds of actual innocence, namely evidence that the defendant did not commit the crime."[65]

Another aspect that defines what cases are seen as wrongful is pragmatic in nature. In the United States, where the innocence movement began, research has focused on cases that innocence projects accepted for review and then successfully litigated. But innocence projects typically filter out cases that would be hard to litigate. For example, the Wisconsin Innocence Project does not take cases in which the applicant currently pursues direct appeal, does not claim actual innocence, has less than seven years to serve of initial confinement, is on probation or parole, played a minor role in the crime, acted in self-defense, claims other affirmative defenses, or was convicted of a sexual assault for an encounter the defendant claims was consensual.[66] The reason is that resources are scarce and that working on cases requires time and money. Innocence projects must make sure the inmate is not released before any of their work can bear fruit. Situations of self-defense and consent in a sexual assault case are difficult to pursue, as their success depends on proving a state of mind in a situation where the act itself is not contested. Therefore, innocence projects look at a specific type of wrongful conviction, one that is conceptually narrower than the term would suggest. An initially false conviction that was overturned upon appeal could also be considered as "wrongful" but is not considered a typical wrongful conviction. The point is that the conceptual understanding of wrongful conviction reflects certain types of cases that the innocence movement addresses.[67] Minor convictions such as traffic tickets that lack a factual basis might as well meet the definition of a wrongful conviction, but they are not counted in analyses of wrong-person factual errors, because they are not based on systemic faults visible in typical wrongful convictions but rather specific circumstances.[68] That is no judgment on the validity of other claims of innocence but simply a reflection of practical limitation.

Finality is a likewise important factor in conceptualizing wrongful convictions. Cases must be "final" in the sense that no other ordinary appeal would be possible. That means that the procedural set up of a criminal justice system influences what conviction qualifies as wrongful. This is particularly important when cases are compared and discussed across different criminal justice systems. In the United States, "the trial is the paramount event for determining the defendant's guilt or innocence," and higher courts "do not sit to correct errors of fact, but to ensure that individuals are not imprisoned in violation of the Constitution."[69] Most inquisitorial systems (as they exist in central Europe) allow for factual appeals that let participants contest the factual basis of a conviction, and such systems often provide opportunities to reopen cases when new evidence surfaces regardless of the amount of time that has passed. For Germany, where that is possible, it can be argued that, for as long as procedural remedies for factual review exist, a conviction cannot be considered wrongful because it lacks legal finality. It would be a matter of justice and fairness to let the defendant present exculpatory evidence. Within the American system, it is not considered a matter of "fundamental fairness" if a court refuses to entertain new evidence eight years after a trial.[70]

Defining a wrongful conviction narrative is complicated further by the fact that the law does not require a proof of innocence for an acquittal or a proof of certain guilt for a conviction. Guilt is a *probability judgment* based on available data. This data rarely comes without uncertainty or contradictions and gaps. Innocence must be considered within the rules of the criminal justice system, and "under those rules, [the] courts . . . decide who is guilty, and conversely who is entitled to claim innocence in the absence of proof of guilt. Without proof of guilt determined by a court, the presumption of innocence defines innocence."[71] This means that innocence and guilt are legally determined in the sense that innocence is presumed for as long as the state does not meet its burden of proving guilt beyond a reasonable doubt. However, "where a defendant has been afforded a fair trial and convicted of the offense for which he was charged, [then] the constitutional presumption of innocence disappears."[72] Under the law, a jury is never scrutinized as to whether it made a "*correct* guilt or innocence determination, but rather whether it made a *rational* decision to convict or acquit."[73] Thus, the narratives that underlie a wrongful conviction differ from narratives in other discourses because they have components that require a "reference to the real world,"[74] but they also allow and even require a degree of imagination because rarely if ever do we have enough evidence to paint a complete picture of a crime; there are always gaps that must be filled in by officers, prosecutors, jurors, and judges—anyone who is involved in the discourse.

Exemplarity of Wrongful Conviction Narratives

Within the context of this book, *wrongful convictions* are understood as *exemplary narratives* in the sense that they do not only represent instances where justice went wrong; they also represent typical and compelling kinds of narratives that have changed our understanding of narrative processes and how law steers them. The concept of *exemplarity* in narrative is typically used when describing the role and function of standardized stories: how they develop, how they bridge between rules and a particular case, or how they become rules themselves. But the scope of exemplarity is broader. "Exemplarity" can be characterized as possessing a dual nature:

> [F]irst, the exemplary signifies that which is archetypal, or has become so, as in phenomena that become so embedded and engraved over time that they serve as paradigms, frames, baselines, and signposts; second, the exemplary expresses and communicates some evaluative content—good or bad conduct, virtues and vices—and this content is presented to guide or incite certain beliefs, attitudes, and/or actions. These are two faces of the same concept, for both contain a little of each other: the archetypal in the normative, and the normative in the archetypal.[75]

Wrongful conviction narratives are exemplary both in their archetypal status—standing as a paradigm for other such narratives—and in their clear evaluative content—where the wrongfulness of the conviction is normatively judged as "bad" and the exoneration is judged as "good." There are two major exemplary subnarratives within wrongful conviction narratives: first as the result of the story of innocence lost, a story that is "squeezed out" as an effect of "the standardizing/simplifying/ diluting pressures of the adversarial system";[76] and second as the larger narratives of redemption and justice (the exoneration narrative). These are the narratives that lead to a wrongful conviction and those that lead out from one. Since the 1990s, both forms of these narratives have developed a pervasive legally paradigmatic status and have become signposts of unresolved issues within criminal justice systems.

Narratives of the Innocence Movement

Cases of innocent defendants being convicted have always existed and been written about[77] not only in the United States but also around the world. As long as cases were considered isolated incidences, they could be dismissed as "ghosts" and "unreal dreams."[78] Only with better and more data did wrongful convictions gain relevance.[79] As exemplary "ideal-types," they were recognized as representing larger, systemic issues. An ideal-typical story helps to exemplify and make recognizable a phenomenon that consists of "a great many diffuse, discrete, more or less present and occasionally absent concrete individual phenomena."[80] The whole concept of exemplarity, as discussed above, depends on the recognition of a variable cluster of factors and features that can but do not need to overlap. They are often indiscrete and dependent on multiple elements. The different treatment of wrongful convictions across time and in different justice systems is arguably an effect of how much wrongful conviction narratives have become ideal-typical or exemplary. Are they an exception, that is to say, isolated incidences in which the system did not work? Or do they represent a broader issue?

The early cases we know of today often featured newsworthy, dramatic elements, like the first known wrongful conviction reported in the United States—the case of the Boorn brothers.[81] In 1812, Russel Colvin vanished from Manchester, Vermont. His brothers-in-law, Jesse and Stephen Boorn, became suspects because they had publicly complained about Colvin. Then, years later, the uncle of the suspects, Amos Boorn, claimed that Colvin had appeared to him in his dream, saying that Colvin had been slain and that his body had been put into a cellar hole on the farm where they all worked. The cellar hole was excavated, and no human body parts were found, but there were items, among them a penknife, that Sally Boorn (Colvin's wife and the sister of the suspects) said belonged to her husband. Days later, a dog unearthed several bone fragments, which three area physicians pronounced human. Rumors suggested that Colvin's body was first buried in the cellar hole and then, years later, moved to different locations. Jesse Born was arrested (brother Stephen had moved to New York). While in jail, Jesse's cellmate claimed that Jesse had confessed that Stephen clubbed Colvin to the ground and that Barney Boorn (Sally's father), who was also present, cut Colvin's throat with the knife. In exchange for the testimony, the cellmate was promised immediate release. When Stephen heard about this, he returned to Vermont to clear his name. Witnesses came forward and remembered that seven years prior they heard the brothers threaten to kill Colvin. Stephen also confessed but insisted that he had acted in self-defense—a contention that, if believed, could mitigate against his hanging. Before the trial, the bones found under the tree were again analyzed but now turned out to be not human. Both were put on trial, found guilty, and sentenced to death (though Jesse's sentence was reduced to life in prison). The conviction was reported in the *New York Evening Post*, and a traveler in New York was reminded of someone with the alleged victim's name. The traveler wrote a letter to the newspaper, which published it. That letter was read by a person who knew that Colvin was not dead and managed to coax him back to Vermont. The Boorn brothers were exonerated.

This was not the only incident of an allegedly dead person returning from the beyond (sometimes too late),[82] proving that justice systems fail in the United States and abroad. Many of what are now considered canonical elements of wrongful convictions are recognizable in these early cases (unreliable forensic evidence, false confessions, jailhouse informants, false accusations by witnesses, and "dreams") but only rarely effect reforms or sharpened innocence awareness.[83]

The year 1913 often considered as marking the beginning of the American innocence movement, when Edwin Borchard published the article "European Systems of State Indemnity for Errors of Criminal Justice."[84] It begins with the lament that "it is strange that society, at least in this country, utterly disregards the plight of the innocent victim of unjust conviction or detention in criminal cases."[85] Borchard seems to argue from the point that errors of criminal justice are a given and that the United States is lacking in its response to these injustices. European criminal justice systems were more advanced in how they compensate the victims of (what will later be called) wrongful convictions.[86] Borchard's article focuses on compensation and not wrongful convictions, but he later dedicates his book *Convicting the Innocent* (published in 1932) to that issue. But Borchard was not alone in examining cases of factual innocence. In 1911, Erich Sello, a German lawyer, published *The Errors of Criminal Justice and Their Causes. A History of Judicial Murder from 1798–1910.*[87] Borchard was aware of Sello's work.[88] In the following years and decades, more studies like Borchard's came out,[89] all based on the case-study model with a focus on presenting rather than classifying or analyzing the issue.[90] Works like Erle Stanley Gardner's *Court of Last Resort*; Jerome and Barbara Frank's *Not Guilty*; Barry Scheck, Peter Neufeld, and Jim Dwyer's *Actual Innocence*; and Brandon Garrett's *Convicting the Innocent* all fit into Borchard's mold.

Parallel to the scholarly debate, the media and institutions external to the criminal justice system have followed wrongful convictions.[91] Spectacular cases like that of the prizefighter Rubin "Hurricane" Carter attracted the attention of mass media. In the early 1980s, Jim McCloskey, who founded Centurion Ministries, a precursor to innocence projects as we know them today, stressed that convicting innocent people is a systemic problem but there was little follow-up. If there was an innocence movement at that time, it was still in its anecdotal stage. That changed with the advent of modern DNA analysis—the "revelation machine."[92] Forensic scientists and lawyers acquired a "gold standard of innocence."[93] In 1989, DNA was used for the first time to exonerate a falsely accused person.[94] DNA "served as a key foundational piece on which the innocence movement was built."[95] While the issue of wrongful convictions was largely a matter of speculation and skepticism before DNA testing, the law and those who apply it were now confronted with gross failure to protect the innocent (and pursue the guilty). This was a paradigm shift because law as practiced and understood in the United States is a discursive process where what counts as a true fact is partly based on forensic science and partly based on procedure. In a famous quote, Judge Learned Hand dismissed the fear that an innocent person could be convicted as being unfounded given the many existing procedural safeguards: "What we need to fear is the archaic formalism and the watery sentiment that obstructs, delays, and defeats the prosecution of crime."[96] For a long time, courts have shared Judge Hand's sentiment that procedural and constitutional protections (as discursive features) give "the accused . . . every advantage."[97] The United States Supreme Court is convinced that the existing "constitutional safeguards . . . make it more difficult for the State to rebut and finally overturn the presumption of innocence which attaches to every criminal defendant."[98] In *Herrera v. Collins*, Justice Sandra Day O'Connor maintains the connection between factual accuracy and procedural protections: "Our society has a high degree of confidence in its criminal trials, in no small part because the Constitution offers unparalleled protections against convicting the innocent."[99] Protections include: suspects need not disclose their defense, are immune from questioning, cannot be forced to testify, and enjoy law's presumption of innocence.[100] The standard to convict is high, and the burden to meet it rests with the prosecutor. The Supreme Court does not think it necessary to take every conceivable step to eliminate "the possibility of convicting an innocent person" because that "would all but paralyze our system for enforcement of the criminal law."[101] This means that truth has a role only within the existing procedure but is not (as in other systems) a value in itself.[102] From an epistemological (and narratological) point of view, the search for factual truth and procedural safeguards are not two sides of the same coin.[103] The force of DNA made clear that, in the light of the existing proceduralism, the law does not allow for innocence review and that officers and courts can get it wrong.

In the spring of 1992, almost a decade after Reverend McCloskey founded Centurion Ministries, Barry Scheck and Peter Neufeld started the New York–based Innocence Project, an organization that aims to help wrongly convicted people through DNA testing. Although the proportion of DNA-based exonerations has been decreasing (the US National Registry of Exonerations currently counts over 3,300 false convictions between 1989 and today, about 20% based on DNA and 80% on other factors),[104] DNA created innocence awareness that did not exist prior to the late 1980s. Law schools across the United States followed the Innocence Project's model and formed law clinics in which attorneys and students reviewed and litigated claims of actual innocence. These clinics and organizations are all connected through the Innocence Network. Public and scholarly interest "snowballed throughout the 1990s and into the new century," already showing strong policy impact like Illinois governor George Ryan's decision to commute the death sentence of 167 inmates on death row because of doubts as to the accuracy of their verdicts.[105]

The Canon and an Ordinary Case

With the innocent movement, research and scholarly study of wrongful conviction cases continued to grow. Most research was inductive in the sense that certain problem patterns emerged and were then further investigated. There was no larger, systematic approach toward wrongful convictions, and issues became clear incrementally, adding to a growing catalogue of typical (often overlapping) sources for false convictions. This frequently replicated list includes eyewitness misidentification, false confessions/incriminating statements, unvalidated forensic science, and official misconduct.[106] These factors suggest a quasi-causal model of factors leading to wrongful conviction, which is problematic in that it centers the focus on individual issues and less on the system in general.

As oft-recited as these factors have become, most are the result of inductive, retrospective reasoning after an exoneration. They cannot be considered causal given the lack of a control group of cases.[107] A study supported by the National Institute of Justice asked what factors are uniquely present in cases that led the system to correctly acquit or dismiss charges against the innocent defendant (they were called "near misses"), which are not present in cases that lead the system to erroneously convict the innocent.[108] The results of the study indicate that 10 reasons explain why an innocent defendant, once indicted, ends up erroneously convicted rather than released. Factors that emerged are the age and criminal history of the defendant, the punitiveness of the state, Brady violations, forensic error, a weak defense and prosecution case, a family defense witness, an inadvertent misidentification, and lying by a non-eyewitness.[109] Other factors traditionally suggested as sources of erroneous convictions—including false confessions, criminal justice official error, and race effects—appear in statistically similar rates in both sets of cases; thus they likely increase the chance that an innocent suspect will be indicted but not the likelihood that the indictment will result in a conviction. The upshot here is that wrongful convictions cannot easily be tied to certain factors.

Take, for instance, a very "ordinary" case that Emily Bazelon reports.[110] It represents some of the canonical factors—which will be explained—but it also shows how much a conviction is a result of a cluster of nondiscrete, interconnected elements.

At around 2 AM on November 27, 2012, Benjamin Joseph, a white man in his mid-twenties, called 911 to report that he had been robbed at gunpoint outside his house in Mid-City, New Orleans. He said that the robbery took about two minutes. He was about 30 feet from a streetlight but claimed he had a clear view of the attacker. That evening, around 8 PM, Yutico Briley, who is Black, went for a walk in Mid-City with three friends. Officers inside a police car said Briley acted suspiciously, "constantly looking over his shoulder" and "clutching his right hip." When they rolled up and asked Briley to stop, he ran. The police caught Briley a block away in a vacant lot. His gun fell from the leg of his pants. He was arrested and booked. At that time Briley's race, clothing, and age matched Joseph's description of the man who robbed him, yet other physical features did not, like Yutico's beard and mustache and his heavier build. The victim was called to the station to look at the possible suspect. Two officers walked Briley to the department's garage. He stood handcuffed, 15 or 20 feet from Joseph, with a light from the car shining on him as an officer pulled the hood of his gray sweatshirt on and off his head. Joseph sat in a car, shrinking into his seat out of fear of "the guy who pretty much threatened my life," he said in court.[111] Although he felt uncomfortable and realized that the show-up (which is different than a line-up) seemed unprofessional, he identified Briley. Briley learned he was being charged with armed robbery. During the trial, Benjamin Joseph described getting out of his car outside his own house, and "the next thing I know one guy has got a gun in my face." The prosecutor showed Joseph the gun Briley had when he was arrested. It was a pistol with no distinctive markings, but Joseph said he was sure it was the gun he had seen the robber holding. Joseph was also shown the hoodie Briley was wearing when he was arrested. It had a zipper. Joseph said in his 911 call that the gunman's hoodie was a pullover. Now he identified Briley's hoodie as the clothing the gunman wore. The trial lasted for three hours. At the end of the afternoon, the jury found Briley guilty. A few weeks later he was sentenced to 60 years in prison.

The case features many of the canonical elements mentioned above. The first is the mistaken identification. In more than a quarter of all exonerations, a mistaken witness identification was seen as a contributing factor.[112] The problem of eyewitness misidentifications has been at the center of wrongful conviction research early on;[113] as can be seen in Briley's case, it was still an issue in 2012 as it is today.[114] A witness (mis)-identifying a suspect and then identifying the person in open court is not just powerful evidence; it also is a powerful event—so powerful that it does not need further corroborating evidence and can even overcome exculpatory evidence. As Elizabeth Loftus writes in her book *Eyewitness Testimony* (published in 1979), jurors believe a confident eyewitness even though confidence does not correlate with accuracy. In the end, there is "nothing more convincing than a live human being who takes the stand, points a finger at the defendant, and says, 'That's the one!'"[115] When asked if Joseph saw the man who robbed him in the courtroom, he pointed to Briley.

The issue of witness identification has been studied on two levels: The first level is that of the witness itself—the so-called estimator variables, factors that are not under the direct control of the criminal justice system, like the physical conditions under which an eyewitness views a crime, including the lighting, vision, and also the aspect of race.[116] Briley and Joseph were of different races, which is important because cross-racial identification is particularly unreliable,[117] making up more than 40% of misidentifications. The lighting at the time of the crime was problematic as well, and so was the lighting during the show-up many hours after the incident. The second level is that of the so-called system variables, which are factors that are under the control of the criminal justice system, including the manner in which eyewitnesses are interviewed and the kind of procedures that are used to obtain an identification. Suggestive photo arrays and line-ups fall into that category as much as officers that encourage and guide a witness during the identification process. Even subtle suggestions by the police can affect a witness's memory of an event.[118] Low-quality memories can be easily replaced with sharper, clearer, not necessarily more accurate ones through police suggestion. In Briley's case, the show-up was problematic, and no one asked Joseph how familiar he was with guns so that he could identify that specific type. Neither was the robbery victim questioned about the perpetrator's clothing. Research on eyewitness identification also points to adversary effects on witness memory: being assigned to testify for one side or the other versus testifying as a neutral witness significantly biases the testimony in the direction of the party to whom the witnesses were assigned. The victim was afraid of the person in the show-up and probably deferential to the police, who appear to side with the victim. Jennifer Thompson-Cannino, the victim-witness in the Ronald Cotton case (discussed below), was praised by the officers as being the "best witness" and "textbook."[119]

False identifications reach beyond the investigative stage. Judges typically know that jurors cannot distinguish between accurate and inaccurate witnesses but usually defer to the jury when it comes to identification processes. Some states adopted jury instructions that provide context for jurors, but some judges fear that "jurors who receive such an instruction [are made] more skeptical of all eyewitness identifications, no matter what their quality."[120] Calling experts to testify about the psychology of memory may produce better results, but the defense generally must find and pay them. In the end, most trial judges do not feel comfortable withholding information and simply admit eyewitness identifications, letting the jury decide what to believe. "If you're the judge, in the back of your mind you might think, how's it going to look to exclude [an identification]? So you leave it for the jury." In the 1977 case *Manson v. Brathwaite*, seven Supreme Court justices said that even if an identification procedure was unnecessarily suggestive, in a show-up or otherwise, an eyewitness identification could be admitted as evidence as long as a trial judge deemed it reliable based on "the totality of the circumstances."[121]

Official misconduct is not an obvious factor in Briley's case but important overall. The National Registry of Exonerations lists official misconduct as a factor in more than half of all exonerations and in more than 70% of homicides. Defining what constitutes police or prosecutorial misconduct is challenging. Attorneys who try to reopen cases most commonly claim that prosecutors concealed evidence from the defense and that prosecutors misled the jury during their opening or closing arguments[122] It is, however, difficult to establish whether prosecutors hide evidence that is "material and exculpatory"—the standard established in *Brady v. Maryland*—and has the ability to show innocence or help the defense.[123] It is likewise difficult to draw a clear line between police and prosecutorial misconduct, since prosecutors might not know what police conceal. However, there is sufficient evidence that police officers influence witnesses through threats or fail to disclose exculpatory forensic data to the prosecutor and defense.[124] The gamut of identified misconduct is wide, including cases in which informants received helpful deals in their own cases but claimed they had not benefited from testimony in any way, or prosecutors and police withheld evidence supporting the defendant's alibi or the likely guilt of someone else. Briley had a previous drug conviction and would be charged as a habitual offender—unless he pleaded guilty. If he did that, the prosecutor would ask the judge for a shorter (12-year) sentence. This exemplifies the enormous power of the prosecutor. With a possibly much longer sentence facing a convicted defendant, prosecutors can influence a case based on their version of the events (and their agenda), disregarding any potential doubts.

An issue related to governmental misconduct and more visible in this case is inadequate defense work. The overload of the public defense system in the United States has been acknowledged as a long-standing and pervasive problem. Solid and zealous representation requires resources, mainly time. Briley knew an attorney, whom he called right after the arrest. In his first call he presented an alibi, asking the attorney to secure video footage from two hotels where Briley had been. The attorney (who required a retainer of $2,500) took three weeks to file for a subpoena to get the video from the motel where Briley was at the time of the incident. Then the attorney stopped his representation, and it also turned out that he had asked the motel for the video for the wrong hours ("It's a tragic mistake," the attorney commented). When the times were corrected, it was too late; the motel had taped over the footage. Proper defense investigation can prevent overcharging and severe punishment and lead to dismissals and acquittals.[125] In a master's thesis, Rosa Greenbaum argues that "investigative failures were far more frequent than other types of legal inadequacies in the NRE's ILD [Inadequate Legal Defense, RG] cases, appearing in 80.6% of cases, while trial errors were found in just 50.8% of these wrongful convictions."[126] This means that the defense, without investigatory capacities, can never be a fully competent counterpart to the state. This points back to the adversarial setup of the American system, where truth is treated as a partisan issue. Briley's representation during the trial was likewise weak. The new defense attorney questioned the police officer about the show-up procedure only in the most cursory manner while confusing "show-up" with "line-up."

Another source of error is false confessions. In 12% of all exonerations, an innocent person confessed to a crime they did not commit. What appears as almost implausible and absurd—an innocent person taking blame for a crime—can be explained by the standard police practice of long, intensive interrogations that eventually break the will of a suspect to the point where they admit to whatever police want them to.[127] Police still enjoy considerable freedom in choosing their interrogation techniques, and anything short of torture is permissible, including deception. Often, suspects falsely confess and enter a plea bargain to avoid a more severe penalty, like death.[128] Younger defendants and those with mental challenges are more likely to falsely confess than other suspects. False confessions quite often implicate other innocent people in addition to the confessor so that the confession can be made the basis for a trial against someone else. If a case goes to court and a recanted confession is introduced, jurors have a tendency to give it considerable weight.[129]

The use of unreliable and unvalidated forensic science has been linked with wrongful convictions as well. Forensic science is not a single discipline; it consists of many subfields like bloodstain pattern analysis, firearms and tool marks, forensic toxicology, forensic odontology, trace evidence, and mitochondrial DNA analysis.[130] Evidence like serology, microscopic hair analysis, and bite-mark examination can make a direct link between a suspect and a victim, whereas other types of evidence, like a shoe impression or a bullet, can do that only indirectly. Regardless of its scientific validity, directly incriminating evidence has a strong capacity to impact a jury's perception that other kinds of evidence do not have.[131] What juries do not hear, however, is an assessment of the reliability of a certain forensic method. A report from the National Research Council established that, "[a]mong existing forensic methods, only nuclear DNA analysis has been rigorously shown to have the capacity to consistently, and with a high degree of certainty, demonstrate a connection between an evidentiary sample and a specific individual or source."[132] With that, many methods like bite-mark or hair analysis that have been used in wrongful conviction cases were considered unreliable. The majority of wrongful convictions have been associated with serology (e.g., ABO blood-typing and secretor status) and microscopic hair analysis, a subdiscipline of trace evidence. ABO blood-typing has a strong scientific foundation and is based on well-founded population statistics; the problem is that the science was often improperly interpreted and conveyed in court.[133]

False accusations against the innocent come from a variety of people like family members, relatives, or jailhouse informants. False oaths and libelous statements and accusations are found in 57% of all false convictions.[134] The focus of innocence scholarship has been on jailhouse informants—a witness who was in custody with the innocent defendant and who testified that the defendant confessed to them. Eight percent of all exonerees in the national registry were convicted in part by testimony from jailhouse informants, concentrated among the worst crimes.[135] As Judge Hand remarked: "Courts have countenanced the use of informers from time immemorial" as a necessary evil "in cases of conspiracy, or in other cases when the crime consists of preparing for another crime."[136] That means that using secret informers is not seen as "per se unconstitutional."[137] The situation in wrongful convictions is different, though, as informants come forward later in an investigation or even after a new trial following a hung jury. Just as in false confession cases, jailhouse informants purported to have knowledge only the actual perpetrator could have, and that information was then tailored to the strategy of the prosecutor.[138] Informants typically received such information from the police or prosecutors in exchange for lighter sentences, partially dropped charges, or other benefits.[139]

Not mentioned as a canonical factor, but present in almost all exonerations, is tunnel vision. It is difficult to quantify its prevalence among erroneous convictions. However, research suggests that tunnel vision is common. Findley and Scott explain that, when criminal justice professionals "focus on a suspect, select and filter the evidence that will 'build a case' for conviction, while ignoring the suppressing evidence that points away from guilt," they are at risk of "locking on" to the wrong suspect and inadvertently leading to their continued prosecution and conviction.[140] Tunnel vision both affects and is affected by flawed procedures. A mistaken eyewitness might convince an officer early in an investigation, and a conviction of guilt can lead to, for instance, false confessions.[141] Tunnel vision is mainly the effect of cognitive distortions that affect the way we interpret our perceptions.[142] Cognitive biases like confirmation bias, hindsight bias, and outcome bias help explain the ubiquity of tunnel vision in even the most well-meaning actors within the criminal justice system. And these actors are not free from emotion, another source of psychological pressure that can foster tunnel vision, which can give investigators greater resolve to clear the case.[143]

Normative features installed in the criminal justice system on all levels contribute to tunnel vision and make it difficult to review cases for factual accuracy. Criminal appeals, for instance, focus only on legal (as opposed to factual) issues; during a trial, alternate suspects are difficult to introduce; and prosecutors have no duty to disclose evidence unless the evidence is "material"—a high bar.[144] In Briley's armed robbery case, the officers, the prosecutor, and the judge were very likely affected by tunnel vision when they disregarded differences in physical features and clothing and assumed the defendant's guilt from the onset.

In Briley's case we can see a mistaken witness identification, tunnel vision, and ineffective assistance of counsel. But these are just the legally visible issues. The larger narrative shows a more complex image. For instance, Briley's initial stop—when he became a suspect in the first place—was not brought up. He was stopped because of the way he held his hands and where he looked. How did racial aspects of policing play into this? It appears that the stop was never questioned, maybe because Briley ran. But even his running from the police requires interpretation. It is not a sign of guilt per se. Carrying a gun meant he was violating his parole, but apart from that he "would have run away no matter what. It's what he grew up learning to do."[145] This cultural narrative explaining why Briley reacted the way he did was not considered. What is said in court can be seen and read, but what jurors think cannot. Here the jurors said they argued over the case and thought it came down to "one man's word against another." One juror noted that multiple jurors voiced doubts about Briley's guilt but that fear of crime and violence was "in the air." Briley carried a gun, and that "played into the idea of, you know, 'This is just someone who belongs in jail.'" This is an expression of narrative character—of a certain "type"—who fits into preconceived cultural scripts. Character and deed become a single, unreviewable issue. The jury, often described as the great leveler, is a community of people inexperienced in the dynamics of the adversarial process, which overwhelms them. One juror noted that she thought she could not make a difference. "I knew he didn't stand a chance, with those people in that room," she told me. "It really haunted me for quite a while. I had nightmares about it." The judge in this case presented his biases more explicitly. When Briley seethed with frustration after Joseph pointed him out, he said, "Man, you are bad, man." The judge reprimanded and warned him, "Don't make me gag you." What does that say about Briley's role in the trial? At Briley's sentencing hearing, the judge lectured Briley: "I can't imagine somebody who appeared more scared than this victim did," the judge said. "The reason why he was so frightened, sir, was because of you. This court is convinced beyond all doubt that you committed this offense. I just don't simply understand what goes on in this town." The judge was convinced beyond "all doubt," and not just reasonable doubt, that Briley was the perpetrator. And this was during a period when the problem of eyewitness misidentification was common knowledge among lawyers and innocence awareness had spread across the United States.

The Advent of Crime, Wrongful Conviction, and Exoneration Narratives

The interest in wrongful conviction stories has seen increased popular interest in recent years. Podcasts like the 2014 *Serial*, which revisited the investigation of the 1999 killing of the Baltimore teenager Hae Min Lee and the conviction of her boyfriend, Adnan Syed, and TV documentary series like *Making a Murderer* have resonated with the popular sense that the legal system is broken.[146] Wrongful conviction literature has become its own genre,[147] with an appeal that goes beyond crime fiction in general. Often, these narratives lie between the poles of purely fictional and nonfictional accounts of miscarriages of justice, and they address the two subnarratives: *wrongful conviction narratives* (what led to the wrongful conviction, stressing the dysfunctionality of the system) and *exoneration narratives* (how the wrongful conviction was overcome, stressing advocacy and perseverance).

A New (Sub)Genre

Wrongful conviction narratives have a long literary history. The act of telling the stories of the innocently convicted began long before the first DNA tests were conducted. The case of the Boorn brothers discussed above is one example. Wrongful conviction stories often provide the backdrop for crime mysteries like Scott Turow's legal thriller *Presumed Innocent.*[148] Other texts, like Harper Lee's *To Kill a Mockingbird*, do not revolve around a crime to be solved but portray how guilt is socially constructed and can easily be transferred to an innocent by changing the narrative. Mayella Ewell's accusations against Tom Robinson are motivated by her own guilt—being attracted to a Black man. Such transferences are often observable in actual cases.

Parallel to the development of innocence projects, investigative exposés of wrongful convictions formed their own genre.[149] Without the publicly narrativized cases of injustice, we would not have learned about the many wrongful convictions and the events that led to them. Rob Warden, a legal affairs journalist and the cofounder of the Center on Wrongful Convictions at the Northwestern University Pritzker School of Law, said that "if it hadn't been for great investigative journalism . . . the innocence movement wouldn't have gotten off the ground."[150] What should be kept in mind, however, is that all texts that represent a case in whatever form oscillate between case reports, fictionalized gap-filling,[151] true-crime fiction, and purely imaginative fiction. David Schmid calls it the "vertical integration between advocacy groups . . . and editorial teams" that turns raw data into fascinating stories.[152] There rarely is narrativization without fictionalization and a certain motivation by authors to present content in a certain way. For instance, as much as *Actual Innocence*—the collection of wrongful conviction narratives that was written by the founders of the Innocence Project and a journalist—claims to be "a work of nonfiction,"[153] its narratives are written with hindsight by a quasi-omniscient author with an awareness of how to tell the stories.

The effects of wrongful convictions are depicted in biographical memoir-style narratives like *Picking Cotton*, cowritten by Ronald Cotton (who spent 11 years in prison for a crime he did not commit) with Jennifer Thompson-Cannino—his former accuser. In most criminal proceedings, suspects and defendants lose narrative agency; their voices are mediated through their attorneys and reduced to procedurally relevant aspects. Sometimes they sit and hear what witnesses and prosecutors have to say about their case silently, almost completely voiceless: "I sat and listened . . . having to stay silent when everyone was just telling a pack of lies about me."[154] The biographical accounts function to speak up after years of enduring an injustice and to reclaim dignity and person-hood. They also write about resilience, persistence, faith, and strength and their journey toward regaining agency while incarcerated. Ronald Cotton states: "In prison, working out and staying strong is a form of surviving. Not only did you need to be able to throw someone down, but also you needed to exhaust yourself or else you might never sleep."[155] That then leads to the exoneration narrative when an innocence project picks up their case and we as readers fear that the evidence might have been destroyed. Even if it is, the memoirs often end by implying resti-tution, healing, a form of reconciliation, and forgiveness. Exonerations rarely provide closure, but for many exonerees "it was an ending."[156]

The recent rise and broad reach of new media outlets like podcasts and online streaming services resulted not only in a popularization of issues of crime; these new forms of narrative also allow the public to become involved in the discourse of perceived injustices permeating the justice system. The intrinsically powerful wrongful conviction narra-tives appeal to the true-crime genre for multiple reasons: they resonate with the noticeably decreasing confidence in the criminal justice system and support the reliance on improved technology and the opportunities that new forms of media and their wide reach provide to (re)investigate cases. One crime reporter noted that there has been "an incredible shift in public consciousness about wrongful convictions and the possibility that someone who's in prison is innocent."[157] Media programs like *Se-rial* and *Making a Murderer* reached audiences of millions. Both became cultural phenomena that initiated conversations about wrongful convic-tions and faults within the justice system.[158] Much of the momentum of the innocence movement is due to the force of innocence narratives, and that momentum is palpable in public responses. Some argue that Adnan Syed's new trial (and recent release) was an effect of *Serial* because it was granted after the podcast prompted public scrutiny of the murder of Hae Min Lee.[159] After the release of the *Making a Murderer* documentary series, over 100,000 people signed a petition seeking a pardon for Steven Avery. In response, one scholar spoke of the *"Making a Murderer* Effect," where barriers that have traditionally impeded access to information are broken down, changing the way mainstream society interprets and discusses the law.[160] There appears to be great potential to advance the public good when independent producers show where individual and systemic biases affect both the application of law and the construction of the case story the law is applied to. Courts, lawyers, and judges lose their monopoly on defining the relevant truth. Debates that were reserved for experts on news shows have entered the public realm, allowing everyone to participate in the justice process.

Yet narratives, documentaries, TV shows, and podcasts merely provide the legal background necessary for their narratives and rarely provide all the raw data for viewers to scrutinize. While true-crime narrative comes with the allure of democratizing and exposing typically hidden discourses, the possibility likely remains that new categories of media narratives on criminal cases, regardless of how well they present "truth," may be distorting their audience's understanding of law and its intricate relationship with facts.[161] That has probably less to do with the audience than the genre of true crime and all narrative genres. Innocence narratives, apart from their value as entertainment, exemplify that there is a danger in a system that routinely keeps information from jurors and controls what they hear.

2

Speaking of the Truth

Law, Narratology, and the Narrative Imagination

> But you know that the language of analysis has not replaced
> the narrative, that Aeschylus and Homer are still to be read,
> and that one who believes that everything can be said in a
> language of theory and system is an impossible fool.[1]
> —J. B. White

I start this chapter with an excerpt from a prosecutor's opening statement during the criminal trial against Richard Danziger in Texas:

> What I'd like to do here today is separate fact from fiction and explain
> why the state introduced so many exhibits and took so long to get you
> to this point. First of all, this is not storytime. Remember, the evidence
> comes from here.[2]

Here are the underlying facts. Christopher Ochoa and Richard Danziger were falsely convicted and sentenced to life for the rape and (in
Ochoa's case) the murder of Nancy DePriest, the manager of a Pizza Hut
in Austin in 1989. On the morning of October 24, 1988, DePriest was
working alone in the kitchen of the restaurant when a person dressed
as a repairman knocked at the rear entrance and was let in. DePriest
was tied up, raped, and murdered by gunshot. The perpetrator then
clogged the sinks and flooded the kitchen to destroy evidence. Since
there was no lead on a potential suspect, police, who believed that a
master key had been used to gain entrance to the restaurant, "set up a
meeting with [the] employees [of the Pizza Hut] and told them to just be
kind of on the lookout for anything unusual."[3] A few days later, Ochoa
and Danziger, who were both working for Pizza Hut at a different location, decided to visit the restaurant where the murder had happened. A

waitress observed both "eating and drinking beer in what she surmised to be a toast to the victim." She then informed the police that indeed something "suspicious" had happened. By asking to be on the lookout for anything "unusual," the staff were invited to put random events into a legally significant narrative when, in fact, such events were—though maybe tasteless—harmless and unrelated to the crime. Would the waitress have contacted the police without being encouraged to look for and create a potential crime story?

Ochoa was interrogated for hours, threatened, and intimidated before he finally confessed to the crime. During the same time, a serologist from the Department of Public Safety claimed that Ochoa could not be excluded as the source of the semen found in the victim, a claim that was misleading because the victim's blood-group markers could have "masked" the perpetrator. Another test included Ochoa (with 16% of the Mexican American population) as a biological source. Ochoa accepted a plea deal through which he managed to avoid the death penalty. His confession was then used in the trial against Danziger. More than 10 years into their sentences, the Wisconsin Innocence Project conducted DNA testing of biological evidence preserved from the crime scene. It excluded Ochoa and Danziger, and both were exonerated in 2002. The actual perpetrator, Achim Marino, was identified and prosecuted. Marino, who was serving time for different crimes, had sent written confessions to newspapers and the governor of Texas over years while Ochoa was in prison. He told police that he was in possession of the murder weapon that was recovered by the police during Marino's arrest. When police conducted a ballistics test, they could not match the gun to the crime, so the investigation did not continue. Ochoa was informed about Marino while in prison but maintained that he and Danziger alone committed the crime. After his exoneration, he explained that he still felt intimidated by the police and therefore maintained the false story.[4]

This case can be rendered in traditional wrongful conviction concepts: there was false and misleading forensic evidence, perjury, official misconduct, and—in Danziger's case—a false accusation contributing to the wrongful conviction. These canonical factors, however, are just landmarks and not the whole path that led to the conviction. They are part of a larger incriminatory narrative that started to build from the moment the crime had been discovered. The factors that lead to wrongful convictions have been widely discussed in the literature, but the underlying narratives that are imagined, developed, contested, confirmed, falsified, and so on have not received the same attention. Danziger's and Ochoa's case (like many others) exemplifies the power of narrative and calls into question the way criminal justice systems arrive at "guilt." Who do we put in charge of developing the case narrative, what is their agenda, how does the law narrate factual "truth," why do made-up—false—confessions develop so much more narrative momentum than truthful confessions? In typical false confession cases, the narrative is a result of abuse, deception, or intimidation. And while that is true for Ochoa, he did not change his narrative even after years in prison, which somehow suggests that, potentially, the confession had become integrated into Ochoa's conception, or narrative, of himself.[5] The true story, even when maintained adamantly, might not change the direction of a case when an initial narrative has taken root.

This case also raises questions that have not been cast into wrongful conviction terminology. The way a case is narrativized depends on elements that are typically exclusive to the literary domain: interpretation, questions of authorship, rhetoric, culture, and the experience of minorities.[6] These elements raise questions such as: How did Ochoa's race play into the investigation? How did both defendants' youth and lower socioeconomic status impact the case? Is Ochoa an unreliable narrator? Is Marino? And who is the author of the main narrative and the many micro-narratives? Is Ochoa the author of his confession? Wrongful convictions raise doubts as to the reliability of the investigative and adjudicative process and require a multidimensional approach to look beyond the (admittedly already) complex canonical factors. The processing of a legal case is not a purely logical, rational endeavor; it is often intuitive with no clear line between representing the "real" and "fiction-making."[7]

The state's opening statement excerpted above is indicative of the commonly made distinction in criminal litigation between "fact" and "fiction"—between the "truth" that "evidence" represents and the "story." With the term "storytime," the prosecutor refers to a meaning of "story" that invokes the image of fairytales read to children and not how that term is used in scholarship and here.[8] He then emphasizes that what will follow during the case in chief is not that "story"; rather it is an evidence-driven discourse. This remark appears as a lawyer's naïve confidence in the evidentiary process. In hindsight, however, it sounds almost cynical. With the benefit of hindsight in this and thousands of other cases, we must question whether "fiction" and "fact" can so easily be separated in the legal discourse when the relevant facts of a case are determined through a process that depends so much on methods of representing events, including oral, visual, and textual. Although juries are told to look for facts that fulfill the legal requirements of the crime in question beyond a reasonable doubt, we see that, in the end, all a criminal conviction requires is a narrative that conveys a plausible, coherent, and acceptable story.[9] This story does not require factual truth; neither is there any way to review whether jurors were convinced beyond a reasonable doubt.

The basic distinction between factual truth (what objectively happened, known by an omniscient observer), legal truth (what a jury or judge legitimately thinks happened), and the corresponding concepts of factual and legal guilt are as fundamental for law and its discourses as they are problematic in the sense that they evoke a false sense of certainty that the representation of facts and legally endorsed fiction-making are not intimately related. In this chapter, I define how legal and factual truth are different and how narrative—playing on preconceived beliefs about types of people and stories—can be misused by unscrupulous authors (or can lead scrupulous authors astray) to posit a legal reality divorced from factual reality.

Narrating Agents and Narrative Stages

The legal determination of guilt or innocence is saturated and inflected by the construction of narratives. The representation of an event involves selecting, omitting, and shaping elements that we as the creators of the narrative find noteworthy or important to convey that story. Criminal cases rely on the assembling, coordinating, but also competition among competing ways of "telling the story" (i.e., narrating). Factual truths must be sought, selected, and ordered into a story that ultimately serves the purpose to inculpate or exculpate. That act of seeking, selection, and ordering—that is, the crafting of legal narratives at every stage—is subject to constraints imposed by procedural and institutional rules, which are meant to provide "formulas by which the law attempts to impose form and rule on stories."[10] It is also given enormous license by those rules. This license is harnessed by different agents within the assemblage of storytellers.

Multiple narrating agents are involved in the construction of a criminal case on multiple stages. A legislature narrates the laws that describe punishable events before police "read" a potential crime scene and write a report, which is then read and re-narrated by the prosecutor, the judge, the jury, appellate courts, lawyers of an innocence project, and other players. It is rarely possible to clearly distinguish between entities that only narrate or only read. Even jurors as passive listeners will re-narrate among themselves what they hear during the trial, though that re-narration rarely becomes public. Juries deliver verdicts but not narratives. The addressee of a narrative is likewise important. Lawyers tune their narratives to their audiences. While an American trial lawyer will use language and rhetoric for a lay audience, a German prosecutor mainly addresses a judge who is not just a passive listener but the entity most actively involved in the development of the narrative in court. Rhetorical flourishes or the use of "themes" are not as common as they are in the United States.

Not all legal narration serves the same function at all times. The prototypical criminal case moves through various narrative stages from the initial suspicion and investigation, over the charge, appearances before court, the trial, sentencing, and so on. On each stage, the case is narrativized differently. Police will collect evidence and data, which are written up in a report, which then becomes the basis for a charge. Although police are bound by rules of evidence, they must imagine the events that led to harm and then collect evidence. Legal stories—the crime stories— are not found, and they are not like the exposed yet still invisible images on a piece of photographic paper that come into existence in the photographic developer. A pure representation of an event (the crime) does not exist, and there are always elements beyond the text or structure that are examined: "In reading or viewing or listening to any narrative, we are at once taking in and adding, tracing and sharpening. There is a continuum here, and at a certain point we find that what we call interpretation is looking more and more like what we call creation."[11] That freedom to imagine is limited on the prosecutorial stage, because now a more solidified case narrative that is supported by evidence must be presented in order for the case to move forward. The criminal courtroom has been described as a place for a contest between competing narratives, out of which ideally the truest (and practically the most plausible) narrative will emerge.

The trial is also the narrative gravitation point in which a multitude of narratives and micro-narratives develop. The dominance of narrative studies focusing on courtroom discourse is due to the adversarial trial's dramatic structure and the adversaries' reliance on conflicting arguments,[12] both of which are missing in inquisitorial trials. It is worth questioning the paradigm of the contest of narratives. This will be addressed in more detail, but as paradigmatic as the contest-metaphor has become, wrongful convictions show the lack of an actual contest of narratives; given the power imbalance between the state and the defense, it might simply be an ideal that is rarely met. After the verdict, a case moves into the appellate stage, where the case narrative is the ground on which courts reason but is not scrutinized. Appellate courts do not review narrative and usually extend deference to the trial court's evaluation of an issue as one of law or fact.

Law's Truths

Law's relationship with truth is complex. While there "is no gainsaying that arriving at the truth is a fundamental goal of our legal system"[13] finding the objective truth is not the only prerogative that agents in a criminal justice system must follow. Because of the consequences of a criminal process, the pursuit of truth is limited by value judgments that regulate what data ("evidence") is available for review and how such a review is conducted. The exclusionary rule (and other rules of evidence), the prohibitions against torture and double jeopardy, the statute of limitations—all protect an individual from a search for truth that is excessively invasive and can lead to potentially unreliable data, even if that data will help uncover the factual truth. Lay jurors, as the typical fact finders, are entrusted with rendering the verdict, but they are trained in neither epistemology nor law. This is atypical in fields that search for truth. There is no lay element in, for instance, the natural sciences, medicine, or history. These discourses do not rely on adversarial testing of narratives before a lay audience like jurors. Competition among scientists and scholars primarily serves the truth and not an agenda, like winning an argument, a conviction, or an acquittal. The American adversarial criminal justice system is based on the idea that the desire to win serves finding the truth and ultimately justice,[14] when, in fact, it might have the opposite effect. Even when new facts are discovered, a false jury verdict is very difficult to review as to its factual content and is protected because claims of actual innocence would have a "very disruptive effect . . . on the need for finality in capital cases" and would put an enormous burden on states that would have to "retry cases based on often stale evidence."[15] This is plainly illogical in other circumstances. A physician who would tell a patient that running more tests because of additional and new symptoms would have a "disruptive effect" on their work acts unethically and likely would face legal consequences. Larry Laudan argues that if "we were serious about error reduction, and if we likewise recognized that juries sometimes reach wrong verdicts, then the obvious remedy would be to . . . permit . . . appeals of both acquittals and convictions."[16] Other criminal justice systems allow for a retrial in favor of a defendant when new evidence is discovered, and they also allow in narrowly defined cases for a reopening not favoring the defendant.[17] This already shows that wrongful convictions cannot be considered without also considering particular legal settings and value judgments within a system.

A cursory glance at case files of the wrongfully convicted reveals that the way law creates the "facts" is narrative in nature, influenced by everyone who is involved in the legal discourse. In the Texas case above, Ochoa and Danziger did not become suspects because of a scientific test like a buccal swab that came back positive—they became suspects because of the "narrative desire"[18] to match someone to the crime. Suspicion is always narrative. It is always the result of an imaginative process through which a story is created. It was not facts that incriminated Danziger and Ochoa and many other exonerees but an envisioned story. Ochoa's confession is the product of police officers who coercively try to match the law with an envisioned scenario from their imaginations. That raises multiple questions that are again narrative in nature. For instance, how much does law pay attention to matters of narrative agency and authorship? Peter Brooks stresses that point when he discusses a report of a consent to a search by an officer in free indirect discourse as an act of narrative "ventriloquism."[19] Is Ochoa's detailed confession of the rape and murder of the victim not similar? Are these "his" words or someone else's? Ochoa, one could say, is with his signature the formal author and the implied and internally focalizing author, but he actually became that author against his will. This is not his story.

When Chris Ochoa took the stand in Richard Danziger's trial, his plea agreement (including the confession) was entered into evidence. When asked whether he would "testify truthfully," he answered, "Yes, ma'am."[20] Ochoa then testified to the events as they were laid out in his confession. During his testimony he had to explain "lies" he had told about specifics of the crime, which shows how much what is true or false become relative, almost absurd in their meanings. Their only baseline reference is the story the state wants to tell through the suspect. And when being asked again, "Did you tell the truth in that statement? . . . Are you telling this jury the truth now?"[21] Ochoa confirmed again[22] and said that no one influenced him in making his confession.[23] He was then ordered to "[l]ook that jury in the eye. . . . Look each of them in the eye. You're under oath. Are you telling them truth?" "Yes."[24] In closing, the prosecutor returns to that eye contact to underscore Ochoa's credibility: "Richard Danziger is a plotter, a schemer. And you know what it comes down to is your ability as human beings to watch the testimony of Chris Ochoa and watch the testimony of Richard Danziger to have made that eye contact with him and know he's telling you the truth."[25]

As we see, a trial is to a large extent a choreographed, agenda-driven event, with limited capability to find the truth. In a criminal trial, the factual truth of a narrative matters to a certain degree only because law's truth—legal truth—is based more on the authority of the decision maker (judges, juries) than on factual certainty. In ordering a certain decision, a court activates a narrative as the correct one, deciding what is "real" in the eyes of the law.[26] Despite the high standard of certainty "beyond a reasonable doubt," a plausible, acceptable story is sufficient for a conviction. Just as in the legal discourse in general, the role of narrative in wrongful conviction cases is not reducible to legal, psychological, or pragmatic questions. Stories (and their narration) serve their own social function, their own psychological purpose.[27] Narratives provide order and help to find order where there were just pieces of evidence.[28] Evidence itself has no existence outside of a narrative.[29]

A Legal Narratology?

That law is narrative—and that storytelling plays a crucial role in all areas of law—has become a truism,[30] almost cliché.[31] Legal professionals, including law enforcement, are trained to construct narratives effectively so that an audience, be it the jury, a client, or a judge, is able to comprehend the arc and purpose of a story.[32] Participants in legal proceedings understand and process the events they make the subject of their legal actions through narrativization, because this is how these actions are brought in line with some larger series of events they take to constitute the legal system and the culture that sustains it.[33] Adversarial lawyers in particular are taught to assemble facts "persuasively" in order to advance and frame their conclusions.[34] Storytelling is firmly rooted not only in legal advocacy and litigation but also in the ways we think about and teach law.[35] The American Bar Association, for instance, suggests beginning an opening statement with a one-sentence emotional theme to serve as an anchor, creating impressions for the jury that linger throughout the trial.[36] The description of the case tells the jury what happened chronologically either from the viewpoint of the plaintiff or the defendant. When giving an opening statement, the lawyer should offer an account that will make the jury want to decide in their favor. Prosecutors are encouraged to make the jury a participant in the story[37] by finding themes that resonate with the average person, by using metaphorical language, or by coming up with catchphrases that can be used throughout the trial.[38]

Storytelling as a *practical* (emotion-triggering) feature is a characteristic of all criminal justice systems, but more so in the American system in particular because judge-driven Continental systems are much more guided by process and hermeneutics than zealous advocacy.[39] As much as strategies of narrative are used as a tool in law and court rooms, they have not undergone substantial scrutiny.

Narrative Within a Legal "System"

Since the late twentieth century, outside the realm of practical law, a new turn in legal and interdisciplinary scholarship developed a focus on the centrality of narrative across many scholarly fields.[40] Legal narratology addresses "the embedding of narrative in the legal discourse"[41] and is described as one of three major subcategories of the Law and Literature movement.[42] Law as a subject of narrative inquiry has attracted scholars from various disciplines: law, linguistics, psychology, literary studies. Although narrative thinking about law in the shape of rhetorical analysis goes back to antiquity, the interdisciplinary and analytical approach to a narrative of the law is a comparatively young area of study. The movement gained momentum when, in 1995, a symposium on legal narratology at the Yale Law School led to a collection of essays that embraced a wide range of issues—trials, sentencing, judicial opinions, confessions, and narrative scholarship.[43] This new field did not develop without criticism.[44] The text that became foundational for the narrative turn was Peter Brooks's much cited *Narrative Transactions*. Brooks stresses that legal narratology is a field sui generis, "not reducible to other kinds of speech and argument."[45] Indeed, as Fish observes, as much as legal systems employ narrative, they do "not wish to be absorbed by, or declared subordinate to, some other—nonlegal—structure of concern."[46] Brooks's leading question is this: If narrative is so central in law, why "doesn't the law pay more attention to narratives, to narrative analysis and even narrative theory?"[47] Answering that question proves difficult and complex. The reason for not having a further established legal narratology is likely affected by three intersecting issues: the hegemony and autonomy of law as a system, the deep imbrication of law and narrative, and the methodological limitations that come with the literary study of fictional narratives.

The first issue arguably affects law's openness to narrative analysis the most. Legal practitioners are generally skeptical of those who pursue narrative inquiries into the law.[48] Courts, their decisions, and the legal discourse within law do not deal, at least not openly, with narrative as argument. Lawyers work within a *nomos*, a normative universe and legal doctrine as an expression of that nomos. Narrative considerations distort the ideal of rationality that distinguishes description from prescription.[49] Law desires that the components of its autonomous existence be self-declaring and not in need of piecing out by some supplementary, nonlegal, external discourse.[50] It is law's self-referentiality (or "autopoiesis"), as conceptualized by Niklas Luhmann, that limits the legal discourse. Outside influences are shielded because, "[l]ike all systems,

court procedures constitute themselves by differentiation, by strengthening borders to their environment."[51] In Luhmann's eyes, agents such
as judges and prosecutors act on behalf of the system and not as individuals who try to understand the nature (or larger narrative) of the
act or the mind and heart of the offender—and often the victim.[52] Thus
a functional dichotomy between law—its doctrines and its application
and execution—and the role narrative plays in it are accepted by legal
practitioners and scholars alike,[53] often unconsciously. Every lawyer
thinks about how they represent their clients' stories in any court, hear-
ings, depositions, but the same lawyers might deny narrative's dogmatic
relevance.[54]

Rhetoric—the discipline whose objects of formal study are the conventions of discourse and argument—faces a similar resistance.[55] Just
like narrative, rhetorical conventions help "constitute ourselves, our com-
munities, and, perhaps, our world,"[56] and yet law operates through the
systematic denial that it is rhetoric.[57] This criticism has been expressed
for a long time, particularly strongly in civil law countries where since
the reception of Roman law a strong belief in conceptual, "axiomatic"
jurisprudence and law as a legal science developed. Theodor Viehweg,
who pioneered the renaissance of law and rhetoric, argued in *Topics and
Law* that lawyers disregard that law operates in the realm of opinions
("doxa") and not truth ("episteme").[58] Rhetoric shapes not only how we
speak but also how we see, how we think, and what we know.[59] In other
words, it shapes and creates legal reality. That reality is not dependent on
actual truth because of the "rhetorical commitments" lawyers make, so it
must be clear that advocacy and argumentation entail an indifference to
truth."[60] Here we can see that part of the rhetorical convention is narrative. As I have indicated, lawyers generate narratives to enhance the intelligibility and the persuasiveness of their argument. They make efforts to
disguise the fact that their narratives are creations and then present them
"as a simple revelation of the objective truth."[61] Facts will be lawyered[62]
for shared rhetorical and narrative purposes: toward achieving certainty,
simplification, sufficiency, and closure. Searching for truth leads in a different direction: away from closure and out in the direction of complexity, contingency, uncertainty, rhetoric, and narrative.

Richard Posner's criticism of the narrative approach is based on the
fear that a more conscious concentration on narrative would blur the

lines between fiction and facts, when law requires a firm link to reality: "This may be embarrassingly non-postmodern, but reality exists. . . . It is my view that the major conflicts of our time are over the real and only secondarily over versions of it and methods for apprehending it."[63] In Posner's view, "reality" would be distorted if what he calls "stories" and I call "narrative" were given more room in court:

> When a defendant in his plea of mercy tells a horrific (and let us as-
> sume truthful) story of childhood abuse and neglect, he implicitly asserts
> a causal relationship between the events narrated and the criminal act for
> which he is to be sentenced; the story has no relevance otherwise. But to
> assert and to prove are two different things. The proof is critical, and is
> not supplied by the story, which may merely be appealing to credulous
> and sentimental intuitions.[64]

Here, Posner appears to argue against a demand for more "emotional-ity"[65] in legal narratives and that "judges should forgo the 'quest after persuasive power or beauty' in favor of 'clear analysis and clear transmission' of their decisions."[66] But it is a myth that there can be a "clear analysis and clear transmission" of verdicts outside a narrative context. Lawyers know (and learn) that "for better or worse, . . . you could argue any a legal point any way you like."[67]

Narrative and Rationality

Courts rarely consider (and might not be aware of) how the representation of facts becomes part of the argument once the fact-finding stage is completed and a case moves to the appellate stage. This is because legal systems—common law but even more so the civil—claim "pure rationality,"[68] operating under the idea that facts are determined and verdicts are the result of reasoning. To put it differently: there are various types of sub-discourses and genres active within the legal discourse. There is the practical discourse of following a narrative agenda and try-ing to persuade jurors not only legally but also emotionally, and then there is the more technical-legal or doctrinal discourse that reasons and presents itself as logical. That discourse is reductive in the sense that it seeks to formulate and develop actual definitions of justice, whereas the literary or narrative is based on metaphors or situational context. The legal discourse reduces the complexity of life to elements that are either given or not given. There is little in between. The vagueness and the many facets of the human condition are difficult to account for in law because vagueness is hard to codify or adjudicate. As James Boyd White defines it:

> [Legal language] operates by reducing what can be said about experience to a series of questions cast in terms of legal conclusions ("legal issues") which must be answered simply "yes" or "no"; it maintains a false pretense that it can be used as a language of description or naming, when in fact it calls for a process of complex judgment, to which it seems to give no directions whatever.[69]

The question "Who is this man?"[70] is rarely asked in legal discourse, which in its pursuit of uniformity and clarity is in danger of "trivializing the human experience."[71] When judges must decide whether someone committed a murder, they do not have to ponder the philosophical, linguistic, or literary connotations of the term "murder." The law defines it, and it also describes what elements need to be proven for a specific action to be considered murder or any other crime. The same is true for procedural questions.[72] In the American criminal justice system, a prosecutor needs to prove *actus reus* (human conduct), *mens rea* (the guilty mind, i.e., intent or negligence), concurrence (*actus reus* and *mens rea* have to concur at the same time), causation, and harm. For some crimes (so-called strict liability crimes) mens rea does not need to be proven, which means that, for example, in a case of statutory rape it does not matter if the defendant thought the victim was of age, if they were in love, if they were dating, or if the victim expressed factual albeit legally irrelevant consent.

These questions might be related to motives and extralegal issues of justice, but they do not pertain to the law itself. What might be a complex cluster of intentions, motives, and circumstances is reduced, compressed, or "sanitized"[73] to a few elements that preclude considerations that are relevant outside the law.[74] The legal narrative is "a kind of two dimensional cartoon rendition of the three dimensional world."[75] For example, whether a pharmacist is killed because he insulted the killer's mother or because the killer does not have the money to buy medication for his very sick wife does not matter for the determination of the crime itself. It might matter during the sentencing process, but they do not play a role unless substantive law explicitly states that certain motives are aggravating or mitigating factors. Law, as with all symbolic systems, makes reality "appear in such and such a way."[76] This reality-making is enforced under the law itself. A judge would not even be able to include extralegal aspects and argue that a case cannot be decided because a law is insufficient in addressing a pertinent issue.[77]

Law can be (and perhaps must be) very rigid, and because of that a judge or jury must disregard elements that might be important to the individuals involved but are not part of the discourse. Criminal trials "are not designed to get at the total truth in all its mystery; they only allow decision of narrow issues of fact and law within the limitations of a moderately effective litigation system."[78] Narrative jurisprudence as a scholarly field moves against that rigidity by opening up the discourse to oppositional stories, which could revolutionize the law and influence legal ethics and humanize the field.[79] But for as long as a specific situation potentially affecting the level of someone's accountability is not allowed a place in law, such a situation—oppositional stories—does not develop any relevance for the discourse.

Another aspect that affects the development of legal narratology is that much of the existing narrative theory is based on fictitious texts, which lack (among other aspects) the ostensibly documentary and normative functions of legal narratives. That makes the direct application of such theories to real-world events and law with its many demands on narrativization difficult. Further, just as in discourse outside legal studies, within legal narrative scholarship the term "narrative" is not used consistently and often represents something else, such as images, conceptions, or ideologies.[80] As Olson argues, the lexeme narrative is invoked very broadly "to describe any manner of phenomena," including "the history of a given legal culture, the aesthetic evocation of a story in a given text, legal-political trends, as well as the history of a given case or legal norm as well as more specific aspects of legal storytelling."[81] Narrative is used more like a placeholder than a concrete concept.

The scope of legal narratives is necessarily broad, including elements that refer to "the real" (for example, a dead body with a bullet in its head); elements that are imagined, envisioned, and constructed (like suspicion or the state of mind of a defendant at the moment of the crime); and elements that deal with law and how it works (legal hermeneutics, methods, etc.). Different areas of law require different narrative approaches. Those that are commonly discussed are trial narratives (the so-called contest of narratives), the narratives of legal "outsiders," and the larger narratives of (constitutional) law itself.[82] It is much rarer that an author addresses the question of *narrative voice*. Who, for instance, is the author of a confession that is contained in a typed-up and signed document in a file? There is the prima facie *intradiegetic* level of the speaker who describes certain events. But what appears to be said by the suspect actually could be *extradiegetic*—as when someone else speaks for the suspect or makes the suspect say certain things—like when a police officer tells their story through someone else. What is an almost natural approach for a literary scholar (asking, *who* is speaking?) is foreign to the lawyer who is trained and used to write and read on one narrative plane narratives that must be internally consistent and contain adequately developed stories.[83] In the legal discourse, texts are not supposed to mean something else.

Looking at the narratives of wrongful convictions makes apparent that little is known about the early stages of a case—for instance, why and how someone became a suspect. Most of the canonical factors of wrongful convictions influence cases in their early (pretrial) stages. These factors contribute to the incrimination narrative when evidence is produced and the first narratives are formed. False witness identification happens early, and so do false confessions, and these then affect how unbiased police pursue the case. Narratology has had its focus on what is transcribed in transcripts or court decisions. The more the modalities of narrative presentation are studied the better we can understand how narrativity influences human consciousness. That requires the deconstruction or "denaturalization" of narratives, so we can see how they are put together.[84]

Categorizing Legal Narratives

Circumscribing narrative categories helps to achieve clarity on the setting and function of specific narratives. A guiding frame is to ask: Who tells whom what when and where for what purpose? It matters who narrates, who the audience is, the object of the narration, and its specific function at that time. Analyzing witness testimony requires a different approach or at least a different kind of narrative awareness than the narrative content of laws or court decisions, constitutions, or law's larger narratives or *grand récit*.[85] It makes a difference if narratives are presented to jurors or judges, and it also matters whether a case narrative is constructed during trial or reviewed on appeal. Similar cases would also be narrated and read differently in different legal systems like common law, civil, mixed, or any other.

Poetic and Nonpoetic Narration

Martinez and Scheffel categorize narratives into four general types: there is narration of real and the narration of imagined events through poetic or nonpoetic discourse.[86] According to this distinction, a police report or a statement of fact in an opening statement or appellate decision, just like the report of a journalist, is written with the intention to provide a true image—a description—of real events, as opposed to the fiction writer who does not make such a claim. Even if (parts) of such a narrative are (intentionally or unintentionally) made up, they would, according to Martinez and Scheffel, still fall into the category of factual, nonpoetic narration because they refer to something that actually happened.[87] What complicates the categorization of legal narratives is that they are historical in the sense that narrators (and narratees) claim (believe) that something has happened in a certain way, and they also must imagine these events at least partly because no narrative can ever be fully complete, stating every detail. Reality is constructed through narrative and "operates as an instrument of mind in the construction of reality."[88] Narrative sequence, plot, and intelligibility are used to make sense of our lives and our world because it is "a basic human operation, learned in infancy, and culturally omnipresent."[89] Such processes are inventive for both the narrator and the listener, so jurors "may not be getting the entire story and they may let their imagination fill in the gaps to the prejudice of one side or another."[90]

The opening statement in Richard Danziger's murder trial, for instance, is nonpoetic and factual but simultaneously makes up a story of a murder that never occurred the way it was described. However, as a broad category, all representations of world events in law can be considered real, nonpoetic discourse. Legal narratives that have a purpose other than describing actual events fall out of the categorization proposed by Martinez and Scheffel. Statutory laws, judge-made laws, constitutions, and contracts do not deal with the direct representation of specific events; they are prescriptive (normative) in nature and pertain to nonconcrete, generalized scenarios. Such texts have been considered to be narrative regardless of their mainly normative function. Most prominently, Ronald Dworkin has compared law to a collective novel: "In this enterprise a group of novelists writes a novel seriatim; each novelist in the chain interprets the chapter he has been given in order to write a new chapter, which is then added to what the next novelist receives, and so on."[91] In civil law systems, judges interpret the law but do not generally "write new chapters." It can be argued, however, that those and all laws narrate in that they describe typical stories that are to be prevented. When a law stipulates that "[w]hoever . . . [e]nters or remains on any land of another after having been notified by the owner or occupant not to enter or remain on the premises"[92] commits trespass, a type of action is described that allows for multiple possible events to be subsumed under it. Although that legal narrative refers to the hypothetical realm and does not represent a real event, it can still be seen as narrative because law becomes a world we live in. Here every "prescription is insistent in its demand to be located in discourse to be supplied with history and destiny, beginning and end, explanation and purpose."[93]

When a lawyer or officer has internalized normative narratives, these narratives become filters through which events are seen and recognized as legally relevant. Scholars have tried to categorize the potential objects fit for legal narrative analysis. Von Arnauld lists legal texts in the broader sense: testimony before court and other offices, legal scholarship, and texts written for the education of law students law are open for narrative analysis.[94] In the light of the wide variety of legally relevant expressions—verbal or otherwise—this seems unnecessarily narrow. Much more than just verbal expressions can be (part of) a narrative. A defendant's demeanor, for instance, is seen as an indicator of credibility under U.S. law[95] and can influence the reading of a case and the creation of masterplots.

Causal Narratives

All legal concepts are (to varying degrees) storied. *Causation* as one of the fundamental elements of a crime must incorporate evaluations of foreseeability, intervening causes, or "reasonableness," all requiring narrative assessments.[96] Just as agents are tied to events through narrative in wrongful convictions, events must then causally lead to harm. Certainly, all criminal convictions employ modes of causation. Wrongful convictions show that narratives explicitly and tacitly rely on notions of causation and, as an effect, can be an instrument to establish a sense of causation when there is none. Causation is not simply a necessary element of the crime; it is the connective tissue that holds all parts of a case together and, arguably, is one of the foundational principles in criminal law:

> The whole criminal law, the way we know it, works since the beginning of our time only and exclusively on the basis of causal connections, which judges—thus everybody—at the same time have to question with all power. . . . Today, many posit the development of criminal law as a progression from "chance" [*Zufall*] to personal "attribution" [*Zurechnung*].[97]

Processes of attribution turn what might in retrospect appear as random into a plausible, causal construct. Little consideration is given to the multiple (often irrational, unpredictable) ways in which harm could have occurred. However, the creator of a legal narrative cannot leave anything to chance or accident or even consider other "absurd" ways of how things happened. A narrative must have connected elements.[98] When a prosecutor presents a case story, events are told in chronological order, which is the opposite order of how the case developed. Story elements become part of a coherently ordered master narrative to make the outcome an inevitable conclusion:

> The point . . . is to retrace how that outcome was inevitable from the "facts of the case." And if we enjoy the mental processes activated by detective fiction and legal argument, it must be in part because of the satisfaction derived from the demonstration of inevitability: it had to be this way, and no other way.[99]

The "inevitability" that Brooks describes is, at its core, a narrative's ability to create temporocausal unity through "rich patterns of causal interaction" between events and subjects, so they appear as related.[100] Narrativity—the sense of a story being told—depends on making such connections, meaning that a reduction of the causality of events reduces narrativity.[101] Even when we know that no connection or causality between events exists, as readers of symbols and narratives we "are prone to a persistent illusion of dependence between certain kinds of events. [C]ertain events seem to be connected, even when all the evidence suggests that they are not."[102] That tendency is stronger when we see a moral force (be it good or evil) behind events.[103] An example that has been used since Aristotle is that of King Mitys, who was murdered and whose murderer was then killed by a falling bronze statue of the king. Even if readers were told the events are unconnected, the narrative form creates a sense of causality that can withstand external information. The "emotional cadence" provided by the juxtaposition of the events is enough to maintain narrativity.[104] "Assigning 'meaning' to such an event generates an implicit tension between a philosophical understanding, which would dismiss the fall as an accident and therefore inessential, and a narrative account, which might posit agency behind the fall." Even if causation is not pointed out explicitly in a narrative, sequential parsing often implies it. *Post hoc ergo propter hoc* is the Latin phrase describing the fallacy that just because there is a sequence of events does not mean they are causally connected.[105]

Causal scripting is another approach to explain why juries may disregard strong exculpatory evidence, like DNA, that has the potential to reduce the level of narrativity necessary for our need of narrative cohesion. Robert Abelson's Script Concept focuses primarily on attitude formation and decision-making but can be applied to criminally relevant processes—like, for instance, the development of suspicion or causation—as well.[106] A cognitive "script" is a "coherent sequence of events expected by the individual, involving him either as a participant or an observer."[107] It is a "hypothesized cognitive structure that when activated organizes comprehension of event-based situations."[108] The events are parsed through the script, which can fill gaps when not enough information about an event is accessible. That can lead to the "false recognition of nonmentioned script events."[109]

Moreover, the sense of causality is influenced by affective responses to a narrative that can influence the extent to which we interpret the events of the story as connected by reason-based relations.[110] Dissonances and doubts make the restoration of a moral balance, a feeling of justice, harder.[111] So in a case where exculpatory DNA does not fit into a plausible and cohesive narrative, it is sometimes put aside. This does not mean that purely reason-based narratives are not thinkable; it means that there is a layer of causation that is connected to how understandable the events are and how much of a reason they provide. One could argue that law is not perceptive to basic scientific epistemologies that demand that "we test the theories against this new evidence. If the data contradict our theory, then we change the theory."[112]

A happening, like a crime, will never be experienced cognitively unbiased—there is always a script and an anticipated narrative that provide order and a causal sequence. If a specific (here: criminal) narrative is expected, noncausal accidents and coincidences are more difficult to be recognized as such because, if police look for evidence, they expect to find it.

Law and Storytelling

Because crimes are reconstructed retrospectively, case narratives rarely develop linearly. At the beginning, there are signs of caused harm (a dead body, a person being robbed, etc.) and maybe some suspicion. The direction that suspicion takes is dependent on available clues and how they are read. In that process a case story might begin to solidify into the initial mold that is filled. Here data might be omitted, dismissed, ignored, or added to gain narrative consistency and continuity. When Jeffrey Deskovic became a suspect (in a murder case discussed further below), a case was built around him—the Gatorade bottle found next to the victim was a potential weapon, the scrap of paper found with the victim was evidence of jealously. Relevance is made, not found. In court, the jury works with the stories as told by either party or (when narrative gaps open) as imagined. In the process of making relevance in criminal procedure, narratives are typically reduced into fewer larger narratives and expanded into many smaller ones. This constant expanding and reducing of narratives plays a role in how the ostensible reality of what actually happened is constructed and therefore how wrongful convictions come about. H. Porter Abbott develops a model of compression and decompression that can be applied to legal narrativization. According to Abbott, "all events, real or imagined, are infinitely decompressible."[113] This means that any event contains multiple events, each of which contains further, finer, interconnected, more complex events.

Criminally relevant events must be considered as being embedded in and being part of an infinite event structure that goes beyond that one particular gunshot or, in legal terms, the *actus reus*. To achieve status as events, it is irrelevant if they take place in the "actual world, in a world mistaken for the actual world, or in a manifestly fictional storyworld."[114] When one event is analyzed, more events (leading to this event, influencing it, etc.) come into view and provide further context. At one point, the main event becomes so complex and interconnected that the term "event" loses its utility. This is the stage of infinite complexity, wherein an event is not identifiable on the background of its determining elements. To be able to narrativize what is happening, the event structure must be compressed and its complexity reduced so that it reaches the "threshold of narratability."[115] If a narrative is further compressed, it reaches the "threshold of tellability," which "refers to the condition of material that renders it worth presenting in story form. It is what gives a story 'point.'"[116] Between the threshold of narratability and tellability, content is still too complex to cast into a story mold, but once at the point of tellability the story is worth telling for its own sake.

At the core of a legal narrative are the rather technical elements whose function it is to align the narrative expectation of the law with the events in question. Substantive and procedural criminal laws define the degree of tellability—the criminal act, the appropriate state of mind (intent, negligence, etc.). This is the narrative that the law requires jurors to be certain of beyond a reasonable doubt. Narrative elements that are "narratable" pass the filter of tellability only if they are relevant for that specific point. Although being part of the whole story, what the murder suspect had for lunch is not relevant for proving the elements of the crime. The threshold of tellability is not firm; it depends on what the agents argue is relevant for establishing the narrative of the crime—the "point." Prosecutors in their pursuit of a conviction try to model (compress) their understanding of the events according to the requirements of that law. That process requires that only the legally relevant elements are narrativized; everything else is (as required by the law) to be filtered out. That filtering process, as technical and methodological it may appear, is a process rooted in the realm of language, rhetoric, and narrative. Broader narratives of power, race, bias, status, culture, and the like come into play, each on the side of the narrator and the narratee, affecting how we tell and hear the case story. When further compressed, a narrative reaches the "threshold of causal disconnection." This threshold is passed when the procession of events is "simply one thing after another, without that sense of causal connectedness that . . . is a necessary . . . condition of narrative itself."[117] Causation (in the narrative sense, not the legal sense) is the common thread that runs through all pieces. The narratee must be able to understand why and how things happened. Motive, for example, is often used to explain behavior when, on the doctrinal level, it rarely plays a role. Narrators compress and decompress events throughout the narrative development of a case. A prosecutor presents an already compressed narrative to the jury, but when jurors fill gaps they must decompress parts of the event structure for a plausible narrative to form. Since they cannot investigate the case or question a witness, the only way to fill narrative gaps is through decompression by imagining what appears plausible. The degree to which legal systems allow for factual decompression—reopening the actual event structure—influences how truthful a system is. As I discuss in chapter 4, inquisitorial systems allow for more factually guided decompression.

The Core: Contest of Narratives

Scholarship on legal narratives still has a strong focus on the courtroom discourse.[118] Although plea bargaining is the far more common practice to resolve criminal conflicts, adversarialness as a concept is still the foundational principle through which criminal justice is thought to be achieved. That alone is striking, since "neither scientists, engineers, historians, nor scholars from any other discipline use bi-polar adversary trials to determine facts."[119] The criminal justice system works under the presumption that "adversarial testing will ultimately advance the public interest in truth and fairness."[120] Jurors, not trained in the law, "bring to a case their common sense and community values; their 'very inexperience is an asset because it secures a fresh perception of each trial, avoiding the stereotypes said to infect the judicial eye.'"[121] The fact-finding prerogative of the jury is the main reason that new facts that arise after a verdict cannot be added easily to a case narrative. Actual innocence or truth in general do not enjoy constitutional protection (as in other systems)[122] and therefore cannot be the basis for such a claim.

The American trial is commonly described as a "regulated storytelling contest between champions of competing, interpretive stories that are composed under significant restraints"[123] in front of an ostensibly impartial and passive fact finder. Courts hold that "[t]ruth is best discovered by powerful statements on both sides of a question."[124] The story element in court is strong, and curtailing it "would be both unworkable and a form of incremental inquisitorialism."[125] Narratives are rendered by continually "switching back and forth from one narrative version of events to the other as the opposing sides seek either to support their own narrative or to undermine their opponents' narrative."[126]

Both parties of that contest have the opportunity to present their points in their opening and closing statements, during direct examination of their own witnesses, and through cross-examination of witnesses called by the opposition. "This openness [to multiple and competing stories] is not accidental but structural . . . for at the hearing two stories are told in competition with one another, and a choice between them—or of a third—is forced upon the decider."[127]

Partisan advocacy on both sides of a case is thought to best promote the "ultimate objective that the guilty be convicted and the innocent go free."[128] But placing elements presented by the adversaries into a story format is a complex process because "a plurality of narrative discourses" are at work at the same time[129] and the adversaries often create their narratives as way to pursue their own narrative strategies with little supervision.[130] That gives attorneys considerable narrative latitude to tell stories that resonate with quotidian, easily recognizable "cognitive routines" that exist in all members of society.[131]

Such judgments need not pass any kind of scientific test; plausibility is all they require. In the trial against Richard Danziger, the investigating officer explained to the jury:

> It's a known fact that suspects return to the scene of the crime to evaluate, or for whatever reason, to figure out if in fact they did leave any clues or evidence for the cops to identify them. I just felt that. I went on my

own gut feeling, I guess. I set up a meeting with [the] employees [of the Pizza Hut] and told them to just be kind of on the lookout for anything unusual that might not mean anything to them but it would mean something to me.[132]

Here, the officer begins with the trope of the criminal returning to the scene of the crime.[133] While there was little to no evidence supporting that claim, at least not when put so generally, the officer relied on the jury recognizing this archetypical schema that would explain why Ochoa and Danziger took the risk to return to the restaurant. Not explaining how both became suspects might have created a narrative gap that might result in doubt.[134] The question of why and how someone becomes a suspect is, surprisingly, rarely addressed in court.

The jury was not informed about whether or not it is true that suspects generally return to the scene of the crime (there is little to no evidence supporting that claim, at least not when put so generally), although this piece was a crucial part of the prosecutor's narrative of the story. Neither did they explain what they meant when they asked the staff to be on the lookout for something "unusual." This is an invitation to conjecture because what is "unusual" depends on the scripts we operate under. A restaurant employee, detective, doctor, sociologist, and so on decode reality differently. The defense could have countered that point but didn't, meaning that the point of how initial suspicion arose remained uncontested. The detective somehow anticipated something would happen. And his prophecy fulfilled itself. The act of "toasting" in memory became dramatized, given relevance so that jurors could signify "about crime through the medium of the trial."[135] Had an ethnographer or anthropologist witnessed that scene in the restaurant, would they have found it "unusual"? The moment when staff parsed Ochoa and Danziger's behavior as "unusual"—when they framed their act of noticing as a narrative of being struck by something out of the ordinary—was the beginning of a miscarriage of justice.

It almost seems as if the prosecutor was aware of Paul Ricoeur's concept of the plot. To present a story is to understand the successive actions and to create expectations concerning the outcome—the "conclusion"—of the story as the pole of attraction.

Looking back from the conclusion towards the episodes which led up to it, we must be able to say that this end required those events and that chain of action. But this retrospective glance is made possible by the te-leologically guided movement of our expectations when we follow the story. Such is the paradox of the contingency, "acceptable after all," which characterizes the understanding of any story.[136]

By presenting a complete narrative during opening arguments, a conclusion is offered to the jury, so all the prosecutor needs to achieve is the acceptability of the proposed series of events leading to that conclusion. The case still must be proven and withstand the defense's arguments; however, a complete narrative is a strong and persuasive road map the legally and epistemologically untrained juror might follow. In Danziger's case, like in many wrongful conviction cases, the defense had little off which to base an alternative narrative. While the contest of narratives metaphor is problematic in the most balanced cases, it proves to be inapplicable in cases of the wrongfully convicted.

Beyond the ideal type of a contest of narratives in court, there are many other kinds of narrative spheres overlapping with and surrounding the core narrative. Here, for instance, there is a narrative about race and gender that goes unremarked but nonetheless frames the events. In this case, a young blonde white woman became the victim of two men, one of them of color. Studies suggest that jurors punish offenders that violate female victims more harshly (the so-called female victim effect). Court narratives exemplify how law forms relations of subordination, which are represented in fields like critical race studies and storytelling, feminist jurisprudence, queer theory, and intersectional legal analysis.[137] As much as race and gender affect the justice system, they are rarely part of the official legal narrative and are often kept outside but shape how defendants and victims are perceived, adding another layer that overlaps with the core narrative.

Wrongful Conviction Narratives

Stated very simply: a verdict that puts an innocent person in prison or on death row is based on a narrative that does not accurately represent the events in question. It is a narrative that suffers from a reconstruction error. Given the dual—factual and legal—nature and function of legal narratives, the narrative can be factually false and legally true at the same time. A conviction is factually wrong when there is no factual guilt but is nevertheless legally true when a jury decides so. In general, wrongful convictions typically fall into one of two categories. First, there are cases in which no crime was committed (for instance, an accident is reconstructed as a crime).[138] Second, the identity of the offender is mistaken, yet a narrative is constructed that incriminates an innocent person. Less often discussed are situations in which the specific event is not disputed but circumstances affect the act of being a crime: affirmative defenses like self-defense fall into this category, as do cases that require (or do not require) a certain state of mind that might be misrepresented (e.g., consent in a case tried as a sexual assault). Such cases are not within the purview of innocence projects' work because of the difficulties proving a state of mind or specific circumstances when it is undisputed that the defendant engaged in the action. False narratives can become the basis for a false conviction in two ways: through an erroneous historical reconstruction, or a coerced false confession. Both types, often sharing similar elements, raise questions as to the narrative reliability of the criminal justice system; both will be addressed in the next sections.

The Imagination of Historical and Legal Reality

That a conviction was false is only known in retrospect—that is to say, after a new, more convincing narrative has falsified or put into serious doubt the elements that were the basis of the initial narrative.[139] Narratives in wrongful convictions (and the wrongful conviction narrative as the narrative of an exoneration) are never mono-dimensional. They represent possible versions of events at various points in time. From a decompressed point of view, both the initial and the retrospective narratives can exist simultaneously in different spheres, and each is just another possible representation of the signs read by the narrators at certain points in time. Evaluations and analyses of narratives must be conscious of what the determining factors and facts of the original and the retrospective narrative are, that each one reduces complexity through edits and omissions so that a specific point can be made—motivated by the narrative agenda. When one stands at the point of the outcome (i.e., the DNA test excludes the client as the perpetrator), hindsight bias makes it easier to retrospectively "plot forward" what now appears a "predictable outcome."[140]

Whether a narrative is true in the factual sense is difficult to tell by looking at the narrative (the text or oral testimony) itself. H. Porter Abbott varies John Searle's oft-quoted remark and argues that "there is no textual property, syntactic or semantic, that will identify a work of nonfiction."[141] What might sound like a true historical account can be fiction after all. This is because a "historian's 'empirical' account and the novelist's imaginative story share the narrative form."[142] Elements of a narrative do not reveal themselves on formal grounds as fictitious to the reader or listener;[143] they are always constructed. That being said, how does the legal discourse as it pertains to the narrative reconstruction of a case differ from other discourses? The main difference might be that scientific procedures can be falsified; narrative constructions, however, can achieve only verisimilitude—the *appearance* of being true.[144]

Just as in traditional history, lawyers act under the pretense that events tell themselves.[145] The legal narrative allegedly develops from the evidence. But that obscures the fact that historical narratives are always a construction. Imagine what the officers found when they arrived at the Pizza Hut where Nancy DePriest was murdered: there lies a dead body among disarray. The kitchen sinks are clogged with towels, the floor is flooded, no weapon can be found, and there is little evidence that would offer a direct and immediate representation of what happened. What the police see are mere signposts of the results of a chain of events that has its beginning somewhere in the past. These signposts must now be merged into a narrative that holds them together and gives them relevance first by the police, then by the prosecutor, and ultimately by the trier of fact. In a criminal case that reconstruction must identify actors and events and, like the historian, must "demonstrate, according to specific rules, that x did y, where x can designate the main actor . . . and y designates any sort of action."[146] Just like the police officer or prosecutor, historians "are concerned with events which can be assigned to specific time-space locations, events which are (or were) in principle observable or perceivable."[147] What distinguishes the historical narrative from the legal narrative is how meaning emerges. In a legal narrative it emerges synchronously and in concert with the gathering of facts.

Hayden White's concept of the *historical emplotment* is helpful to explain how meaning develops, how evidence must be first placed in a temporal order—a "chronicle"[148]—and is then organized into a story, a "process of happening."[149] Through this process, "[t]he historian arranges the events in the chronicle into a hierarchy of significance by assigning events different functions as story elements in such a way as to disclose the formal coherence of a whole set of events considered as a comprehensible process with a discernible beginning, middle and end."[150] Although the story in this sense already includes aspects of significance, it does not explain how and why things happened and what the meaning of the events is. According to White, this takes place in the next step where, through emplotment, stories are compared to archetypical or stereotypical stories such as "romance" or "tragedy."[151] Events are imbued with meaning and transformed into an intelligible whole.[152] The conceptualization of a case history is not linear in the sense that each step neatly and seamlessly follows the other after its completion. Facts might still be gathered while the first version of a story is already emplotted, and this narrative might be changed and revised because of new facts or new ideas about the case. Historical narratives (including those portrayed in court) are read "with the expectation that each thing mentioned is going to be important: which is an attitude conceptually ruled out when we believe ourselves to be reading a chronicle."[153] Here we already see how much a reader's mindset and narrative expectation matters. Unlike historians, police are not trained to reflect on why they found a specific piece of evidence; historians do so often when they distinguish among events, their mention in a chronicle, and their historical explanation.[154]

Advocates try to emplot their stories into simplified, easily recognizable types to communicate efficiently in court.[155] Since every trial and case is different, there is not a single archetype that matches all possible scenarios (not every case is a tragedy or a narrative of greed, violence, or hate), so it is one of the main tasks to identify a theme that is recognizable and resonates with jurors. As mentioned earlier, the American Prosecutors Research Institute suggests prosecutors find recognizable themes that resonate with the average person (juror):

One of the most important strategy decisions you make is selecting a proper theme. The theme is the general storyline of your case. Choose a theme that resonates with the average person. Whenever possible, choose a theme that motivates your jury to convict. Create a catch phrase that captures your theme that you can use throughout the trial. Advertisements, quotation dictionaries, slogans and proverbs can be helpful. You should be able to present your theme in a few short words or phrases. An easy way to start developing a theme is to say "This is a case about . . ." and finish that phrase.[156]

In narrative terms, such themes can be compared to narrative archetypes, schema, or masterplots, which are recurrent skeletal stories that belong to a culture. Masterplots can exert an influence on how we take in new information, causing us to read narratives unconsciously in a specific way.[157] This, of course, has little to do with encouraging jurors to look for truth. Richard Danziger's trial transcripts note what has already been a theme in Ochoa's confession: Danziger wanted to have "a little fun" with the victim.[158] Especially during closing arguments, "having a little fun" is just one line in the transcript away from the description that "the robbery turned into rape, to a brutal, quick, fast series of events that eventually led to the death of Nancy DePriest."[159] This portrays the defendant as a specific type or character and at the same time develops a theme—this is a case about someone who thinks rape and murder are fun.[160]

This again shows a difference to the ideal historical discourse. "Historians may be minimally characterized as seeking to make, and successful when they establish as true, statements about the past; and historical knowledge, on this minimal view, is had when one knows that s, and s is about the past."[161] A successful historian is one who establishes true statements about the past. Being successful as a prosecutor, police officer, or even a defense attorney only partly depends on making true statements about the past. Justice in the formal sense can exist without historical truth (assuming that finding the truth about past events is possible at all.)

White's process of emplotment does not claim reliability: if two historians were given the same historical fact pattern, they might not emplot it in a similar way.[162] In the legal discourse, however, it matters whether one jury would see reason to impose the death penalty and another would not. Narrative accounts do not consist of factual statements (White defines them as "singular existential propositions") alone; they also consist of poetic and rhetorical elements "by which what would otherwise be a list of facts is transformed into a story."[163] That is true for criminal cases as well, which are "little more than highly stylized dramatizations of reality."[164] "Dramatization" means that each side in a case "misses or chooses to ignore some potentially important aspect of the incident in question."[165] This is a potentially perilous process, as James Boyd White notes, because a historian (or officer, or prosecutor, etc.) "will fit the story to his theory" in that the "narrative will become a sort of self-justifying example, a rigged proof."[166]

The reason an event happened is typically distinct from the reason an event is mentioned in a narrative.[167] The motivation for Chris Ochoa and Richard Danziger toasting to the victim's memory is different from what it signified later in the criminal case. What makes an event relevant for a narrative are specific cultural expectations by those who read them.[168] At this point, the historical and the criminal discourse depart conceptually. Although all criminal cases are different, a prosecution case "must employ the same underlying story strategy in every trial,"[169] and this strategy "must attempt to represent the defendant's action within a coherent set of scenes, agencies, and purposes as the action develops over time."[170] The stereotypical or archetypical representation of a case helps to redefine facts and makes it easier for the legal fact finder (i.e., the jury) to create connections that are "satisfying, familiar, or pleasing—connections that maybe stronger than the facts, norms, or logic of the matter would suggest."[171] In other words, prosecutors need to tell a specific story convincingly. They do not engage in a form of historical discourse[172] that allows for different story-meanings. Prosecutors do not go to court to test a narrative; they go to court to win their cases.[173]

Crime is not only a legal but also a cultural phenomenon; thus lawyers are (trained to be) aware of cultural and doctrinal factors that drive a case narrative. A historian is aware of the "cognitive asymmetries which go with narrative structures, namely that the narrator has to know things his characters . . . do not know: he knows how things came out."[174] But the law and those who execute it work with normative and factual assumptions about what a character must have known, could not have known, should have done, or should not have done, and those assumptions require a form of retrospective narrative imagination.[175] To put it differently: the historian is very aware of how meaning is created and that they need to distinguish between aspects the historian knows but the character did not.[176] Criminal cases must be solved, and detectives in their pursuit of an acceptable narrative look for clues that at the same time develop and confirm their stories. Historians do the same, but they can admit to gray areas without jeopardizing the persuasiveness of their narrative. A criminal case needs resolving: Charges are either filed or dropped; a defendant is either convicted or acquitted. There is no middle ground. At least theoretically, a historian could say "*non liquet*"—there is not enough data to conclude one way or another—whether the evil duke was poisoned or died of natural causes. It might even be this gray zone of uncertainty that attracts historical, scholarly analysis. Law does not allow for much ambiguity because it must come to specifically prescribed results. Law is concerned with finality and legal certainty and, at least in the context of wrongful convictions, much less with the truth.

The Fictions of Factual Representations: Narrative Imagination

The roots of most wrongful convictions can be found in stages of the proceedings leading up to a trial or plea agreement. During that time, detectives and prosecutors develop an image of the crime through a process that is largely driven by imagination, inspiration, and intuition. "Investigation" is described as "an art and not a science. . . . The element of intuition or felicity of inspiration in the choice of methods has its effect on the outcome despite the most methodical and exhausting treatment of a case."[177] Reconstructing a potential crime requires reading situations, interactions, and "things" (which may become evidence), much of which is a nonrational process. Officers found "signs" of Danziger and Ochoa's guilt in their behavior, which, like all human behavior, cannot be traced to one single cause. But random behavior can through imagination become part of a crime narrative. Jeffrey Deskovic went to a murder victim's wake and appeared disturbed;

James Richardson rescued a three-year-old girl from a burning house in which police later found the mother of the child murdered. He was a suspect because he was at the scene. Suspicion can arise even from comments. For instance, during recross examination of one of the investigating officers by the defense, the detective pointed out that it is unusual for a person to present an alibi when they are not under suspicion:

> Q: Sergeant Boardman, if I knew that I were suspect in a homicide investigation, and you had approached me in the course of that investigation, and I felt that I had an alibi, would you find it surprising that I told you I have an alibi?
>
> A: I think that's an unusual reaction to have if you haven't done anything wrong.
>
> Q: You mean to tell me that if I'm accused of crime, and I know for a fact I was in Omaha, Nebraska[,] when that crime was committed, and you come to me as police officer investigating that crime, that you had find [sic!] it unusual for me to say to you "Hey, I was in Omaha."
>
> A: First off he wasn't accused of a crime, and second, the words "She's my alibi" are significant to me in that that's an unusual reaction. That's not a word that you would use. You might later in conversation say, "well, I remember I was in Nebraska that day," or "I remember I was with so and so that day."
>
> A: Do you think it's fair inference that if a person tells you that they have an alibi that they feel that they're a suspect?
>
> Q: I think that it's a fair inference to say that there is something there that they feel guilty about that they need to immediately tell you that they have an alibi before any questions are ever asked.

There could be many explanations for Danziger to bring up his alibi when being approached by the police—anxiety, the need to clear his name right away, potential involvement in the crime, and many more. What is an "unusual" statement is very subjective and context specific. Police were looking for leads in the case, and that alone can lead to cognitive bias.

Earlier in the trial, one of the officers was asked about Ochoa's first interview:

Q: And what physical reactions did you observe from him (Ochoa) that day?

A: As I began talking to him and addressing the murder, Mr. Ochoa began shaking and then he began a small rash, started on the left side of his neck and it increased and covered the entire left side of his face. He was gasping for breath. And he showed extreme anxiety. He had sweaty palms and he was very, very shook up.

Here, potential guilt seems to manifest through Ochoa's body by turning his skin red and taking away his breath. This description evokes images of the medieval ordeal where through divine intervention guilt or innocence were made physically observable. At the time of Danziger's trial, the jury had heard Ochoa's confession, so this statement might be read as if there had been actual signs the officers noticed and followed up on without addressing other potential explanations for such a physical reaction. Just mentioning it in court adds to the already established suspicion narrative. And it also adds to the "police-generated mythology of the interrogator as a human lie detector."[178] Factual guilt or innocence do not manifest themselves in a way that they could be diagnosed externally. Innocent people were misclassified as suspects for showing too much and too little emotion, for having physical responses when being confronted by the police, or for simply acting in a way someone considers "unusual."[179] Officers adjust their scope of normality so it fits their narrative expectations, not realizing that normality is a context-specific and fluid concept. Details like a rash, a toast to the memory of a victim, or simply observing that someone does not "look right"[180] might draw the attention of law enforcement (or, when retold, a juror), but absent further "specific reasonable inference[s]"[181] they cannot establish legitimate suspicion in a criminal investigation. Most investigative work requires making such inferences—inferences that remain invisible to a juror's eye. Here the transcript shows the many micro-narratives that in the end add to the larger narrative each side is developing and are integrated into the "historical explanation."[182]

Referential narratives, like historical or legal, are subject to judgments of truth and falsehood,[183] their producers affirm that the events did occur with a certain degree of probability, while fictitious texts are immune to that.[184] This is why the historical discourse "came to be set over against fiction, and especially the novel, as the representation of the 'actual' to the representation of the 'possible' or only 'imaginable.'"[185] But the "dream of a historical discourse that would consist of nothing but factually accurate statements about a realm of events"[186] is unreal, especially in the legal domain because what sets the prosecutor apart from the scientist or historian is that they can present their cases *as if* there is no other alternative, at least not a likely one.[187] While legal narratives are concerned with a (re)construction of a true image of historical reality, law allows a presentation based on presumptions, meaning that it presents its narratives *as if* they represented reality and assumes that what underlies a verdict is *as if* it had happened, whereas literary fiction does not make the same claim[188] because it differs in the kind of meaning it creates.[189]

The way meaning is created in a criminal case is often considered to be driven by data like fingerprints, biological evidence, camera footage, store receipts, and testimony. Verdicts are supposed to be based on "facts," so that juries, just like in Danziger's case, can "render a true verdict on the facts and the evidence."[190] Facts, however, only signify within the context created by the narrator. A blood stain on a knife can mean many things and must be imagined as being part of a crime narrative before it becomes evidence and makes a case "real."[191] Facts only become evidence when they are turned into signposts of a crime story. As such, they are part of a process that resembles fiction writing, or a "fiction-making operation."[192] Facts then "exist only as a congeries of contiguously related fragments. These fragments must be put together to make a whole of a particular, not a general, kind."[193] It would go too far to conclude that legal reality is foremost a radically constructed entity. It is not, but it is not a typical factual representation either. Police, prosecutors, jurors all "imagine" and fictionalize, and wrongful conviction narratives show that the process of imagination is not bound by the truth. The process of "fusing events, whether imaginary or real, into a comprehensible totality capable of serving as the object of a representation is a poetic process. . . . [T]he techniques or strategies that they use in the composition of their discourses can be shown to be substantially the same, however different they may appear on a purely surface, or dictional, level of their texts." In that sense, "verbal artifacts histories and novels are indistinguishable from one another."[194] The trust that facts can be determined by expunging "every hint of the fictive" misses that the legal, historical, and literary discourse provide images of a "reality."[195] This is the point when legal and literary parts overlap and when elements of the case might be, as Dershowitz calls it, "dramatized," which means that (in retrospect) these elements didn't bear any relevance (like Ochoa and Danziger's toasts) or vice versa: "[F]act finders employ the canons of literature and interpretation in the search for truth, generally without any conscious awareness that they are doing so."[196]

Klein and Martinez argue that the reader of a factual narrative expects the presentation of a real (*wirklich*) event and not one that is possible (*möglich*).[197] This dichotomy might oversimplify the reality of most factual discourses. Within the adversarial system, prosecutor and defense are expected to present something real, even though they often do not know all the pieces of a case. And neither do they need to present a convincing story. Beyond the role of expectations, the aspect that sets apart the legal narrative from the historical narrative is its purpose. While the "prosecutor should not make a statement of fact or law, or offer evidence, that the prosecutor does not reasonably believe to be true, to a court, lawyer, witness, or third party,"[198] there are no neutral narratives in law, at least not in the pretrial or trial stage. These narratives accuse and charge, or question and excuse, much more than other factual narratives.[199] Ideally, history is "set over against fiction, and especially the novel, as the representation of the 'actual' to the representation of the 'possible' or only 'imaginable.'"[200] That, of course, as White notes, is a dream, but at least that discourse has an awareness of distinction between the realm of events and the realm of meaning and significance. By contrast, in law what is an imagined event can be turned into legal reality. The image of reality constructed by the novelist is no less real than that referred to by the historian or the lawyer.[201]

Impossible Contestations and Authorship

In this final section, I return to the myth of the narrative contest to focus on situations when no contest is possible. Trials before an impartial fact finder are the exception in a criminal justice system that relies heavily on plea bargains and the confessions that make them possible. In those confessions, two kinds of authorship can be distinguished: the confessor, and those who make them confess.[202] When judges accept plea bargains and their underlying confessions without much scrutiny, we can see that law has a mono-dimensional understanding of authorship (the one who signs is the one who speaks), when in fact there are multiple authors talking. Literary scholarship has long been critical of such a mono-dimensional perspective, most notably the work of Roland Barthes, who argues that

> [w]e know that a text does not consist of a line of words, releasing a single . . . meaning . . . , but is a space of many dimensions, in which are wedded and contested various kinds of writing, no one of which is original: the text is a tissue of quotations, resulting from the thousand sources of culture.[203]

Confessions (and other legal texts) can be read as the product of multiple authors. In an opening statement, for instance, the prosecutor uttering the text can be seen as the "scriptor"—just like the officer or prosecutor who writes down a confession—while the utterance itself is the product of many voices.

Christopher Ochoa's confession[204] to the rape and murder of Nancy DePriest spans over five densely typed pages. It is very detailed, including precise descriptions of the purported events and how he and Richard Danziger committed them. The document is typed on a form made for statements given to the police. It includes preprinted sections with fill-in-the-blank spaces for the case file number, name and age of the interviewee, name and rank of the officer, and place and time of the interrogation. Except for the printed sections, the typewritten part is in all capital letters. The actual statement is prefaced by Ochoa remarking that this is his second statement to the detective because he "didn't give a complete and truthful statement" to the officer before. In the following text, which does not have a single paragraph break, Ochoa recounts the crime. His account includes indirect speech ("[H]e asked me to take him to his girlfriend's residence"), direct speech ("Richard then stated to me 'I'm running a little low on cash and I'm thinking about ripping off one of the Pizza Huts'"), but no free indirect discourse, the technique of presenting a character's voice partly mediated by the voice of an author. Direct speech, as used here, makes the crime appear more real and personal. It makes a difference if someone says "he then said he would kill her" or "I will kill her." Ochoa's confession is a narrative construct—put together by the officers—but it appears as intradiegetic narration—assembled by Ochoa himself.

The statement includes many details suggesting that Ochoa saw and noted things that only the actual perpetrator could see.[205] He also described the elaborate plan for the robbery, where the two men entered the Pizza Hut, what the victim said when she saw the two men, in which direction her head fell, and where the blood splattered after she had been shot. The testimony included the brands of clothes both men were wearing and where on these clothes blood from the victim was located after the crime. The judge who formally endorsed Ochoa's plea bargain described the testimony as "very compelling."[206] Not only was it emotional; it also contained details police said only a witness to the crime could have known. It would have been difficult for the judge to spot an incorrect element.[207] Given the uncontested facts, the judge had little reason to verify whether it was possible to access the restaurant through the backdoor without a key—which Ochoa claimed they did.[208] Moreover, since the initial plan was to just rob the store, why did the events escalate, leading to Danziger and Ochoa raping and murdering DePriest? The confession did not explain that. Once Ochoa and Danziger had the money, and without any transition, the document continues: "Richard then started to look at Nancy, and he looked at me and stated, 'Let's have some fun. . . .' Richard then told Nancy 'I'm going to have some fun with you.'" Nothing in the confession suggests the two were planning or even considering rape, but the next sentence after Danziger's statement is that Ochoa "grabbed Nancy from behind by grabbing her shoulders." Ochoa wrote that he was "reluctant, but Richard was persistent, and I finally agreed to join him and go in with him on the robbery." Without any explanation or even verbal remark, Ochoa now becomes complicit in the rape. In Ochoa's confession document, only after Danziger had already raped DePriest did Ochoa tell him that he wouldn't rape Nancy but did it regardless. Afterward he asked Danziger "Are you satisfied?," making it appear as if Ochoa committed the rape to comply with Danziger—who at no point threatened or forced Ochoa.

Ochoa later explained that his confession, including Danziger's implication in the crime, was the result of police pressure and fear of the death penalty, citing periods of time when officers harassed him and threatened him with the consequences of not confessing.[209] Part of the agreement was that he testified against Danziger. Danziger was incriminated through Ochoa's confession. When he was tried and confronted with Ochoa's statements, Danziger tried to explain the reason why Ochoa incriminated him:

> Q: Richard, how did you feel when you were sitting over here listening to Chris Ochoa sit up in that witness stand and accuse you of this crime?
> A: I was pretty pissed off
> Q: Why?
> A: Because you sit here for 15 months for something you didn't do, you get pretty pissed off, too. I couldn't do nothing couldn't jump up and do nothing. I couldn't do anything. I couldn't do anything.
> Q: This is your opportunity to tell the jury your side of the story.
> A: That's what I'm doing.
> Q: Richard, did you sexually assault ND at the Pizza Hut?
> A: No, I didn't.
> Q: Were you present when Chris Ochoa sexually assaulted ND?
> A: No, I wasn't.
> Q: Were you present when Chris Ochoa murdered ND?
> A: No, I wasn't. I was sleeping. . . .
> Q: Why would Chris Ochoa tell these lies? . . .
> A: To get out of capital murder, to get out of anything, because of the fact I went there with him to drink beer.
> Q: You think you're just being framed?
> A: By him, yes.
> Q: And the cops have joined in?
> A: Yes. I didn't say those statements that they stated, no, I didn't.
> Q: And all these people that said they didn't tell you about the caliber of the weapon—
> A: Everybody knew about the crime scene.

In retrospect, these statements are of striking clarity—and they are also factually true. Ochoa's confession, however, was a construction that developed a powerful narrative momentum that trumped Danziger's testimony, turning truth into its opposite.[210] An innocent defendant can rarely contest an incriminating narrative—there simply is no counternarrative, no shadow story except for denying involvement in the crime and explaining where they were (if they remember, that is). Even when multiple witnesses or evidence like DNA exclude a defendant as the potential perpetrator, a prosecutor's narrative can still be powerful enough to sway a jury.[211] Testifying alone comes with great risks. First, defendants face the delicate task of conveying innocence and compassion for the victim at the same time.[212] If they have a criminal record, it might be introduced, and jurors could "type" the defendant negatively. If an innocent defendant testifies in court, they can often only deny their involvement in the crime, which might trigger further negative responses. In Danziger's case, the prosecutor brings up the theme of the "conspiracy theory" (a conspiracy between Ochoa and the police), which must sound odd and implausible to the jury. Immediately after Danziger mentions that many people knew about the crime, the prosecutor asks him: "Why did you misrepresent to the jury how hard you've been working?" and then asks him if he ever thought about raping a woman. A minute later, the prosecutor again tries to put Danziger at the scene of the crime:

> Q: It worried you when they took your shoes didn't it?
> A: It didn't worry me. I was wondering why they took my shoes, yeah.
> Q: Weren't you afraid you might have left a little spot of blood on them?
> A: No, I wasn't afraid of a single thing because I wasn't there, that's why.
> Q: You're pretty sure you hadn't left sample of your semen.
> A: I wasn't there to leave a sample that's why.

Given the dynamics of an interrogation in a courtroom before a jury untrained in law and litigation techniques, Danziger faced the difficult task of challenging the veracity of an already established story. It is difficult if not impossible to distinguish the narrative that is in line with the facts from the one that is made up. The prosecutor appears convinced that Danziger is complicit in the murder, and the trial is not the place where the state would change its story. Legal reality can be created through narrative, and such a narrative does not reveal itself as being true to reality or not. Ochoa and Danziger spent 13 and 12 years respectively in prison because the narrative developed a momentum as powerful as physical evidence.

While the first-person narration, the use of direct speech, and Ochoa's signature make Ochoa appear to be the actual author of the confession, the text itself does not carry signs that would prove this one way or another. Although no one would expect that the confessor would type up the confession, readers just trust that these are his words, his thoughts, his way of expressing his guilt.

A legal narrative is, in this regard, a tissue of multiple citations from all stages of the process. But even beyond the actual textual narrativization, a legal narrative includes elements of individual and departmental cultures, of biases, beliefs, and opinions. Take, for instance, witness testimony in court. Witnesses provide evidence that is supposed to shed light on the events in question. But witnesses, whether called by the state or by the defense, serve a certain role, and in the United States they rarely enter the courtroom unprepared. To establish the timeline in Nancy DePriest's murder, a witness who delivered produce to the Pizza Hut was asked about how long it took him to drive to the Pizza Hut.

> A: Yes, ma'am. It should have taken approximately 20 minutes.
> Q: Now, are you a time-conscious person?
> A: Yes, ma'am.
> Q: Do you wear a watch?
> A: Yes, I do.
> Q: Is there any little trick you play on yourself with your watch to make sure [you're on] time?
> A: I run it about five minutes fast continually.
> Q: And you're aware of that and you know that.
> A: Yes, ma'am.

Without already knowing that the witness adjusted his watch, the question about the "little trick" would have come as a surprise. It is no surprise that prosecutors and police speak with witnesses to ensure they support their narratives, but that means that witnesses do not speak—author—freely. But doesn't the evidential value of an assertion that a witness makes rest on the fact "that it cannot be desired by the witness to be either defending or incriminating the person charged, because the witness does not comprehend the context that is to be clarified"?[213] Gadamer argues that a "pure" assertion corresponds with a witness who "has to answer questions without knowing why one is asked them."[214] Adversarial trials are not an ideal place for pure testimony. Most of it is offered in the service and under the guidance of one side or the other, so its reliability must be doubted.

In a similar vein, a confession like Ochoa's can be considered a monolithic utterance. That is, the multiple narratives that have informed and influenced the narrative are now an integral, indiscernible part of it. Ochoa had little if any influence on how the text was composed. He was intimidated and deceived and therefore did not provide his statements freely. In an interview conducted by the University of Wisconsin Law School, Ochoa described how his statement was pieced together:[215]

Q: How else did you know about what had happened at the crime scene?

A: He would ask me "Did this happen, did that happen, was it this color of a certain item, wasn't this here, that's how he. . . ."

Q: OK, so that's how that statement was taken.

A: Yeah, he was just giving me leading questions like this.

Q: And what would happen if you said the incorrect thing?

A: Well, you know . . . [on] Monday they took two statements, one on tape, he wanted me to be an accomplice, and he went through it all and then once he was satisfied, then I just repeated what had done on tape. Then he wasn't satisfied with that, then he wanted me to [garbled] and when he started talking that [way] that's how he would ask me if I wasn't answering the way I was supposed to, he would stop the tape and start it and then there was a lot of stopping 'cause I was stuttering a lot and it started and stop and started and stopped. At that point, one of the officers got very frustrated, he threw the chair at me, he threw it at my head and it hit the wall, just missed my head, and this guy's a pretty big guy, I mean these guys are big, I was really small at the time. He caught it right before it fell to my head and that's when Hector Blanco said "Well, here let's just type it and we'll help you out." And that's exactly how, and he typed it and I have never to this day read the statements. I signed it, he brought witnesses to sign it, and I was terrified, when he threw the chair, I thought these guys were gonna hurt me bad. But this was terrifying for me, he was giving me a choice, death or . . .

Q: So basically at this point, had you implicated Richard?

A: Yeah, he made sure I implicated Richard.

Q: What did you tell him that Richard had done?

A: He wanted me . . . He asked "Did Richard pull the trigger," Richard did this, and he would type it. Richard told you he did this and he did that, whatever, and at this point I just wanted to get it over with. He kept on saying "We'll give you, you'll do your time and go home 'cause if you don't, you're gonna get the death penalty, you'll die for something you didn't do. Do you want to die for something you didn't do? I don't want you to die for something you didn't do," stuff like that.

Once written up and introduced in court, a statement is seen as authored by one individual. In literary studies it is common to explore the background voices, texts, contexts, and histories that inform and inflect an author's words so that the concept of the single-person, one-name authorship has been questioned. But law treats the document bearing Ochoa's signature as if it stems from Ochoa and no one else when in fact it must be clear that—using Genette's terms—the recipient (the factual receiver of the words spoken or written) and the addressee (the narrator's image of the one to whom the message is sent) are different. Ochoa's confession does have an addressee and appears to be a sober, factual report of the crime. But no interaction in an interrogation room is ever free. Police are not mere recipients of the suspect's words—they channel them with future recipients (prosecutors, judges, etc.) in mind.

Authorship and questions of textual origin are rarely, if at all, scrutinized in court.[216] Returning to Brooks: "Appellate courts are to some degree the enforcers of rule-governed storytelling. Yet they don't talk narrative talk. They are conspicuously lacking in the analytic vocabulary and tools of literary 'narratology,' for instance."[217] The trial is paramount in constructing the case narrative,[218] after which law finds only some specific narratives to be problematic, mainly those that involve a violation of the Constitution that negatively influenced the trial. The "law's recognition of its repressed narrative content and form generally comes in a *negative* manner, as denial. The bar of repression keeps the narrativity of the law under erasure."[219] This means that, unless parts of a narrative appear constitutionally problematic, there is no review. One can go even further and argue that law does not care much about narratives (jurors do) because law regulates only how and if individual facts make it into court but leaves the ultimate construction of the narrative to the participants. In an investigation, statements of witnesses or suspects are often transcribed through free, indirect discourse or narrated monologue as a way to disperse or avoid responsibility.[220]

Criminal justice systems assign different authorial roles to the participants in the legal discourse. Systems differ in how they determine who can speak, who must listen, who can ask questions, who must answer, or whose voice is heard and whose isn't. The more a narrative is co-authored by the suspect or the victim, the more each one can contribute to the discourse without having to fear penalties and the less they are reduced to a mere object of the proceedings. In Germany, for example, a suspect on the stand or during an interrogation cannot commit perjury; even a lie would not be penalized. English courts, conceptually closer to the American system than other European systems, do not tolerate trickery and deceit to the same extent than their American counterparts.[221] Legal cultures vary in how much they allow the suspect to add to "the tissue of citations" and the subject of the text itself. Given the overall narrative power vested in law enforcement and state authorities in general, a suspect's status as a subject capable of creating their own narratives is reduced. Authorship is more than simply being able to add facts to the narrative: it includes a degree of agency and autonomy. This autonomy is diminished when suspects are instrumentalized against themselves. As Christopher Ochoa's confession shows, he was objectified to the extent that the sentences he later signed were not his. He may have spoken the words, but he did not author them.

3

The Evidentiary Power of Stories

Narrativizing Guilt in an Adversarial System

And as he thought, he also decided he would write a note as
if his wife was still alive. So, he wrote a note, pretending she
was still alive, and left that in the bathroom.[1]
—*State of Texas v. Michael Morton*

The construction of a legal narrative is a multitiered and multifaceted
process. It goes through various phases—investigation, indictment,
trial, appeal, post-conviction—each time guided by a different narrative agenda and focus and with a different audience in mind. Especially
at the beginning of a case, meaning must be created; certain phenomena are read—processed—before being turned into a narrative that
has a certain meaning ("what happened"), and then it must be decided
whether or not that narrative is of legal relevance. An elderly woman
who had been treated for a terminal illness is found dead in a bathtub,
a hair dryer still in her hands. Is this the scene of a tragical suicide or
murder? Such a scene can be read in various ways, often depending on
who the (first) reader is. The woman's doctor, whose number is noted
next to the phone, is called. The doctor knew about the illness and how
the deceased struggled with it. She might not look for clues that would
point toward a homicide. A medical examiner might have taken a different view, might have looked for other injuries, like the tiny needle
wound.[2] The creation of meaning does not happen in a vacuum—it is
guided initially by some form of imagination, instinct, or intuition and,
later, once an event becomes a case via the narrative blueprint a legal
system provides. This blueprint, and the narrative freedom it allows,
shape how cases are constructed, and that blueprint is at least partly
responsible for wrongful convictions.

The Narratological Framework of Wrongful Convictions in the United States

The innocence movement has resulted in a decline of the confidence in the Anglo-American adversarial system.[3] Even beyond the United States, "[a]ll around the common-law world," serious doubts have been raised regarding the reliability and accuracy of adversarial criminal trials.[4] While the adversarial system itself is rarely mentioned as a causes for wrongful convictions, it forms "the context [and] the backdrop" of wrongful conviction cases.[5] The (American) adversarial criminal justice system and its underlying narrative blueprint allow for a degree of narrative latitude that makes wrongful convictions more likely or even enables them. This is in contrast to the German inquisitorial system in which, despite the existence of lay judges, the addressee of a case narrative is the court, which mainly consists of professional career judges who are charged to find the truth of a case and trained to disregard any argument not relevant for legal analysis. That carries its own problems and does not, as chapters 4 and 5 will show, prevent miscarriages of justice; however, it makes a difference if judges are the only audience a trial attorney has to address because it affects what kind of relevance is created. Criminal trials in the United States, at least the ones that deal with serious cases, are not about reconciliation or rehabilitation; they are about retributive justice, which affects the legal discourse and how attorneys present their cases. What is thought to be at the heart of the adversarial trial (and process)—zealous advocacy for one party and the trust in a legally inexperienced factfinder—could also be the reason for often untruthful storytelling. In such a setting, the narrative itself gains quasi-evidentiary power for the factfinder.

The Narrative Blueprint

Law-Guided Storytelling

Almost all wrongful convictions are based on narratives that have roots in the early stages of an investigation when an initial narrative is created and consolidated.[6] Throughout every stage of a case—the investigation, charge, trial, appeal, post-conviction—narrators select, omit, and shape elements that they find relevant or important to convey the idea of that story; any and every story "is a reduction, a fiction made from a certain point of view."[7] Narrators must tell a story that matches the narrative mold of a substantive criminal law, a story of theft, rape, murder, and so on, and that story can be told only through elements that are procedurally admissible. Despite such limitations, investigators still enjoy significant narrative freedom in how they put together signs, clues, and evidence. But in contrast to (other) evidence-based sciences, there are few established practices that would provide epistemological guidance—like the method of *differential diagnosis*. Police, prosecutors, and jurors think in terms of common plausibility but not statistical significance. In other words, people who tell their wives that they are disappointed in their behavior do not necessarily kill them. It might seem culturally plausible but not statistically predictive. When a jury hears an opening statement, they listen to a highly refined narrative, which is the result of weeks of investigation. Rarely does a prosecutor explain how the defendant became a suspect. Sometimes it was just a coincidence, sometimes a hunch.

Lawyers, police, witnesses, or anybody even remotely involved in the criminal process cannot tell their stories of events or people freely and as they find relevant. Every (criminal) justice system provides a narrative blueprint, a kind of "preordained forensic narrative."[8] This blueprint is based on the law's formal, positivistic approach toward elements that can make it into the legal discourse and which can't. These blueprints define and regulate what stories ought to be told (i.e., the crime as defined by the law), how evidence in its support ought to be gathered (evidence that is not excluded by law), who is in charge of constructing the initial narrative (police, prosecutors, investigative judges), who controls how narratives are presented in court (the adversaries, judges), who are the narratees of the narrative that develop the master narrative (the narrative that becomes the basis for the verdict), and how a narrative can be reviewed factually and procedurally after a verdict.[9]

In contrast to fiction, law's voice is supposedly "detached"[10] because law requires facts that can be subsumed under an element of a crime filling the narrative mold provided by the system. In general, crimes require a form of act (*actus reus*), a guilty mind (*mens rea*, like intent, negligence, or recklessness), concurrence between the two, causation, and harm. Aspects that are outside these requirements are considered irrelevant for the subsumption (applying the law to facts) under these elements. The prosecutor in Michael Morton's case urged the jurors to just look at the elements of the crime, explaining that "the details and the surrounding things of the case are not required to be proved beyond a reasonable doubt. . . . The reasonable doubt, if a jury has one, has to relate directly to part of the crime."[11] But most trial discourses are all but technical and detached. An inquisitorial trial judge might be better equipped to filter out "surrounding things," but in the United States when a jury retires for deliberation (right after an often complex instruction on the law), the task they are assigned—to distinguish between what are the necessary elements and what is unrelated—can become overwhelming. All of the doctrinal parts of a case are obvious in a trial system run by lawyers, whereas the adversarial approach can and must be less technical so a lay decision maker can understand.

Criminal justice systems vary in how they pursue these objectives but distinguish between substantive and procedural elements: to be punishable under a particular statute, a specifically stipulated story (and only that story) has to be told in which all the elements of that crime are present.[12] For instance, for theft in Wisconsin, police and prosecutors must present a story in which someone "[i]ntentionally takes and carries away . . . movable property of another without the other's consent and with intent to deprive the owner permanently of possession of such property."[13] The law requires a narrative that matches this description, and any police officer investigating a case in which someone is found riding some else's bike must investigate all these requirements: Whose bike is it? What if the rider says it is theirs but it turns out the bike the stolen bike and the rider's bike are the same model and color? What if the rider claims they are late for class and planned to return the bike later? If true, none of these scenarios would lead to punishment under this statute. What if the stolen items are groceries that someone needs to feed their poor family? The law rarely requires an explanation of the motivation (poor family, in this case) of the alleged offender.[14] Motivation makes an action plausible—it is the narrative "caulk" between the technical elements of the crime; however, in contrast to intent, it is not a generally required element of the crime.[15] But as will be discussed below, motive (or what is imagined to be the motive) can quickly limit the scope of what police or the fact finder in court see and is a highly powerful narrative device.

Criminal procedure is another regulating element. Evidence obtained in violation of the Constitution—for instance, through a search without a warrant or exception—will prevent the court from using it as part of the narrative incriminating the suspect, regardless of this person's factual (true) guilt. But if all procedural rules are followed, and a jury finds a defendant guilty of a crime they factually did not commit, this defendant is legally guilty despite their innocence. How criminal procedure focuses on factual (as opposed to legal) truth influences the likelihood of wrongful convictions. In contemporary procedural thinking, two concepts of truth are discussed: the correspondence theory, and the consensus theory.[16] The *correspondence theory* of truth sees truth as being correspondent to a fact (*adaequatio rei et intellectus*).[17] Here, truth consists in relation to reality[18] and is a relational property "involving a characteristic relation . . . to some portion of reality."[19] The *consensus theory*, in contrast, stresses "the process of justification of claims to knowledge."[20] Truth is what would be agreed upon or established in a dialogue. "Truth is regarded as no more than the ideal end of a properly structured inquiry."[21] Adversarial systems have traditionally been associated with the consensus theory of truth, meaning that truth is the narrative the fact finder arrives at after hearing all sides of a case. It is to a much lesser degree the result of an inquiry.[22] This means that the more procedures allow for discourse, the more pronounced the role of narrative becomes.[23]

Adversarial Storytelling

The American criminal justice process relies on adversarial (i.e., opposing) parties for the adjudication of a case and establishing guilt. This stands in contrast to inquisitorial or "nonadversarial" systems existing in continental Europe, where an authoritative, neutral officer is entrusted with collecting relevant evidence that is later introduced in court to recreate the "truth" of a case.[24] In the United States, a case develops from the bottom up, meaning that the adversaries (prosecutor and defense) address their narratives to a jury (the narratee), which is more or less a passive listener and does not actively investigate the case story.[25] The narrative that underlies the verdict is not put in writing, and there is no text that would correlate the established facts with the law. German judges, for instance, must write down a statement of facts in a verdict, providing an accessible narrative for the decision. That already shows how differently narrative discourse is organized. Just the question of who the addressee (Genette's *narrataire*) of a verdict (oral or written) is shows how different narrative dimensions can affect the whole system.

In the adversarial system, two adversaries in what is best described as a "regulated storytelling contest" present their versions of the events in question to an impartial fact finder, typically the jury. The judge functions as a referee, controlling but actively engaging in the discourse. After trial, the jury members deliberate and come back with a verdict. There is no representation of which version of the events they believed. They come back with a verdict, not a narrative. In an inquisitorial system, the judiciary is charged with developing a truthful narrative. Although prosecutors and police collect evidence, it is a judge or a whole bench of judges who must inform themselves about the events. If there are gaps, the judge can ask for more information, hire experts, and so on. After the trial, the judge renders a verdict that summarizes all the facts relevant for the verdict and sentence.

Also in the adversarial system: the burden of presenting a persuasive and complete narrative is on the prosecutor, who must convince the jury beyond a reasonable doubt of a specific narrative. The defense need not develop a likewise inclusive narrative; it is sufficient to present a "shadow story"[26] through which the defendant can show, for example, that it would have been possible for someone else to have committed the crime. Lawyers in adversarial systems are trained to keep the story dimension in mind[27] and are often committed to winning the contest ("keeping score"[28]) rather than discovering the truth.[29] They look for a narrative that will convince the untrained jurors.[30] Factual "truth" and accuracy are not prerogatives of adversarial storytelling,[31] at least not to the same degree as they are in more inquisitorially oriented systems—because *the* truth is not partisan. As has been argued, "the criminal trial is organized around storytelling," and "in order to understand, take part in, and communicate about criminal trials, people transform the evidence introduced in trials into stories about the alleged criminal activity."[32] This setup influences the whole criminal process and not just the trial.[33] Although "[t]he adversar[ial] system is a foundational feature" of the American legal system,[34] the term "adversarial" is nowhere defined. The system works by the use of a number of interconnecting procedures that set up the process as a whole.[35] One often quoted and agreed upon characterization is that the American adversarial criminal trial is "a regulated storytelling contest between champions of competing, interpretive stories that are composed under significant restraints" in front of an impartial fact finder.[36]

> This openness [to multiple and competing stories] is not accidental but structural . . . for at the hearing two stories are told in competition with one another, and a choice between them—or of a third—is forced upon the decider.[37]

Comparable to ancient drama[38] with the courtroom being similar to the classical Athenian theater, the American trial rests on the assumption that factual "[t]ruth is best discovered by powerful statements on both sides of the question."[39] Partisan advocacy is thought to promote the "ultimate objective that the guilty be convicted and the innocent go free."[40] The contest-of-stories paradigm is based on the ideal that there are two equally founded stories that can compete against each other, one of which will be more convincing to the fact finder. This paradigm, however, is an insufficient metaphor for many reasons, which become particularly clear in cases in which innocent defendants are tried.

The adversarial system vests authority in a neutral decision maker (the judge or jury), who renders a verdict in light of the materials presented by the adversarial parties (the state and the defendant). This material is presented in a highly structured, forensic procedure.[41] The parties have the responsibility of investigating the facts. The prosecutor seeks evidence supporting his or her view. The defense does not have to prove innocence but needs to show potential "other" stories. In the pretrial stage, prosecution and defense are (ideally) equally active. However, the defense need not collect a single piece of exculpatory evidence due to the burden-of-proof requirement, which the state must meet. During the trial, each party is supposed to determine the facts and the law in a way most favorable and persuasive to its side and to challenge the arguments and presentations made by the opponent.[42] The United States Supreme Court shares the view that facts are best proven dialectically through a complex process of persuasion and holds that truth "is best discovered by powerful statements on both sides of the question."[43]

Narrating Agents

Apart from regulations, storytelling is a process undertaken by the participants in the legal discourse.[44] The shaping of the narrative is a continuous process; it is geared toward a trial as the place where narratives are ultimately developed and presented to the fact finder. But each stage comes with its own narrative agenda. Wrongful convictions show that this process is often not about establishing the truth—it is more "a display of possibilities. Sometimes, it's about what it looks like."[45] Police officers, prosecutors, defense attorneys, judges, and juries construct stories in that they reduce and put together factual elements of a case. All of these players "are free to signify"[46] and assign meaning through the criminal process in general and during the trial in particular. That process of narration usually begins with the police, who select and omit elements they observe at a crime scene and begin forming an initial narrative—whether consciously or not. In wrongful conviction cases, these narratives of suspicion and guilt provided little room for doubt. One can argue, as Herbert Packer does, that police act under a (factual, not normative) "presumption of guilt" that, once a suspect is identified, makes it harder to see exculpatory evidence:

> Once a man has been arrested and investigated without being found to be probably innocent, . . . [and] once a determination has been made that here is enough evidence of guilt to permit holding him for further action, then all subsequent activity directed toward him is based on the view that he is probably guilty.[47]

Another reflection might also exist on the prosecutorial level, as, for example, the American Prosecutors Research Institute in its Basic Trial Techniques for Prosecutors course suggests: "Most jurors want to reach a fair and just decision. Your [prosecutors'] job is to help them achieve that goal by finding the defendant guilty. You must sell yourself and your case."[48]

In narratological terms, the story of a guilty suspect is archetypical. Once detectives act under a presumption of guilt, the innocence story becomes an atypical and unlikely one. Because of the operational confidence in the screening process conducted by the police, it is assumed that a defendant is typically guilty. Beyond these more conceptual considerations, there is also the reality of biases against suspects and defendants of a certain race, ethnicity, gender, sexual inclination, religion, or other characteristic. Such cultural masterplots embed an unfairness that is difficult to adjudicate.[49] Law's ability to curb the effects of cultural inertia in criminal proceedings is limited. Racial bias, for example, knowingly or subconsciously influences decision-making within the criminal justice system at every stage, with every interaction. The law, however, rarely recognizes racial motivations as legally relevant. Police stopping an African American driver might be motivated by race, but for as long as the officer pursues an actual traffic violation, even if they wait for it to happen, the reasonableness of a traffic stop is not affected.[50] Race is among the many narrative subcurrents that influence the larger narratives in a criminal case. The existing narrative blueprint might in effect make such subcurrents irrelevant for the decision.[51] The Michael Morton case, discussed more fully in the next section, is an example of how such narrative subcurrents are introduced in court but were difficult to counter. It might even be those subcurrents that raise suspicion in the first place and trigger the development of tunnel vision, a cognitive process that "leads investigators, prosecutors, judges, and defense lawyers alike to focus on a particular conclusion and then filter all evidence in a case through the lens provided by that conclusion."[52] Through that process of tunnel vision, crucial evidence (and the actual perpetrators) can be missed. Both the filtering and reconstruction processes work hand in glove. Reconstruction is not limited to the later stages of the process, like the indictment.[53] Even the first piece of (what is considered) evidence needs to be contextualized and immediately becomes part of a narrative. The trial itself also follows a story model. What is recounted at trial is not "reality" but a rigidly structured narrative, the telling of which is accomplished through a question-and-answer set piece.[54] At the end, a jury or a judge forms a master narrative. With no objective fact finder involved in the process through which the narrative is shaped, "plausibility"[55] and persuasiveness,[56] not accuracy, guide the establishment of the factual basis for a decision:

> The drawing of inferences from one fact to another is clearly contingent upon the acceptability to the drawers of such inferences of the consequences of their findings of fact. . . . For the inferences from one fact to

another is not a matter of "proof" in the scientific sense . . . but rather involves a relationship of plausibility. And plausibility is constructed . . . in terms of narrative models which in their structure may be universal but in their content are socially and culturally contingent, models which reflect both common experience . . . and the social and cultural values which inform such collective representations.[57]

The jury plays an important role in the development of the narrative but is not well equipped to evaluate the quality of evidence or to look at the coherence of a narrative, to mention two examples.[58] The ordinary person probably knows more about how the world of nature is constructed in terms of "causes, probabilities, space-time manifolds, and so on" but knows "too little about how we go about constructing and representing the rich and messy domain of human interaction" (or the narrative, for that matter).[59]

In the adversarial trial, the prosecutor (who has an almost unsurpassed narrative dominance) provides the first coherent narrative of the case that a jury hears in the opening statement.[60] In the contest between competing versions of plausible narratives, structure is important. Opening statements provide a framing narrative that maps out the story and helps guide the jury through complicated evidentiary procedures by framing alternative, embedded narratives. This is the first time sense and order are provided, and the "plot, beginning and end, major and minor characters, heroes and villains, motives, [and] a moral" are introduced.[61] In the trial against Richard Danziger, an innocent defendant, the prosecutor explained the purpose of his opening statement:

> What I say here is not evidence in this case nor is it argument. It's an opportunity for the state to present what we expect the evidence will reveal during the course of this trial. It is a road map, an overview, of how we expect the trial will go. This will be a lengthy trial and we would anticipate that some of the issues may become somewhat convoluted throughout the course of the trial. So this is an opportunity for you to get an overview of what we expect to happen.[62]

Opening statements can develop a strong force in that they prime how jurors match evidence with the narrative of the opening statement.[63] One could describe the development of a case narrative through all stages as a whole series of matchings.[64] Because prosecutors present first, they determine the account that becomes the preferred version of events.[65] There is a significant amount of research that shows how brains respond to stories on the neurological and cognitive levels. Narratives with a dramatic arc catch our attention, which leads to an increase in cortisol.[66] Oxytocin is correlated with prosocial behavior, which can be triggered by a narrative—perhaps the one alleged by a prosecutor who promises to make society safer. The neurochemical effects of emotionally engaging narratives last beyond the time it takes to tell a story and can inspire post-narrative actions.[67] On a cognitive level, narratives stimulate the brain in areas that produce an affective response.[68] Readers of a narrative (whether fictional or factual) make many unconscious operations (processes) that enable them to "leap from symbols on a page to elaborate models of narrative worlds."[69] The products of these processes are representations that get stored, for some duration, in one's memory.[70] But the creation of such representations is a complex undertaking that requires involvement from readers, who use memory structures (like a specific script) or schemas to enhance their narrative experiences.[71] This experience and the arousal that accompanies it is stronger when a complete narrative is presented, one that the receiver can resonate with.[72] Michael Morton's note, for instance, can be read within the context of the crime and triggers a schema of a person who puts his own satisfaction over the wishes of his wife. An officer at the scene and a juror in court can make such connections unconsciously and might not even be able to explain if and how they read such a symbol.[73]

Prosecutors might be at a considerable advantage, especially in cases of innocent clients, because they must present a complete narrative, whereas the defense does not need to and often cannot. Moreover, the prosecutor can also address how the jury should look at the evidence. The following quotation, taken from another wrongful conviction case, illuminates how a legal standard like "beyond a reasonable doubt" can be primed:

> Now Ladies and Gentlemen that's all the state has to prove in this case. And we only have to prove it to beyond reasonable doubt. We don't have to prove it to an absolute certainty. So don't get off on some tangent about

wondering about other things, wondering why this didn't occur or that didn't occur or something else. What I just told you is all the state has to do. And all the state expects to do.

Through these remarks, the prosecutor not only diminished the standard of proof ("only . . . beyond a reasonable doubt") but also explicitly discouraged jurors from looking for alternative scenarios or explanations of the events in question. Prosecutors, with their official authority, can change a juror's understanding of the standard of proof—something that is in the hands of the judge.

Jurors expect that elements introduced in court add up and are part of a complete narrative. This expectation is in line with what sociolinguists call the "logic" of a conversation, in which listeners generally suppose that speakers observe what Paul Grice termed the "cooperative principle."[74] Grice suggests that there is an accepted way of speaking that we all recognize as standard behavior. When we produce or hear an utterance, we assume that it will generally be true and relevant, have the right amount of information, and will be couched in understandable terms.[75] If, however, an utterance does not appear to conform to this model, then we do not consider the utterance as nonsense; rather, we assume that an appropriate meaning is there to be inferred, that the logical gaps we experience can be filled. As listeners we suppose that the information provided in conversations is relevant simply because it has been provided. Looking for the atypical story, here the innocence story is neither trained nor part of the adversarial trial system. Other justice systems that put fact-finding and the reconstruction of the story not in the hands of two adversaries but in the hands of impartial and professional judges might be less prone to dramatization and simplification and thus more likely to be responsive to an atypical story.

One final point: a jury verdict is difficult, if not almost impossible, to review, since facts and "flaws" in the narrative are hard to notice.[76] Jurors, like everyone else, "crave meaning,"[77] and they organize and interpret trial evidence as they receive it by placing it into a story format, which helps to create meaning. During their deliberations, jurors develop their own version of the events and the meaning of the evidence that was presented in court. To put it another way: they "re-story" the case narrative into their own version, a version that might even differ from juror to juror. The side that can offer a narrative that the juror accepts as the best explanation of the evidence presented, and is the closest match to his or her own narrative, will win that juror's vote in the end.[78] This is in line with how cognitive psychologists believe we create meaning—by lacing experience into cognitive frames called "schemas" or "scripts."[79] Like the reader of a novel, the jury makes sense (of the "text") by identifying the story and then seeing the presented narrative as one particular presentation of that story.[80] Narrative gaps will not be filled by asking for more proof but rather by establishing "a relationship of plausibility."[81]

> [The] array of competing stories drives the listener to the edge of language and of consciousness, to the moment of silence where transformation and invention can take place, and a new story . . . can be told.[82]

The trial is the place where the factual basis for a judgment is established,[83] but a judgment can be legitimate even if the master narrative is not factually true. It only needs to be a product of legitimate storytelling—that is, *legally* true. Justices reviewing a case for procedural errors can be sensitive readers of narrative accounts, but narrativization is not a procedural issue.[84]

Masterplotting Michael Morton: A Contest of Narratives?

On August 13, 1986, Michael Morton got ready for work early in the morning. He usually left the house at 5:30 AM for his job as a manager in a grocery store. It was the day after his birthday. Before he left, he placed a note for his wife, Chris, near the bathroom sink. The note read:

> Chris, I know you didn't mean to, but you made me feel really unwanted last night. After a good meal, we came home, you binged on the rest of the cookies. Then with your nightgown around your waist and while I was rubbing your hands and arms, you farted and fell asleep. I'm not mad or expecting a big production. I just wanted you to know how I feel without us getting into another fight about sex. Just think how you might have felt if you were left hanging on your birthday. ILY—M [I love you—Michael]

In this note, Morton expressed his disappointment about his wife's falling asleep after they celebrated his birthday the night before. He had rented a sexually explicit video that he planned on watching with her. But Chris was tired and did not reciprocate his romantic expectations. At work the next day, Morton wondered why his wife hadn't called as she usually did, though he did not think much of it. He became worried when, after work, he wanted to pick up their three-year-old son, Eric, from the babysitter's and was told that he hadn't been dropped off. Morton realized that something was wrong. He called his home, but instead of hearing his wife's voice, a male answered the phone. It was Sheriff Jim Boutwell, who told Morton to come home. When he arrived, he learned that his wife had been murdered. She was found by a neighbor who checked the house when she saw Eric outside. Chris's body was found on their bed under a comforter, with a wicker basket and suitcase on top of it. Chris suffered severe head trauma caused by multiple blows with a blunt object. There was some disarray, but apart from her purse nothing was missing, not even the engagement ring and wedding band, both lying visibly on the nightstand. There were no signs of forced entry; the sliding glass door in the dining area was not locked.

These were the initial moments of a criminal investigation that would lead to Michael Morton's arrest for and then conviction of his wife's murder, a murder he did not commit. Morton spent nearly 25 years in prison, serving a life sentence before he was released and officially exonerated in 2011. DNA evidence that had been with the police since the day after the crime was analyzed and implicated another man who committed a similar murder two years after the murder of Chris Morton.

The reasons for Michael Morton's wrongful conviction can be rendered in canonical terms: police and prosecutorial misconduct (one-sided investigation, withholding evidence), unvalidated forensic methods (time of death estimate based on the stage of digestion of stomach content), and tunnel vision. But what was the reason for the early focus on Morton? How could the jury be convinced that Michael Morton was a murderer? Like many, this (and each) wrongful conviction case is complex, more complex than the case summaries on websites or in newspaper articles might suggest. Usually, case documentation consists of hundreds and often thousands of pages of transcripts, briefs, decisions, and other material. All of these connect to laws, precedent, arguments, notes, and concept that come with a multitude of smaller and larger narratives, each one signifying something specific, weaving together a narrative fabric that extends outward from the core events,[85] including aspects internal to the case and external—like precedent, rules of evidence, and the like.

Michael Morton's case exemplifies how narrative affects questions of guilt or innocence. A close reading sheds light on the simple question: How, in the absence of directly incriminatory evidence, is it possible to convince a jury that Michael Morton committed a crime that never happened the way it was charged?

Jurors, as the ultimate factual decision makers, do not think in legal terms. They do not consider theories behind legal doctrine or ask whether an act concurred with the appropriate state of mind. They are not supposed to undertake these sorts of things. Jurors represent the wishes and feelings of the community, "the "passionate elements in our nature," and are by intention of the Framers not permanently attached to the sovereign and the professional administrators of the law.[86] Jurors hear about the law only when every witness has spoken and every expert has testified—that is, after they have already formed an opinion and thought about a crime narrative. From a doctrinal point of view, the driving force in establishing guilt in a system with lay fact finders is not evidence; it is the narrative that conveys motive and personality. Even the power of evidence is relative. Although the perceived strength of trial evidence and the credibility of testimony are seen as the strongest predictors of jury judgments,[87] evidence is dependent on the narrative it tries to prove. A gun itself does not tell a story. Michael Morton's wrongful conviction stands for many and is exemplary in that it shows that a narrative masterplot—the creation of a character and type—influences the outcome of a case at least as much as other kinds of evidence. In the following section I will discuss how the masterplot developed through the three stages of the Morton case: suspicion/investigation, trial, and appeal. I will also argue that the prosecution dominates the narrative and that there rarely ever is an actual contest of narratives.

Suspicion

Suspicion typically forms early when officers are called to a potential crime scene and start reading what they find.[88] The prosecutor in Morton's case explained that the

> information officers learn at the scene has the relevance of bearing upon whether they had probable cause to focus at that time on Mr. Morton as a suspect in the case. . . . Any bit of information they learn through hearing it, from witnesses that they interviewed prior to talking to Mr. Morton or observations that they made at the scene goes to the matrix of probable cause or reasonable suspicion to focus on a person.[89]

That "matrix" of probable cause is a combination of scripts and expectations, information, and other mental constructs. When police asked, for instance, whether the neighbor who found the victim's body heard something like shouting or yelling from the Morton's house the night before, that question follows—consciously or not—a script, a potential story: a possible fight between husband and wife that became deadly.[90] This is when a happening is legally embedded, when an event becomes a case.

When the sheriff and his staff entered the house, they found the body of Chris Morton and observed some disorder—a dresser with most of the drawers pulled out, which is a potential sign of robbery—but they also saw that not all valuables (jewelry on the nightstand, a camera) were taken. There was also Morton's note to his wife, which could be read as a sign of frustration or even anger—a potentially strong motive for a crime. The sheriff thought that Morton became enraged, then killed his wife out of sexual rejection and built-up frustration. The tossed suitcase, the missing purse, and the valuables left behind were seen as staged, as if Morton wanted to distract the police by pointing the finger to an unknown (nonexistent) intruder. Morton became a suspect probably even before he arrived home when police had spoken with the neighbor who found the body. Although the investigation was still preliminary (latent fingerprints and the unlocked sliding glass door hadn't been found yet) and the sheriff still believed Chris Morton died of a gunshot,[91] the initial core narrative of a fight over sex that escalated into murder had been formed.

Throughout the whole case, the state based its story on circumstantial inferences, mainly from testimony on Morton's character and personality. Later, it had to be explained to the jury how someone with no record of violence, someone who left the house at 5:30 AM to support his family would kill his wife over an almost trivial incident, leaving his son, who had just recovered from heart surgery, motherless. This is a gap in the narrative that needed filling because there was no development toward violence, no criminal record, no other manifested signs of the ability to commit a brutal murder. Had there been a video or a reliable eyewitness to the crime, Morton's potential motive would be of much less relevance. However, absent such evidence, the "why" of the crime replaced the missing factual support. The less evidence exists, the more motivation and the creation of a personality matter—both are established through masterplots.

The concept of *masterplot* is not sharply defined in narratology but generally refers to stories that we "tell over and over in myriad forms and that connect vitally with our deepest values, wishes, and fears."[92] People's values and identities are linked to masterplots, which can have (especially in an adversarial setting) a strong rhetorical impact. A narrative based on a masterplot resonates with a listener's own understanding of the world. Masterplots tie narrative strings together, include types and characters, and can develop a strong moral force. They evoke an image of the world in which right and wrong and good and evil are easily identifiable and may make it difficult to weigh evidence dispassionately. That is true for the main suspects in a case, but it is also true for witnesses or experts who testify.

The sexual nature of the crime is in itself a strong motif, which is present in many wrongful conviction cases. In Michael Morton's case, it was combined with an alleged lack of emotion, aggressiveness, selfishness, and detachment. When examined during the trial, an officer reported that "the first thing Mr. Morton said, 'Are they both dead or what?'"[93] The sheriff added that, after Morton had learned that his wife was dead, there "was no particular reaction at all."[94] Morton was perceived and later presented as lacking affection, as uncaring, as being detached. His alleged coldheartedness would become a main pillar of the state's case, with multiple witnesses testifying to Morton's emotionless character.[95] Throughout the trial until closing arguments, the prosecutor asked the jury, "[W]hat would a normal person think unless you're the killer and know what happened"?[96] This alleged connection between not being "normal" and being the murderer was a dominant theme. Although people react to tragic news in many ways, there are certain normalized psychological expectations that we assume are intuitive and part of universal human nature: grave news require an empathetic response, tears, a breakdown, or some other form behavior that jurors understand as typical for such a situation. If that is missing (and putting aside whether a "normal" response actually exists at all), jurors might develop emotions against the defendant that affect their judgment.[97] When the prosecutor said that "maybe" Morton had a little bit of panic in his voice when he first spoke with the sheriff on the phone, and that his cool reaction is "just not the way human beings, any human being would react," Morton is dehumanized and loses all empathy. The Supreme Court held that being able to "know the heart and mind of the offender and judge his character, his contrition or its absence," is crucial in determining the defendants blameworthiness.[98] By that, the Court assumes that inferring someone's emotions is possible when in fact it is not—at least not that easily.[99] In his own account of the initial moments of the investigation, Morton says that "[w]e all think we know how we would react to devastating news. Some of us believe we would cry, others might reason that they would feel faint. Still, others believe they would scream and collapse. . . . When I learned of Chris's death, I had collapsed but not spectacularly there on the lawn."[100]

Minutes after Morton had arrived home, the sheriff sat down with him and read him his Miranda warnings.[101] Miranda warnings are required when a suspect is subject to interrogation and arrested (not free to leave). An arrest requires probable cause, meaning that it must be more likely than not that, in his wife's case, Morton had committed the crime. Within minutes and without even having inspected the crime scene thoroughly (but having read Morton's note), the sheriff suspected Morton to be the perpetrator. He asked him whether there had been violence in the marriage and if Morton ever had an affair.[102] On the stand, the sheriff added multiple micro-narratives that further incriminated Morton. Why, for instance, would Morton ask if his ".45 [is] missing" if the gun hadn't been involved somehow in the crime? When Morton initially spoke with the sheriff, he inquired only about his son (potentially already knowing that his wife is dead—"are they both dead?"). Maybe Morton already knew that his wife was dead? That is how it was presented to the jury. Signs that would exculpate Morton were not considered—unintentionally and purposefully. Nothing in the record suggests that police were looking for alternative explanations or listened to Morton, who protested his innocence. There was no competing narrative offered by anyone except Morton himself. During these first moments, the incriminatory narrative could develop uncontested. The record does not show any reflection as to other potential scenarios, which supports the argument this chapter makes that the trust in a contest of narratives is unjustified. Crime narratives develop or can develop almost completely uncontested until they reach the trial stage.

This incriminatory framing narrative was perpetuated throughout the investigation, trial, and appeal. Parts that fit this narrative would be introduced into the official narrative, whereas parts that did not were left out. For instance, Morton had no criminal history; by all reports he appeared to be a loving father and husband. There were fingerprints of an unknown source on one doorframe and a footprint in the yard that did not match Morton or anyone else living in the house. Neighbors told the police that a green van was repeatedly parked on the street behind the Morton house and that its driver walked off into a wooded area that bordered the Morton lot. Police records also show that Christine Morton's missing credit card had been recovered after the murder. It was used by a woman who was not Chris. Then there was a bloodstained bandana recovered by Morton's brother-in-law from behind the house. Also, Morton's son told his grandmother that he saw a man in the house and that the murderer was not his father but a "monster," stating that his "Daddy was not home" when the crime happened. None of that information had been turned over to the defense,[103] which certainly was a gross Brady violation (whereby prosecutors must disclose exculpatory evidence to the defense) that later opened the door for a retrial.

Apart from evidentiary aspects, one could also wonder about the logic of the sheriff's narrative. If Morton had in fact killed his wife, why had he not disposed of the note, which would clearly incriminate him? Why would he leave his toddler alone at home, not to speak of exposing him over hours to the dead body of his mother? Why did he not call in sick, remove the body, and cancel the babysitter? These all could be signs, clues, and evidence for a different narrative: someone else—a stranger, maybe a relative—could have entered the house and killed Chris. In these first moments, a story forms in the minds of the detectives, and then the "things" (like the note, the valuables left behind, etc.) are used to support their narrative; they become evidence. If this were crime or courtroom fiction, one would expect the defense attorney to rise and untangle the logical inconsistencies of the state's narrative. But the prosecutor reminded prospective jurors that this "isn't going to be Perry Mason. Nobody is going to get up in the middle of the trial and shout, 'I did it,' like they did for Perry. It just doesn't happen that way."[104] In cases of unidentified perpetrators, the defense is in a weaker position because unless it can present someone who says "I did it!" they are confronted with an at least somewhat plausible narrative that is difficult to dismiss by implying it was someone else.

This turns the ideal of contest of narratives into a myth, at least in wrongful convictions, because rarely is there an alternative story to tell. Much of the existing narrative scholarship assumes that the person charged and tried committed certain acts that then need to be folded into a set of legal criteria. Bennett and Feldman in their seminal and influential work, *Reconstructing Reality in the Courtroom*, introduced the idea of "story" as a communicative and interpretive device.[105] Their analysis and arguments are based on the premise that, through "telling and interpreting stories, the actors in a trial present, organize, and analyze the evidence that bears on the alleged illegal activity."[106] But what if what is called "evidence" is already the result of an interpretation? All the subsequent interpretative stages float in the sense that the interpretation, organization, and analysis of information presented in court are baseless. Bennett and Feldman's approach (as a stand-in for others) is based on an ideal-typical scenario and is not cognizant of potentially false accusations. In a typical case, the defense has, according to Bennett and Feldman, "more numerous" strategic options than the prosecutor.[107] "[S]tory operations are so powerful that the proper choice of a defense strategy can transform a seemingly airtight prosecution case into a doubtful one."[108] The strategies through which that can happen— challenge, redefinition, reconstruction—all require a form of an alternative event, whether it is imagined or supported by some evidence. But as the Morton case shows, to provide traction as a challenge-type story, the defense can easily be overwhelmed by the already plausibly presented incrimination story.

The Trial Narrative

After the state's opening in the Morton case, the defense did not propose a counternarrative and only later pointed out that there were unidentified fingerprints and footprints, that there had been a way for a stranger to enter the house, and that there were loose connections between (what the state considered to be) evidence and the narrative. It also seems that the defense counsel became emotionally involved in the trial, concluding in closing, for instance, that if the jury believed the state's story, then "you need a subscription for a lifetime to the National Enquirer."[109]

Deciding the question of legal guilt involves a complex process: evaluating events as they are represented and, in the case of the jury, turning them into a master narrative as a basis for the verdict. A trial transcript cannot fully reflect how the defendant, witnesses, and attorneys are perceived as people, with facial expressions, demeanor, voice, appearances, and so on. What happens during a trial is also the result of a long preparation on how each side intends to present their narratives, as well as the ones who will listen. The jurors chosen for the panel are selected through a process that influences how narratives are heard. Each side tries to filter out jurors who would potentially read the case to their side's disadvantage. The bias in a jury is also a narrative bias, in that jurors react differently to certain archetypical narratives. Pretrial motions are filed with the aim to include or exclude certain pieces of evidence that might add to certain narratives. This means that, once the trial begins, there is little information or data that has not already been thought about.

In his opening statement, the prosecutor presented a "road map," the "big picture" of how everything "fits in."[110] He told his version of the story: how, when the family came home from the birthday dinner, Michael wanted to have sex with his wife, who said "no" and wanted to go to bed. She said "no" again in the bedroom. Morton went to the living room, where "he viewed that sexually-explicit videotape and he got madder and madder."[111] Morton is already being presented as an insensitive and intolerant type, not being empathetic to his wife, who is tired after she had worked all day and Morton himself had the day off. He watched the video and is reminded of what this evening could have been, so he gets mad and, in his alleged rage, "got some sort of blunt object, probably a club, and he took that club and he went into the bedroom and he took it and he beat his wife repeatedly to death. The blows are to the face."[112] Mentioning the face invokes the image of a man dehumanizing his wife, taking away her identity because she had violated what Morton thought was rightfully his. In the hours after the crime, according to the prosecution, Morton piled the comforter and drawers from a dresser on top of his wife. "And as he thought, he also decided he would write a note as if his wife was still alive So, he wrote a note, pretending she was still alive, and left that in the bathroom."[113] At this point, the note was contextualized and integrated into the state's narrative: it was allegedly written after the crime so as to mislead with the impression that Chris was still alive—a way of trying to deflect his involvement in the crime.

The defense chose not to make an opening statement and thereby allowed the state's framing narrative to go unchecked. The defense could have presented a different image and ask that, if Morton took the time and care to write such a note (it looked clean, with neat handwriting), then why was he as the alleged murderer so careless otherwise? If he wanted to let the scene look like a burglary, why didn't he take more items of value, open drawers and cabinets in other rooms, break a window, put a screwdriver to a lock? Narrative gaps are not as easily noticed, especially when there already is a plausible, complete story. But the absence of certain narratives is as important as those that are narrated. Later in the trial, the prosecutor only briefly touched on these inconsistencies, describing them as "mistakes" that Morton made.

The Evidence

All the evidence admitted in Morton's case was circumstantial. The probative value of circumstantial evidence depends on the connection to a conclusion of a fact. It does not, like direct evidence, support guilt without any kind of inference. Circumstantial evidence always requires narrativization; its very quality as evidence depends on an inference that is always context-specific.[114] In a criminal case based entirely on circumstantial evidence, facts that underly the inferences must be established with certainty and must be inconsistent with the innocence of the defendant and must exclude "to a moral certainty"[115] every other reasonable hypothesis. Courts require that the inference of guilt from circumstantial evidence must be "the only one that can fairly and reasonably be drawn from the facts."[116] But readings from evidence are potentially infinite, and more than one fair and reasonable reading is possible. Wrongful convictions put into question the epistemological methods that decision makers (unconsciously) apply when making such inferences. Such readings draw on different notions of probability and causation, and idiosyncratic and consensual views of the way things happen can simply fail to account for unusual but real combinations of facts and events.[117] It seems that, despite developing doubt as to the infallibility of circumstantial reasoning, the way in which lay decision makers decide is unaffected by warnings about the inevitable process of human interpretation that destabilizes and potentially corrupts the probative value of circumstantial evidence.[118]

In Morton's case, there were only two pieces of incriminating evidence that did not pertain to Morton's character: traces of a potential murder weapon, and expert testimony regarding the time of his wife's death. The remaining evidence was tightly connected to Morton's character and type.

Since no weapon was found directly linking Morton to the crime, and since Chris's purse and Morton's gun were missing, the prosecutor claimed Morton disposed of everything on his way to work. On the examination of the victim's hair, "several wood chips that were blackened on one side"[119] were found. They could stem from the murder weapon or, as an expert said, particles that were attached to it. Morton admitted that he owned two billy clubs, but they weren't black. He kept one in his car for self-protection because of the hours he worked. Friends saw it in his truck and described it as being dark or black. The prosecutor made a connection between the club and the piece of wood. A link between that small piece of wood and Morton's club was contested by the defense with the argument that any hard wood turns dark when weathered and that no direct connection between the club and particles found on the victim could be made. The technical considerations took a narrative turn when Morton was asked: "How do you protect yourself with it?" He answered, "You swing it." The prosecutor replied by stating: "You swing it and smash people's heads open, right?" Morton said, "Yes."[120] Despite the inconclusive connection between Morton's club and the pieces of wood, the prosecutor drew Morton into an image that resembled the victim's injuries.

Just as inconclusive was the expert evidence that tried to determine the time of death. The expert for the state explained that, based on what was left in the victim's stomach, she could have died before Morton had left for work. The expert for the defense argued that there was no reliable scientific data and research to make such a claim. This expert cited studies that show that digestion is a highly individual process depending on many variables and that no reliable time-of-death determination could be based on stomach contents. The expert even provided support from cases he examined in which such estimates were proven wrong. But methods and data are embedded in narrative and mean only as much as the context they are put in. The prosecutor was not successful when discussing the technical side of the argument but then asked the expert why he was so resistant to committing to a time frame in which Chris could have died. When the expert explained that the existing science warns about making any such predictions, the prosecutor quickly discredited the expert as having been unwilling to cooperate, charging a lot of money, and being in the business of going "around the country testifying against" other forensic pathologists.[121] A technical, methodological exchange turned into one about the character of the expert within seconds by adding a micro-narrative. Morton's transcript shows many such "micro-narratives . . . that sprout out everywhere you look, pulling credibility from one overarching narrative to the other in a rhythm that carries through the entire collective event."[122]

Truth is something interchangeable depending on whose side one is arguing. The prosecutor normalizes and makes it appear "natural" that disagreeing with another expert is not a factual and scientific matter rather than a professional and rhetorical matter. It is difficult to say how much influence such frames have on the jury's creation of its own narrative, but they exemplify how narrative discourse can be controlled and steered and how medical or technical evidence in general is dependent on how it is narrativized. Several wrongful convictions I have analyzed had strong exculpatory evidence during the trial (including DNA) that was explained away by the state. The cases of Amanda Knox, the Norfolk Four, Billy Wayne Cope, and the Central Park Five all had exculpatory DNA evidence available before the trial, yet all the defendants were convicted.[123] The prosecutors in those cases proposed speculative theories to explain away the exculpatory DNA. In the case of Terrill Swift, a young man accused of raping and killing a woman, the DNA found in the victim excluded him and his codefendants, but a confession out of "terror and exhaustion" would be what the jury eventually believed.[124] Even 17 years later, when a known rapist and killer was linked to the DNA, the prosecutor did not immediately dismiss the case. "DNA evidence in and of itself is not always the 'silver bullet' that it is sometimes perceived to be," said the prosecutor.[125] Psychological research suggests that, "without a prosecutorial theory, a confession with exculpatory DNA may have the same effect on jurors as a case in which the defendant has never confessed."[126] That again stresses the relevance of the narrative.

The prosecutor in the Morton case presented a fulsome, oxytocin-inducing narrative of how the murder could have been committed. The defense's counternarrative was pale in comparison. It was based on the argument that someone else committed the crime (for which the defense had little proof). The defense noted that the state missed certain pieces of evidence and that existing evidence was not properly contextualized. For instance, Sheriff Boutwell confirmed during cross-examination that the "sliding glass door at the rear of that house was unlocked." There were also unidentified footprints outside the house, which the prosecutor argued were made by the funeral director, who was pulling a gurney. The defense asked why they were never linked to a person involved in the investigation: "Don't you go get the gurney man?"[127] A neighbor testified that it would have been possible to access Morton's house without being seen, and police found fingerprints that were never identified. These were attempts to disqualify, to poke holes in the state's story, showing that it was a shadow story, a story that is "incomplete, missing key elements . . . hidden in the shadows."[128] But the defense's narrative had more of these shadow elements. During closing arguments, the defense attorney reminded the jury that "the Defense has no burden. If Mike didn't do it, who did, puts a burden on the Defense, and we can't answer that question because we don't know.

If I had an answer for you, I would have given it to you. I don't know. I don't know the answer. And the law says I don't have to prove it."[129] Jurors are "not here to solve the crime. You are here to solve the case, but not the crime."[130] The danger of a false conviction was brought up, and jurors were reminded of "recent examples of that in our own state which are fairly terrifying to us personally."[131] Such a possibility was dismissed in the state's closing argument: "Their theory that some psychopath came in there out of the blue—would somebody like that really cover a body up to gain more time?"[132] The idea of a burglary was ridiculed:

> I mean, that's ridiculous to think there was some sort of burglary here. Why would somebody stage a crime scene, ladies and gentlemen? Would some psychopath come in there and have some reason to stage a crime scene? Why would he want to make it look like a burglary?"
>
> The only person who has a motive to stage a crime scene is somebody whose fingerprints are there that we know is there, and that's the Defendant. He lived there and he staged that crime scene. And if you look at those pictures, four drawers out of the entire house are ransacked, four drawers, nothing else is touched. What's the first thing, a real burglar would have done? He would have grabbed that diamond ring. He would have grabbed the watch. He would have looked in the jewelry box, not in closed drawers.[133]

Here, the defense's narrative is qualified as a shadow story, missing key elements and being implausible. In hindsight, the state's description of what is implausible is what had in fact happened, but in the context of their framing narrative, it must appear as unlikely. And it connects the motive for the crime with the coverup, the staged burglary, via the X-rated tape.

Type and Personality

In the absence of any directly incriminatory evidence, Morton's personality became the focus of the trial discourse. Federal and state rules of evidence generally limit the degree to which so-called character evidence can be introduced in court. Rule 404(a) of the Federal Rules of Evidence prohibits any use of evidence of a person's character or character trait "to prove that on a particular occasion the person acted in accordance with the character or trait." However, Sec. 19.06 (now Art. 38.36) of the Texas Code of Criminal Procedure stipulated that in prosecutions of murder "the state or the defendant shall be permitted to offer testimony as to all relevant facts and circumstances surrounding the killing and the previous relationship existing between the accused and the deceased, together with all relevant facts and circumstances going to show the condition of the mind of the accused at the time of the offense." That means that Texas does not treat relationship evidence as character evidence or does not see it as prejudicial.[134] Despite a debate between the parties about this issue prior to the trial, the court allowed relationship evidence to be introduced and thereby opened the door to present a masterplot characterizing Morton's personality.

Throughout the trial, Michael Morton was portrayed as emotionless, offensive, selfish, aggressive, callous, even perverted when it came to his sexual needs.[135] The only time the state admitted that he showed visible signs of emotion was when a detective "was questioning him rather closely about his whereabouts and what he had been doing."[136] The second witness, a neighbor, portrayed Michael and Chris's marriage as unhappy. They "disagreed at least a couple of times a week about one situation or another."[137] That also included a disagreement about marigolds, which Chris had planted in the front yard against Michael's objection. The witness also reported how Michael angrily cursed his wife in front of others: "We were out on the deck [in] late . . . April, early May. Chris and I were having wine coolers, and Mike was sitting out there also. It was towards the evening, and Mike called her a bitch and said, 'Bitch, go get me a beer. Hey, bitch, go get me a beer.'"[138] According to the testimony, Chris tolerated this: "Well, Chris—she'd either go, 'Oh, Mike,' or she'd say, 'Oh, don't mind him. Oh, don't mind him.' And I'd say, 'You want me to go or something?' She'd, say, 'Oh, no, no, sit down, sit down. Oh, don't mind him.' That's how she would always do it."[139] When Morton testified, he said that calling her that name was a "running gag" from college, and witnesses for the defense testified that Morton cursed his wife "jokingly" and that she would curse back. Morton stated that the cursing related to the "relationships that our friends had.

We had some friends of ours who had a very unbalanced relationship. He was very domineering over her. He would tell her to do things, and she would hop up and wait on him. And we didn't live that way."[140] That is the opposite of how these words were perceived by neighbors and probably the jury.

The idiosyncrasies of a relationship are difficult to translate into a setting that requires a binary answer to most questions. Is using curse words a sign of a dysfunctional relationship? A former neighbor disagreed and testified that all that cursing and the arguments about sex "was just the way they were. It was done in fun. It wasn't done in abuse as far as I could perceive."[141] "But other people might perceive it differently?" was how the state responded. This play between various types of characterizations was visible throughout the trial. None of this had any relevance for the crime and the reconstruction of the events. There were many instances in which the prosecutor added to Morton's characterization as a selfish and unemotional character type. Elizabeth Gee, the second witness for the state, recounted that, two days after the funeral, Michael "was weed-eating her marigolds,"[142] the flowers the couple fought over before. Such micro-narratives provide vivid imagery for the jury. The jury foreman said in an interview that from this moment on he "didn't like Michael Morton." "I'm assuming the entire jury felt that way too. Whether he was a murderer or not was still to be determined, but I knew that I did not like him."[143] Even more, that narrative was interpreted as behavior signifying guilt. In his closing argument, the prosecutor asked: "What spouse, after the day or two after his wife's funeral, would go out, something they fought about, and weed-eat down the marigolds? You may go out and take one and press it in a dictionary, you might do a lot of things with those, but you sure wouldn't weed-eat them down unless you'd killed her."[144] Here, the flowers are turned into a metaphor: they are brutally cut down, just like the life of Chris Morton. Chris Morton becomes part of a an archetypical "victim story," a story that adheres "to an unspoken norm that prefers narratives of helplessness to stories to stories of responsibility, and tales of victimization to narratives of human agency and capacity."[145]

But in other ways, Chris was not helplessly lost in the relationship. She had agency and success (in her job, for instance), which in turn was held up as a mark against Morton, a thorn in his ego. That shows how schemas and typical stories are not mutually exclusive when they fit a larger framing narrative. The relevance of both is not just to evoke sympathy; it is also to prove causation ("unless you'd killed her"). Such oppositionists' stories typically contain assertions of causation because the story would have no relevance otherwise.[146] The state made a similar inference when it introduced into evidence how Morton slept in the bed in which the murder was committed. "You slept in that waterbed with your wife's blood underneath the mattress the day after she'd been murdered, is that right?"[147] Morton confirmed it, and in the closing statement the prosecutor drew a conclusion: "And the only possible conclusion that can be drawn from that set of facts is that that Defendant murdered his wife because no human being who had not murdered his wife could possibly react to those sets of facts and sleep in that bed that very next night."[148] Here, through Morton's uncanny ability to sleep in the bed in which his wife was murdered, his guilt manifests itself externally; it is visible to others, just like Lady Macbeth's sleepwalking, her washing of her hands, or Claudius's choleric temper after seeing the play of the murdered king in Hamlet. Through such narratives, causality is created.[149] To clarify: this kind of causation is different from legal causation, the element of the crime. The state must prove that the defendant intentionally and knowingly caused the death of an individual.[150] That causation was implied given the lack of direct evidence. The causation here is of a narrative nature, in which an event is naturally or metaphorically linked to a character trait or certain action.

Morton's unnatural character was brought up again during the state's closing statement. The prosecutor reminded the jury of the call Morton made from the babysitter's. "You call home and somebody wants to know who you are, so you say, 'Mike.' 'Mike who?' 'Morton.'—And you don't react? Any person would react[.] Any mother, any father who unless you knew exactly what was going on, unless you were trying to keep yourself under control."[151] Only when he "finally remembers that he's supposed to have a little bit of panic in his voice"[152] does he show some emotion. The defense presented witnesses that provided context and testified that Morton has not been showing his emotions in general but that he showed feelings at certain points—the funeral, for instance. Jurors, however, were put off by Morton's "perceived woodenness"

when he testified.[153] One juror said that "I would have been scream-
ing, 'I could never have done this! I love my wife!'" Another juror came
to the same conclusion: "He just did not come off as genuine, because
there was no emotion there."[154] The jurors' expectation of some form of
normal emotional display appeared to have gone unmet. The schema of
normalcy also pertained to Morton's sexuality and his frustrated desires.
He wanted more than the normal; he rented an X-rated video for the
couple to watch. One juror said she "was repulsed" by the film: "I kept
thinking, 'What kind of person would watch this?'"[155] The sexual motive and Morton's deviation from what is normal sexuality was stressed
by the prosecutor going so far as to suggest that, after beating his wife
to death, Michael had masturbated over her lifeless body.[156] Through all
this, Morton was portrayed as a sexual and emotional outsider, as someone whose guilt was visible in his detachment from "deeply inculcated
beliefs"[157] within the dominant culture and accepted moral values. Michael Morton is not the only one on trial; but also any kind of behavior
that deviates from the values and beliefs that permeate an ideal-typical
society. Existing cultural inertia exclude counternarratives that would
normalize Morton's behavior.[158] Such narrativization is in line with the
law. There are no legal objections to this kind of storytelling, and it is
only through narrative that the margins of cultural power—in one direction or the other, for or against the defendant—come to light.

The defense de-dramatized the state's narrative by trying to disconnect the cursing, the rejection, and the videotape from the murder narrative. Its masterplot was that Morton was of normal character and that
his behavior was not deviant.

Nobody ever saw him lose control. Been married seven and a half years.
How many times do you' think your wife said no in seven and a half
years? I'll bet you more than once. And they want you to believe that on
that day following his birthday, that Michael Morton, having looked at a
sexually provocative film ... he just got crazy. And then what he did is
he went crazy and he went in and he beat her and beat her and beat her
to death, and then he masturbated over her, and that's how this hair gets
on the top of it. That is absolutely ludicrous. If you believe that, you need
a subscription for a lifetime to the National Enquirer.[159]

Through all this, Morton's response to the rejection is put within the range of behavior that is acceptable within a relationship. Just because a husband is rejected does not mean he kills his wife. Life is not a dramatic narrative in which each action and element is part of a larger purposive story.[160] Rejection does not lead to watching a video, does not lead to rage and death. The same applies to the evidence found on the victim and in the bed:

> I mean, where would you expect to find your husband's pubic hair or head hair except in his marriage bed? Is that proof beyond a reasonable doubt that Michael Morton killed his wife? They even tie it in with the semen stain, right? They go, "There, that proves he beat her in the head and then he masturbated and then this hair fell because there's this stain over here." Well, what do we hear about that? We hear that we got no idea how long that stain's been there. We don't—not one stain, but two.[161]

Motive as the "ulterior intention beyond the penal harm"[162] is not an element that the law requires the prosecutor prove, but it helps the jury understand the crime and the defendant. Jerome Hall, in his *General Principles of Criminal Law*, stated that "hardly any part of the penal law is more settled than that motive is irrelevant."[163] But distinguishing motive from intent is difficult, and many legal decision makers see moral significance in what drives someone to commit a crime. Why would a husband kill his wife, the mother of their son, so brutally? He had no history of violence, and there was no indication of a dysfunctional relationship or a marriage about to fall apart.

In cases of innocent defendants, the defense is confronted with the task of practically solving the crime if it wants to present a narrative that is as strong as the state's. It is hard to speak of a contest of narratives, since only the state has the practical means and is under the legal burden to provide a complete narrative. Arguably, the defense's narrative burden is even higher than the state's because a shadow story, as could be seen in Michael Morton's case, is often incomplete or not persuasive.[164] Regardless of how unlikely the state's crime story was, it presented the fuller narrative—one that could be considered plausible. The state withheld crucial evidence that might have spoken to Morton's innocence or, at the least, raised greater doubt. But even the parked van, Eric's testimony, the bandana, the footprints, and all the rest could have been explained away as unrelated, as the result of trauma and denial, and so on. The jurors heard how confident the prosecutors were, that there "is no question in this case but that the murder and the beating death of Chris Morton was an intentional and knowing act. There's no question but that the cause of death was, in fact, those blows struck by the blunt object to the head. There's no question that, in fact, that blunt object was a deadly weapon. It certainly was capable of causing death, as, in fact, it did."[165] The jurors deliberated for less than two hours, though eleven of them were ready to convict at the start. "I was certain of his guilt," the foreman said later.

Appellate Narratives

Once the defendant is tried and sentenced, the case narrative is solidified in the record. In general, American appellate courts do not sit to correct errors of fact but rather to ensure that individuals are not imprisoned in violation of the Constitution and procedural rights. This is why appellate courts are much less attuned to the narrative dynamics of a case: they do not need to be because "the trial is the paramount event for determining the defendant's guilt or innocence."[166] State appellate courts can, however, review the creation of a case narrative based on the rules of evidence and criminal procedure. But they do not second-guess the triers of fact; they judge the framework in which the verdict was reached.[167] Whether or not evidence was sufficient for a conviction is determined by the so-called Jackson standard,[168] which requires an appellate court to "view the evidence in the light most favorable to the verdict and then determine whether any rational trier of fact could have found the essential elements of the offense beyond a reasonable doubt."[169] The Supreme Court gives "full play to the responsibility of the trier of fact fairly to resolve conflicts in the testimony, to weigh the evidence, and to draw reasonable inferences from basic facts to ultimate facts."[170]

Many systems across the world have traditionally used such a two-tiered approach, with only a few allowing for appeals based on newly found evidence.[171] This makes it very difficult to present a counternarrative that might contradict or call into question the master narrative. Instead of considering a multitude of potential counterfactual stories by reassessing the evidence, an appellate court asks, based on the record alone (that which is not in the transcript does not exist[172]), whether "no rational trier of fact" would have convicted beyond a reasonable doubt. In circumstantial evidence cases, a process of elimination must be used. If the evidence supports an inference other than guilt beyond a reasonable doubt, such a finding is not rational.[173] That is based on the presumption that properly selected judges and properly instructed juries act rationally.[174]

While courts in appellate criminal review maintain the trial court's prerogative to establish the facts and therefore limit counterfactual evaluations to the Jackson minimum, other courts often deal with counterfactuals. In cases of civil liability, courts regularly must engage in counterfactual imagination—for instance, what damages must be paid when a young person is killed in an accident. What job with what salary would that person have pursued? What kind of promotions would have increased the salary? Would that person have had children and taken time off from full-time employment?[175] Here, courts imagine a potential life narrative. On the appellate level, such imagination is limited to procedural evaluations, but that does not mean that appellate decisions are completely free of narration. They provide a narrative within its own right with its own quality. For instance, the appellate court's case summary in its opinion in the Morton case begins with this sentence: "The story told by the evidence at trial is a chilling one."[176] The detached voice appellate courts use—letting the evidence speak, as opposed to the jury or anyone else—creates a sense of objectivity that, as we know, does not exist. The case summary includes parts that were elements of the state's masterplot, like the semen stain on the bedsheet and that Morton slept in the marital bed the night after the murder, the blood still beneath it. The summary ends with the statement that "he cut down some marigolds she had planted, about which they had argued."[177] Why would an appellate court include these story elements when they have little bearing on the merits of the appeal? This is not to argue that the appellate court was biased and repeated these parts to set a certain tone, but it might show that there is no innocent, objective review of procedural issues on the appellate stage. Morton raised six points of error, which the appellate court had to decide. All six points were overruled, and the judgment of the trial court was affirmed.

In his appeal, Morton argued that the note to his wife was inadmissible. Regardless of an actual error in admitting the note (which the appellate court claimed was not made), even if it had been, it would have been a harmless error.[178] An error (including evidentiary but also errors of professional conduct) is procedurally harmless when "there is a reasonable probability that the complained of evidence might have contributed to the conviction or the punishment assessed."[179] Such an assessment requires the re-creation of an imaginary past,[180] through which the appellate court must eliminate the potential error and then play out an alternative (counterfactual) evaluation of the evidence. Such an assessment is difficult because judges must first put themselves in the shoes of the jurors and then evaluate in the context of the Fourth Amendment the counterfactual scenario,[181] which describes such processes as making a "retrospective prophecy," which is "a construction of the story of the past by way of its outcome, what it was leading to." Only if the appellate court can imagine even remotely a possible counterfactual scenario where the trial outcome would have changed, the error is not harmless.[182] That means *e contrario* that Morton's note had no effect beyond a reasonable doubt on the outcome of the case. The appellate court supported the harmlessness of the note as follows:

> Evidence of Morton's guilt included Dr. Bayardo's testimony concerning the time of death, the arguably faked burglary scene, testimony about the Mortons' arguments about sex, testimony that Morton slept in the bed the night after her murder, that he cut down marigolds she had planted, evidence of a semen stain on the sheets and a pubic hair on Christine's hand consistent with Morton's blood and hair types.[183]

This reflects the narrative the state presented in court. The phrasing is peculiar in the way it lists evidence without fully acknowledging or denying its probative function. To say it was an "arguably" faked burglary scene, or that there was testimony that Morton "slept in the bed the night after the murder," distances the court from the narrative, but at the same time it lacks a reflection on how the case was constructed and what counts as evidence and what is questionable. The court does not seem to want to get involved; it simply stated there was other evidence.

It is difficult to speculate what narrative would have prevailed without the note. Maybe the defense's expert would have raised enough doubt for the jury to acquit. The jury heard that the state considered the note a confession, "because it describes the nightgown as being up around Christine's waist, which is how the body was found,"[184] but in the eyes of the appellate court the note had a mere supplementary function. Most of the elements that would make the note harmless refer to the masterplot the state developed. In the eyes of the court, this narrative had enough momentum so that the note did not add much, when in fact that is questionable. What would a jury have thought at that time without the note? What kind of story would the state have been able to construct absent the theme of sexual frustration that the note introduced? In this case, the harmless error doctrine faces similar objections than the inevitable discovery doctrine that Brooks discusses. It requires a retrospective probability judgment against an already established narrative. There is "no principled way for courts to determine whether a harmless error counterfactual (without the evidence the same result would have been obtained) is true."[185] This is particularly salient when the framing narrative hinges on that piece of evidence. The appellate court supposed that "the other circumstantial evidence the State presented also supports a finding of guilty beyond a reasonable doubt."[186]

Morton also challenged the admissibility of two minutes of the videotape that were shown to the jury "on the basis that its probative value was substantially outweighed by the danger of unfair prejudice." The section of the tape shows "sex scenes between a burglar who breaks into a house and the woman who lives there." It is the connection between sex and a burglary that the trial as well as the appellate court found relevant in that the "tape was some evidence of Morton's motives of being sexually frustrated and of covering up the murder as a burglary."[187] It would have been difficult to read the connection between the content of the tape and the actual crime scene as a mere coincidence (which, in retrospect, it was). Although the appellate court saw the relevance of the videotape to the burglary motive as less probative as it was to the sexual motive,[188] it gained a dramatic quality in that it created "bad man" evidence.[189] But just because a husband watched a sexually explicit video with a burglary theme does not mean he killed his wife out of sexual frustration and then staged a burglary to cover up the murder because that's the next thing that came to mind. In Morton, the appellate court upheld the use of the tape with the argument that "this is a circumstantial evidence case and the probative effect of establishing a motive for a husband to have brutally beaten his wife to death outweighs the prejudice which showing two minutes of the video tape might have produced."[190] There is something circular to that argument, because it appears that, when a crime is severe enough, prejudicial evidence can always be used to connect the defendant (who still enjoys the presumption of innocence) to that crime. On the contrary, it could also be argued that, especially in cases that carry the potential of a sentence of death or life in prison, any kind of prejudicial evidence or conjecture as to a potential motive should be kept out. Appellate courts do not pick up on the narrative elements of the case. The trial judge was aware of the potentially prejudicial nature of the video but thought that "just a short introduction of the thing [or] just a few minutes" can be justified.[191] After the trial, the one juror noted that she "was repulsed" by the video Morton had rented: "I kept thinking, 'What kind of person would watch this?'"[192] Her repulsion is not just an expression of distaste—it aligns her with a community, one that Morton is not part of. Her affect is an expression of belonging to one group and displacing Morton to another.[193]

The narrative developed against Michael Morton fits the schema of a "culturally familiar and cognitively plausible explanatory pattern"[194] that jurors brought to the courtroom: violence as a response to sexual rejection.[195] When the case was eventually overturned, it became clear that that it was the unlikely story, the unexpected story, that happened. Morton's case shows how narrative and not "evidence" provides the thread on which the details of the case are woven. It is difficult for judges of higher courts to disassemble and reconstruct narrative elements based on a filtered narrative. As much as appellate courts are "the enforcers of rule-governed storytelling," they do not talk in narrative terms.[196] The question of narrative accuracy is de facto unreviewable. Although the Supreme Court recognized that wrongful convictions do happen, it considered executive clemency as the appropriate remedy.[197] But factual innocence is a legal and not executive issue. It should be treated as such.

The Evidentiary Power of Stories

Is the note Michael Morton left for his wife evidence? As a text it is evidence—of his frustrated expectations, an underlying imbalance in the couple's needs and desires, but maybe also for the ability to express emotions and wanting to communicate them with his partner. Beyond the text itself, however, does the note signify what the state suggested—a fight about sex that ended in death? In a formal sense, the note was offered into evidence as State's Exhibit 16 and therefore became part of the evidentiary fabric presented in court to argue for Morton's guilt. In retrospect, however, the note is of no evidentiary value in explaining the crime. It is an artifact of an imagined story unrelated to the brutal murder. The way the note was treated in court—as a quasi-confession—calls for a reevaluation of the legal concept of legal evidence.

The quality of a "thing" as evidence depends on the context it is looked at, and it is too simple to say that a wrongful conviction "is fundamentally a failure of evidence."[198] It is a failure of reading and interpreting signs. Morton's note coincided with a murder; the note created a narrative field that affected how the place, words, and things were interpreted by the detectives, the prosecutors, and the jurors. Except for Morton himself there was no one in the trial who could read the scene truthfully; neither there a "Juror #8" from Reginald Rose's play *Twelve Angry Men* who would point out that the evidence is not so unique at all, that coincidences happen, and that a thing does not carry meaning in itself. In addressing the jury, the prosecutor explained that the note was "every bit as good as a confession and that was something the Defense attorneys never, ever wanted to talk about, was this note because they realized how important it is."[199] A confession is among the most powerful pieces of evidence in a criminal trial, and the state—by telling the jury that the defense tried to exclude it— increased the narrative weight of the note (or "dramatized" it, in Dershowitz's terms) even further.[200] The image evoked in the note with Chris's nightgown up to her waist and the similar way in which she was found created a narrative connection that supported the state's case,[201] but in hindsight it was coincidence after all.

The innocence movement is often described as being in sync with an evidentiary revolution.[202] Since the 1990s, smaller and smaller amounts of biological material could be collected and analyzed, which made it possible to connect and disconnect people to certain places, times, and crimes. Although initially the innocence movement was largely associated with DNA exonerations, those types of cases are (and have been) the exception. As much as DNA has been celebrated as a way to prove that a jury erred, DNA by itself does not tell a story—police officers, lawyers, juries and judges do. Like any other piece of potential evidence—the murder weapon, the fingerprint, an eyewitness account, or any other kind of evidence—DNA must be contextualized and integrated into a narrative by those who participate in the legal discourse.[203] It is through narrativization, and not through DNA or any other kind of evidence, that a specific legal reality is ultimately created in criminal proceedings.[204] Court narratives develop a force that goes beyond the evidentiary and can be so strong that even, when DNA clears a convicted person, prosecutors and police might still cling to the original narrative of guilt.[205] In cases where DNA that was found in a victim shows that it does not match a suspect, it sometimes is explained away by, for instance, arguing that the victim was sexually active with someone else, the mysterious "unindicted co-ejaculator."[206] That illuminates how the power of a narrative is based less on its substantive accuracy and more on its formal authenticity—that its parts are introduced.[207] Stories can reveal truth, but they are indifferent to it; their momentum comes from the "sequence of . . . sentences, rather than the truth or falsity of any of those sentences."[208] Wrongful convictions can and will happen for as long as criminal justice systems do not consider the narrative dimensions of the cases they adjudicate. Studies have shown that juries, which are fact finders in most of the cases that led to wrongful convictions, tend to dramatically overvalue direct evidence (such as eyewitness testimony) and undervalue circumstantial evidence (like DNA).[209] Jurors can easily be persuaded to give little to no weight to circumstantial evidence,[210] which means that a convincing and well-crafted narrative presented in court can trump DNA and other types of scientific circumstantial evidence.[211] A number of false convictions fall into this category, in which exculpatory DNA evidence existed at the time of the trial but could be minimized for its probative value by the prosecutor. One example of a case in which a narrative was more influential than DNA is that of Jeffrey Deskovic, who in 1991 was convicted of the rape and murder of a classmate. DNA found at the crime scene excluded him as a suspect, but according to an official report on the case the prosecutor convincingly "developed strained and shifting theories to explain that evidence away."[212]

Evidence always points beyond itself—it is a reference for something someone seeks proof for. Falsification as the ultimate test for the truth of a theory is left to the other side. Most problematically, a jury cannot falsify; it can only agree or disagree with the falsification of a party. This means that the very concept of evidence must be reconsidered in light of false convictions, especially the use of that term in court. In Morton's trial, the prosecutor warned the jury that the "evidence you're going to hear and see during this trial is not going to be easy evidence to look at. There are some gruesome things that you will hear about and see during this trial."[213] The state already suggested that what the jury will see is evidence when in fact it needs to be shown that whatever they see is *facta probantia*.[214] The narrative as presented in court develops a force that equals that of scientifically sound evidence. What evidence there is is in the hands of the adversaries. The prosecution in Morton, for instance, said that "medical science shows this Defendant killed his wife"[215] when in fact it didn't. And the defense was conscious of the circumstantial nature and almost quipped about the lack of relevance in the closing statement:

> Let me tell you the evidence they did give you. Here's how they prove it to you. "You wanted your wife to lose weight, didn't you?" Oh, my, my, my. "You were jealous because she made more money, aren't you?" "You're really upset and angry because she's a success and you were a failure." "You called her a bitch, didn't you?" And this is one of my very favorites. "And you didn't like her dog." Come on. Come on. Is that the kind of evidence you want to convict a man in this country on, that kind of evidence, huh, on marigolds, on him staying in the bed?[216]

Does cursing and cutting flowers signify normal or abnormal behavior? Does it signify guilt? The relevance or irrelevance of the marigolds, the note, and other things as potential evidence for the case depends on the outcome of processes of imagination and interpretation.

> What evidence would you expect to find at the scene other than a dead body? You're going to find his mistakes. You're going to find his abnormal

behavior. That's what you're going to find at the scene, and that's what we've brought you. We've brought you the mistakes that he made trying to cover it up, we brought you his abnormal behavior, and we brought you scientific evidence that shows that she was dead before he went to work that morning.[217]

Is Morton like Meursault in Albert Camus's *The Stranger*, whose crime is indistinguishably connected with his character and what people think of it? When the defense attorney in *The Stranger* asks, "Come now, is my client on trial for burying his mother or for killing a man?" the prosecutor answers: "Indeed . . . I accuse this man of burying his mother with crime in his heart!"[218] The profound, fundamental, and tragic relationship between "these two sets of facts"[219] is what drove Morton's trial, so one could ask whether Morton was on trial for murder or for what others thought was inappropriate behavior? Both are connected, influencing the creation of evidence.

The American adversarial system with its reliance on lay fact finders must control what fact finders hear and see, especially since there will not be a record of how a jury arrived at its conclusions. Evidence must be excluded only if it is inflammatory and might influence a jury to an "unfair" degree, but in general adversarial storytelling rests on the assumption that stories should be presented fully with context and that a "syllogism is not a story, and a naked proposition in a courtroom may be no match for the robust evidence that would be used to prove it."[220] Evidence, in the eyes of the Supreme Court, "has force beyond any linear scheme of reasoning, and as its pieces come together a narrative gains momentum, with power not only to support conclusions but to sustain the willingness of jurors to draw the inferences, whatever they may be, necessary to reach an honest verdict."[221] Telling a "colorful story with descriptive richness"[222] is required and important so jurors are not puzzled by "gaps of abstraction." Jurors are not expected to engage "in an atomistic weighing of probabilities at trial."[223] They are encouraged to consider "law's moral underpinnings" and to look at the story as presented by the prosecutor:

> When a juror's duty does seem hard, the evidentiary account of what a defendant has thought and done can accomplish what no set of abstract

statements ever could, not just to prove a fact but to establish its human significance, and so to implicate the law's moral underpinnings and a juror's obligation to sit in judgment. Thus, the prosecution may fairly seek to place its evidence before the jurors, as much to tell a story of guiltiness as to support an inference of guilt, to convince the jurors that a guilty verdict would be morally reasonable as much as to point to the discrete elements of a defendant's legal fault.[224]

What is puzzling about this part of *Old Chief v. United States* (1997) is that it has "virtually no application" to the holding, because the Court considered Old Chief's prior felony conviction as an issue of legal status, not evidence.[225] But the Court felt it necessary to underscore a concept of evidence and legal discourse that is storied, that places as much value on purely factual elements as it does on their larger context. It almost seems as if the Court was concerned about jurors being "puzzled" by technical stipulations and had to stress that they are "active, curious, and intelligent processors of information"[226] who are allowed to create narrative relevance of what is brought before them.[227] And yet the Court does not provide much clarity, leaving open what kind of "morality" it has in mind, what "human significance" means, or what makes a story "colorful." Is that an appeal to juror's emotions,[228] to their intrinsic, unreviewable sense of justice (which is a community's sense of justice), or to a higher, natural, law? Or is it a way to acknowledge that jurors might be easily overwhelmed by abstractions and technical considerations?

The Court, like the criminal justice system in general, trusts that a jury is motivated not only by its duty to decide a case correctly but also by its interest in learning what happened.[229] It might be naïve to assume that all a correct decision requires is the law and a sober perception and understanding of the events. But in American legal thinking, legal guilt is more than just the sum of the elements of the crime. Jurors do not merely process facts. Above all "the jury evaluates stories not as specific strings of evidence but as gestalts that hang together coherently or fail to do so."[230] To create a complete picture of a case, jurors should be able to appreciate the full brutality of the crime, and they might even find it suspicious if those images are missing. Hearing and seeing it all make the jurors "become fully human."[231] Juries can create their own stories from the facts provided, "and if some important item of evidence seems missing or is under-emphasized, they may hold this failure against the party responsible for it."[232] But how does the jury know what is missing? The line between appropriate gap-filling, conjecture, and undue speculation is blurry. Cognitive psychologists have shown that preexisting schema (in the form of scripts, masterplots, etc.) influence how gaps in information are filled, and when quizzed they will remember hearing story-consistent facts they were never told.[233] That ideal of jury decision-making and the processes that lead to it must be weighed against the cases where jurors found the wrong person guilty. The point here is that American criminal trials are governed by highly complex rules[234] and that the complexity is part of the narrative the jury should consider.

The difficulty of the argument that the prosecution can prove its case with narrative richness until it reaches the limit of Rule 403 of the Federal Rules of Evidence is exemplified in Michael Morton's case.[235] In a circumstantial scenario, the narrative is a force as strong as evidence. The jury in Morton saw the "colorful" crime scene photos and heard the prosecutor's detailed narrative that was anything but a "syllogism." There were no limits set on the jurors' imaginations. The final narrative had the "gestalt" of Michael Morton brutally murdering his wife. The conviction is the result of a narrative that had a specific "human significance." What sounds idealistic in *Old Chief*—the trust that the jury will be "getting it right"[236]—is a problem in this and many other wrongful convictions and trials more generally. The stress on Morton's alleged reprehensible behavior might have reversed the process of first finding guilt and then asking whether it is "morally reasonable." It is this unregulated area of a (comparatively) free narrative discourse that contributes to false convictions and plays with paradigms of evidence that no other factual science allows.

Conclusion

Partisan adjudication through a contest of narratives has been considered a successful means that supports two equally important functions of the American criminal process: establishing legal guilt, and dispute resolution. Unlike inquisitorial proceedings, the adversarial structure of the American trial "maximizes the ability of individuals to participate in

legal processes"[237] and to resolve the dispute between them.[238] "The procedural elements of party control, party commitment to winning, and
jury fact determination are viewed as conducive to fairness because they
lead to a potentially equal contest before an unbiased decision-maker."[239]
Decisions based upon a fair battle between two equal contestants might
be accepted more willingly and might give the participants and the
public a greater sense of fairness and justice than decisions that are produced in an inquisitorial system, even if it means that "truth-discovery"
is an "incidental by-product" of a trial.[240] That statement is probably an
exaggeration, but it makes clear that the process of reconstructing truth
follows and is part of a common and culturally rooted understanding
of justice. "Americans have a strong distrust of concentrated authority, and have always sought to impose various 'checks and balances' on
state power."[241] In that regard, the American idea of truth is not fully
compatible with the German idea of material truth as reflected in the
correspondence theory.[242] Although other goals like due process, fair
proceedings, and finality are also objectives of criminal procedure, none
of them can be achieved without establishing the true facts of the case.[243]
Truth in the American understanding is formalized and not so much an
ontological fact as a social and discourse-oriented concept.[244] Here, the
jury simply announces its verdict and leaves no written opinion that
could be challenged or reviewed later. As long as the decision is "arrived
at through a process which itself conforms to fundamental, dominant
social beliefs and attitudes,"[245] it will (ideally) be accepted as just by the
community. Legal judgment "involves more than a set of formal procedures for resolving disputes in a society. Formal justice procedures
(rules of evidence, uses of case law or opinions, etc.) must engage some
parallel form of social judgment that anchors legal questions in everyday
understandings."[246]

The case of Michael Morton, like so many other wrongful convictions, puts into question the common and rarely disputed trope of the
"contest" of narratives in court[247] as a truth-promoting crucible.[248] There
is hardly ever an actual contest of narratives in court.[249] The criminal
process, including the trial, produces a plurality of narratives that relate to each other but are not in a direct contest. Transcripts show how
within even the briefest exchanges between prosecutor and witnesses or
the defendant narratives that relate to facts switch to character or cred-

ibility. That is true for all cases, not just wrongful convictions, but they exemplify that issue clearly.

First, there never was a narrative that contested the state's version of what happened. The state had a fully developed case narrative, describing what allegedly happened when, who the actor was, his intent, and his motive. There was no counternarrative, no alternative narrative that could compete with the one offered by the prosecution. The only narrative the defense presented was that Morton was not the perpetrator and that he had already left the house when the murder was committed. If this is a competing narrative, it is weak in that it simply states that things did not happen the way they were imagined by the state. How can one tell a story convincingly that "I wasn't there and didn't do it"? To say that one is innocent is not a narrative. Arguing that one was framed and falsely incriminated (as, for instance, Richard Danziger did in his trial) can evoke the trope of the guilty always claiming innocence or not being willing to accept accountability or show remorse.[250] Even cases in which witnesses testified that the defendant was with them at the time of the crime, rich incriminatory narratives proved to be stronger. Although the heavier narrative burden is on the state, jurors expect a counternarrative even when the defense is not required to present one. The prosecutor's burden comes with the advantage of presenting a comprehensive narrative that the defense need not and sometimes cannot counter.

Second, the contest metaphor is premised on an ideal speech situation, one in which both contestants are on a level playing field. Such an ideal discourse situation must be, in the words of Jürgen Habermas, free of coercion/authority (herrschaftsfrei).[251] A discourse is without coercion, for instance, when the participants are structurally equal and all work toward one common goal—like finding the truth. This is not the reality in court or in the legal process more generally. Attorneys strive for authority over the discourse situation, and in the criminal discourse one side (the state) typically has a narrative advantage and more resources available than the other. On this point, a few critics would argue:

> Neither scientists, engineers, historians nor scholars from any other discipline use bi-polar adversary trials to determine facts. . . . In matters of importance, we want an active investigative body capable both of testing any credible hypothesis and of amassing evidence from any source relevant to

them. . . . In trials, party control of evidence acquisition and presentation limits the number of possible hypotheses presented and restricts the evidence which is available to assess these hypotheses. For this reason, trials are generally thought to be less reliable historical fact-finding procedures than more active investigative procedures.[252]

While the quality and validity of an argument can be addressed efficiently through a dialectical discourse,[253] questions of fact cannot. The "cherished belief" that "truth might emerge if the mutual and misleading distortions of the two equally matched and similarly purposed adversaries annihilated each other" is a "hopeful supposition derived from advocacy ideology."[254] But in a trial, dispute resolution and moral judgment are likewise important functions within the contest of narratives. They hinge on the actual existence of such a conflict, on the factual possibility of guilt. When an innocent person is tried, there is no possibility of guilt. Yet the framework of the trial allows for the presentation of "guiltiness" arguments outside of factual guilt, which, makes wrongful convictions a typical risk of such proceedings.

The criminal process is as much about factually true reconstruction as it is about the construction of legal reality. The real and the imagined mix, and there is no simple way of safeguarding the proper and true reconstruction of a crime without making fundamental changes to how stories are told and how they are heard and processed.

4

Storytelling in an Inquisitorial System

Truer Stories?

The German criminal justice system is based on the basic tenet that truth as a constitutionally protected value is not up for debate, should not be "bargained," or be subjected to adversarial negotiations.[1] If the factual basis of a verdict ever comes into question, laws allow for a reconsideration of the facts at any time. A second, similarly strong feature of the German system is the belief that accuracy in law and its application is achieved by particular methods of subsumption (applying the law to facts). Both aspects are deeply engrained in German legal culture. Does that lead to truer narratives and more accurate fact-finding? Aren't narrative undercurrents active in any the legal discourse? If so, how do they potentially affect the veracity of a verdict?

The number of known miscarriages of justice in Germany is significantly lower than in the United States, but some scholars and practitioners worry that the state of criminal procedure in Germany might be "worse than expected."[2] Cases of wrongful convictions and even wrongful executions in Germany have been known and written about long before the onset of the American innocence movement. In the first half of the twentieth century, Rudolf Olden and Josef Bornstein published a report titled *Der Justizmord an Jakubowski* (The judicial murder of Jakubowski; 1928), in which they reconstruct the case of Josef Jakubowski, who was accused of having murdered his stepson. Olden and Bornstein provide an analysis of the case that was narrative in nature. They show how the court constructed a framing narrative that included a strong motive, personality, and character so that, despite narrative gaps, the conviction appeared to be based on a plausible (albeit made-up) story. This case is an early example that the inquisitorial ideal—the official inquiry into the true facts of a case—can fail.

A Different Narratology?

Many elements of the German criminal process are similar to the American, including the institutions, actors, and stages that cases pass through (investigatory, trial, appellate, post-conviction). But because of the specific functions of institutions and procedures, these processes are differently embedded. Most notable is the distinct role of trial judges who, in their pursuit of truth, control the development of the master narrative like no other party.[3] Any approach to a narratology must be system-specific and consider the uniqueness of narrative structures and the many instances in which procedural details affect how a narrative is constructed and perceived.[4] That means that narrative scholarship developed in the American adversarial common law system cannot easily be transferred to a civil law system.[5]

American narrative stereotypes have influenced the public's perception of criminal procedure even in inquisitorial countries. An adversarial model of trial and procedure with rhetorical duels between adversaries featuring a hero lawyer like Atticus Finch or Perry Mason often provides the backdrop of legal procedures in TV shows or movies—even in films set in Germany.[6] Studies show that defendants and lay assessors (Schöffen) are surprised to learn that criminal procedures in Germany differ significantly from what they see on TV.[7] In a German court, opening statements are dry and factual; arguments between lawyers are mediated by the judge and rarely show any rhetorical fireworks; there are no theatrically voiced "objections" to attorneys' arguments; and trials provide little room for dramatic interjections.

The reduced space for narrativity in German procedures might explain why narratology as a transdisciplinary method has not gained the same standing or developed the status of a discipline in inquisitorial systems as it has in the United States.[8] Apart from the law *in* literature movement—which enjoys some popularity,[9] claiming a long tradition of interdisciplinarity in Germany[10]—comparatively little research has been focused on the function of narrative in German law,[11] and the existing research works with varying concepts of narrative that are rarely made explicit.[12] The bulk of legal narratology (explicitly or implicitly) references the adversarial trial because it claims some universality,[13] which one "must quibble with."[14] To be useful, narratological scholarship, like any kind of comparative work, requires an understanding and openness for each system.[15]

How then does the German inquisitorial blueprint and the "frame of telling" it applies differ from the American? In this chapter, I highlight two features that mark and set apart the German system, each influencing the narrative discourse. First, Germany is part of the "civil law" tradition, the legal tradition that is based on codified law and a highly methodological idea of interpretation. Second, German criminal procedure is "inquisitorial" in the sense that, in contrast to an adversarial system, judges, not attorneys, are charged with finding and communicating the truth of a case.[16] German criminal procedure follows the principle of official investigation (Amtsermittlungsgrundsatz), which mandates police, prosecutors, and judges investigate all aspects—the true facts—of a case, including those that favor the defendant. Both elements affect legal narration through all stages of a case. Although, overall, transparent methods and the official search for truth safeguard wrongful convictions, these methods mask that in the end the underlying case stories are the result of narrative processing. Almost every German wrongful conviction shows that imagined crime narratives developed a momentum that could overcome such embedded protections.

Narrative and the Paradigm of Law as Science

German law is conceptualized as a discipline that employs a rigid and transparent methodology. The creation of a statement of facts in a verdict or other legal document has been described as a regulated hermeneutical process that sets the judge-driven Continental system apart from its common law counterparts.[17] This is primarily a result of the reception of Roman Law and the development of highly technical doctrine that led to the fading of the earlier understanding of law being embedded in narrative discourses that employ extralegal components.

Jacob Grimm, the German philologist and jurist who is best known for co-editing *Grimms' Fairy Tales,* claimed that law (Recht) and poetry (Poesie) "arose from the same bed."[18] In his treatise *Von der Poesie im Recht* (On poetry in law, 1816), Grimm develops a concept of law rooted in the belief that there is no sharp line between the factual (law) and the fictional (poetry, poetics, literature).[19] The histories of law and poetry are linked to a more general history of language.[20] The order of things as represented in language applies to law as well.[21] But beyond these etymological roots, Grimm correlates themes (i.e., narratives) found in folktales and myths with common law principles. Law and narrative, according to Grimm, are closely connected, because the "most natural and most common actions meet deep meaning."[22] Narrative and law work hand in glove and are naturally and functionally connected.[23]

This "natural" connection between law and narrative, which appeared to have been strong throughout the Middle Ages,[24] weakened during the reception of Roman Law. With the developing dominance of legal positivism and the ideal of an almost scientific rationality during the second half of the nineteenth century, law emancipated itself from popular cultural sources and was considered as being distinct from narrative or rhetoric. Since then, law as a means of rational control of social processes had much reduced poetic and narrative content.[25] Narrativization and the representation of facts became limited to the very specific needs of law so that "the humanness of the story is obfuscated even if it remains stubbornly and spectrally present in the case."[26]

Throughout the nineteenth century, civil law jurisprudence was inspired by the idea that the legal order could be rendered as an almost logical system that produces reliable results. In deciding a case, the judge extracts the relevant facts from the raw problem, characterizes the legal question that these facts present, finds the appropriate legal provisions, and then subsumes the facts under the law.[27] Law as a discipline is no longer Jurisprudenz (*prudentia iuris*)—a dogmatic discipline focused on careful, judicious decision-making—but Rechtswissenschaft (juridical science).[28] While Jurisprudenz is open to acknowledging the role of narrative and rhetoric, the Rechtswissenschaft is much less so. If law is logic, then narrative's only purpose can be to reduce the pure, unstructured, and unlimited events of the real world into what is relevant for the doctrinal analysis. That allows for unemotional and reliable decision-making. Common law countries also employ methods for interpretation and argumentation, but with the advent and dominance of legal positivism in German law, legal thinking has continuously stressed aspects of rationality and expediency and developed a professional consciousness rooted in logical decision-making. That has reduced law's poetic or narrative content.[29]

Codification of law is the defining characteristic of a positivistic civil law system, which means that the accepted theory of sources of law in the civil law tradition recognizes statutes, regulations, and (to a minor extent) custom as sources of law. Legal reasoning ideally progresses through a process of deduction from the abstract norms of codified law to the particular case.[30] *Stare decisis*—the power and obligation of courts to base decisions on prior decisions—is generally inconsistent with the separation of powers because it in effect acts as a legislature in that it creates laws and is therefore incompatible with civil law systems.[31] A judicial decision is binding only *inter partes* and, at least in theory, is not considered "law" because judges are not lawmakers in the sense that they could reason from case to case.[32] Those who apply the law "are bound fundamentally by the solution to the problem and decisional criteria determined by the legislature."[33] Judges must, however, sometimes interpret the law evolutively when, for example, questions of equity arise.[34] But they are particularly limited in criminal law, for "judicial supplementation of the law would conflict with the principle of legal certainty: 'Certainty in guidance' suffers when existing law is not strictly observed."[35] The interpretation of statutes and the development of legal doctrine represent a complex process that assumes status as a science in itself.

Rudolph Sohm, a leading German scholar in the nineteenth century, argued that the "scientific process, by means of which principles are discovered that are not immediately contained in the sources of law, may be compared to the analytical methods of chemistry"[36] to achieve a maximum of objectivity.[37] Zippelius, in his introduction to legal methods, makes the same argument by comparing scientific (wissenschaftliche) with jurisprudential (rechtswissenschaftliche) methods.

Elements of the German legal system came to be thought of as "natural data," which could be studied in order to determine the more general principles. Hans Kelsen, the most prominent and influential representative of German legal positivism, maintained that the pure theory of law

answers the question of what the law is, not what it ought to be. The latter question is one of politics, while the pure theory of law is science. It is called "pure" because it seeks to preclude from the cognition of positive law all elements foreign thereto.[38]

The science through which legal meaning is established "seeks the real and possible law, not the just, and in this sense. it is radically realistic and empirical. It declines to justify or condemn."[39] It strives for the same "exactness and objectivity with which natural science can determine the content of the physical laws of nature, or jurisprudence the content of any given positive legal order."[40] The impracticability of such a pure legal positivism has been widely acknowledged,[41] and German law actually encourages judges to develop the law further (with limitations in criminal law). Legal methods and legal argumentation often allude to logic and are therefore thought not to be permissible for arguments outside of that realm (like narrative). When legal positivism became more dominant in the second half of the nineteenth century, speech and narrative were limited to answering questions of legal requirements, which were either fulfilled or not.[42] Although German legal scholarship is now more open to discourses that are critical of traditional methods, law as a discipline is still seen (or at least imagined) as applying precisely delineated methods to fields that have exact borders. These borders are considered necessary for achieving legal certainty (Rechtssicherheit), which is particularly crucial in criminal law.[43] An openness to or acknowledgement of storytelling would defy law's promise of certainty. Only certainty and an unemotional approach toward law are ways to arrive at justice.

> Non-lawyers consult their feelings about justice and then express this feeling in an often ill-considered way. It is the task of the criminal lawyer to develop a distance to his or her sense of justice. . . . The decisions rendered by the criminal lawyer are then clearer and more easily reviewable.[44]

While an American trial lawyer must consider what a jury would think a "just" outcome of a case might be, a German lawyer is trained to either ignore the perspective of popular justice altogether or to translate it into acceptable legal terms. This does not mean that German judges would not think in terms of public opinion; rather, the legal discourse is based on the paradigm of juridical science; that paradigm, not popular justice and storytelling, guide legal reasoning. However, ideal-typical American lawyers also do everything within their power to speak in the objective and authoritative tones of reason, science, and the law.[45] That is probably less an effect of the system than it is practice.

At the center of the science paradigm stands differentiation between *factum* and *ius* or *narratio* and *argumentum*.[46] The narrative and the facts of a case must be discerned from law itself.[47] This differentiation appears self-evident to the modern jurist.[48] The free depiction of events is not known to contemporary criminal procedural law.[49] Events are narrated in a formal, highly stylized way. Facts, whether in an indictment or as discovered during an investigation, are reduced to legally relevant elements. Only through the legal method of subsumption are facts and the law merged, a process that comes with an alleged accuracy similar to other sciences. This method is common to all areas of law (and probably universally applicable to other legal systems that work with statutes) and is the first methodological technique law students in a civil law system learn. Through subsumption, "each abstract element of the statutory elements of the case . . . through an attributable fact . . . is put into effect. That means each statutory element of the facts of the case determines a fact that can be 'subsumed' under it. Thus, the statutory order of legal consequence applies to the submitted facts of behavior."[50] According to a Justice at the Federal Court of Justice, the process of subsumption is less related to finding the truth than "pure legal reason."[51] In the end, the outcome appears as the result of a syllogism and not a narrative endeavor, upholding the traditional presumption that there is a "strict divide between the facts and their legal evaluation."[52]

> Criminal procedural law . . . is not interested in factual descriptions [*Schilderungen*], but only in factual determinations [*Feststellungen*]. Descriptions cannot be the basis of conviction or acquittal; only determinations provide such a basis. Therefore, there is no narrative in the criminal process, at best legally clarified storytelling, that is: determination.[53]

Through this process of determination, the legal narrative is "stylized"[54] (stilisiert)—certain facts are excluded, and other facts are privileged. Descriptions as whole, especially unguided narratives, are considered alien to the law, because law depends on the reduction of complexity to make elements of the real world subsumable. During the process of subsumption, a lawyer glances back and forth (Hin- und Herwandern des Blicks) between the norm and the facts. The norm is interpreted with a particular case in mind, and the legal norm and the facts are then synchronized in a step-by-step process. Von Arnauld calls this "the lawyer's alchemical art,"[55] and Bruner speaks of "legal ingenuity,"[56] euphemizing, one could say, the discretion that lies within the process of interpretation and subsumption, because the glance does not move between static facts and a static norm. The law that can be found in the narrative changes in correspondence with how one looks at the facts and the law.[57] Lawyers have leeway in how narratives are constructed, or at least much more leeway than the supposedly scientific methods of German juridical science appear to allow. At this point, the lawyer controls how and if a specific factual scenario fact pattern is or is not applied to a norm. "The legal interest cannot tame the facts. The facts, aptly reported, can mitigate or generate legal interest."[58] This is a fundamental narrative (and rhetorical)[59] process that every participant in the legal discourse internalizes. It is a filter that all police officers apply to events they observe or construct.[60] The fact pattern is not independent of the goals and interests of the participants and cannot be considered isolated from the law.[61] Subsumption as an interpretive process to apply the law is a narrative process. To maintain that it is pure reason would be "ideology."[62]

Hannken-Illjes describes a case that exemplifies this process.[63] A person rode a scooter, which was typically propelled by foot but also has an engine attached to it, on a public road. This person was approached by two police officers who suspected a violation of an insurance law that stipulates: "Who uses a [motor] vehicle on public roads or places . . . although the insurance required for the vehicle . . . does not or no longer exists, will be punished with imprisonment for up to a year or with a fine."[64] The person did not have insurance. In their report, the officers wrote: "On [date], the officers . . . were in [city] to clarify specific facts. At that time, [suspect] was found in a public space driving a scooter type X. The engine was running, and the motor vehicle was steered by the suspect. When the suspect saw the officers, he dismounted and shut off the engine. . . . The vehicle had no license plate."[65] In this report, the officers provided a narrative that already subsumed what they investigated under the law—without mentioning that they did so. The suspect used a motor vehicle, on public roads, without insurance. The officers' narrative is meant to treat the incident as a criminal case and is addressed to the prosecutor, who later indicted the suspect on the mentioned charges. During the trial, the suspect claimed the engine was defective and the scooter could consequently be used in only the traditional way—which would mean that no insurance was needed. The judge found the officers' testimony more credible and convicted the person.

This run-of-the-mill case shows that, contrary to common belief, *narratio* and *argumentum* are in fact tightly connected.[66] The officers approached the scene with a normative schema—the preconceived story of someone driving a vehicle without necessary insurance or license as expressed by the law. From that point on, the discourse is framed by the underlying law in a way that the narrative discourse becomes part of the legal argument, because statutory (criminal) laws contain narrative structures.[67] At the end, the master narrative (in the written verdict) and the legal argument are indistinguishably interwoven.[68] They are visible and meld together as one in the verdict, but they are initially imagined by the officers. Law in that sense provides an *a priori* framing narrative, a narrative expectation, comparable to a casting mold that needs to be filled. Behind statutory definitions of crimes are ideal-typical, abstract narratives that are penalized by law. Learning the law means learning to imagine these typical narratives and their modalities and variations. German law students spend most of their time solving and discussing legal hypotheticals, which are stripped of anything that adds "fluff."[69] Ideally, every element of a hypothetical fact pattern will be used in the analysis of the case. Students expect that nothing irrelevant will be presented in the case, potentially leading to a narrative expectation when being confronted with actual cases.

Legal scholarship and theory rarely recognize that forms of narrativization (including the selection and connection of narratives) with their ties to literary forms of storytelling have the ability to overlay and influence "legal logic."[70] However, in many practical areas of criminal law, observations, expressions, expert testimony, and judgments are combined and funneled into narratives that have certain (legal) meanings. The criminal process must be understood as regulated "narrative play"[71] wherein the presiding judge, as an enforcer of the law, provides the participants with specific narrative positions (Erzählhaltung) and then weighs the different perspectives. All the while, the opening and closing statements and the verdict must be seen as texts authored by just one entity. A verdict must appear as being cast as a single piece.[72]

The presumption that lawyers can produce a seamless subsumption of facts and law is difficult to uphold. In Luhmann's words,

> [l]egal reasoning may regard the product of its activity as "rational," but that does not mean it [legal reasoning] deduces from rational principles; and it does not mean that it appeals to a thinking potential that is equally available to all people.[73]

By that, Luhmann questions the purely rational character of legal argumentation in general, claiming that much of the process of argumentation serves to create coherence and unity within the system and, through that, to present what is inconsistent as consistent.[74] In the narrative context, Luhmann's point invites a critical approach to legal reasoning, including factual representations, because these also serve the purpose of creating consistency within the process. Claiming, for instance, that a prosecutor was guided more by a narrative desire or the need to explain a certain situation would refer to methods that are external to the law. That, however, would be in opposition to the "operational closedness"[75] that all law requires for its legitimization.

Likewise, Joachim Hruschka criticizes the claim of a purely rational legal process. He was a criminal law scholar who, in his mid-twentieth century work *Die Konstitution des Rechtsfalles* (The constitution of the legal case; 1965) expands and applies—though not explicitly—Luhmann's theory to legal reasoning within the civil law tradition. Hruschka applies what Luhmann argues on the level of the system to the process of legal fact-finding and judging. Although he never uses the term "narrative," his arguments support a narrative reading of the application of law. And despite Hruschka's focus on judicial fact-finding during the trial stage,[76] his "meta-juridical" analysis applies to all stages and to everyone who perceives and processes events with the objective to eventually evaluate them legally.[77] Hruschka argues that any statement of facts is already the result of a process of organization and interpretation.[78] Similar to Hayden White's concepts of chronicle and emplotment, Hruschka distinguishes between what he calls a "Lebensverhalt" (the event in its entirety and "absolute infinity")[79] and the resulting statement of facts

("Sachverhalt").[80] The entirety of the "abundant concrete circumstances of fact"[81] is the mere possibility of a statement of facts (of a crime), meaning that there is not just one possible reading of a situation; there are always multiple possible readings.[82] Every representation of an event focuses on this particular event, but there can never be any neutral representation, because there is always a certain meaning assigned through the description. The historical fact—even if it is already understood as a structured description of facts—must be distinguished from the meaning that is projected onto the event with the explicit or implicit purpose of creating structure.[83] It would be "naïve self-deception" to believe that legally relevant aspects could be retrieved or extracted from life events and situations without a pre-rational cognitive interest at play that serves the pragmatics of the specific task, like imagining and seeing a crime in a particular event.[84] Perception and categorical processing are combined in the judge's explicit or implicit statements, which can be used for further legal conclusions.[85] This means that a statement of facts always mirrors the interests of those who construct them. "The 'judge' must know what they want to know. Because the investigation is not based on finding something by chance—one looks for something."[86] Recognizing, selecting, and interpreting are closely tied to what someone is looking for.[87] Only with the possibility of a crime comes the possibility of a criminal, which (in epistemological terms) stresses the importance of legal questions over factual.[88] When the interpretation of life facts is connected to the application of law,[89] a legal case is never a legal case in and of itself; it is created out of the necessity to regulate certain life situations and the way they are seen by a judge. In other words, the idea of a crime existed and was created long before it has actually happened.[90]

Even in the positivist system of law, laws are applied through language and speech and are interpreted by lawyers who ask whether or not specific events fit the normative mold those laws provide. That process of fitting elements into the normative mold depends on narrative imagination of both the law and the events, thereby affecting the whole process from investigation to final verdict.

The Inquisitorial

When the interpretation and application of law cannot be thought to be outside of narrative, neither can the processes that guide how facts are found. In the German system, discovering the truth (the story as it happened) is one pillar of justice, and the criminal process in its totality is the vehicle to acquire truth and achieve that justice.[91] According to German legal thinking, this concept of justice exists *a priori*, since there cannot be justice if there is no material truth.[92] Public officials like prosecutors or magistrates are charged with conducting an objective investigation to determine the factual basis of a case.[93] The police are likewise required to investigate cases with the objective of finding both incriminating and exculpatory evidence. The process is not designed as a storytelling contest between two participants but as an official and impartial inquiry into substantive truth.[94] As a result, the creation process of narratives is shifted to different entities.

A universal and uniform understanding of the "inquisitorial process" does not exist because criminal justice systems following the inquisitorial approach do so with great variation.[95] Sometimes inquisitorial systems are described as being "non-accusatorial,"[96] but given that accusatorial elements exist in inquisitorial systems, the term "accusatorial" does not sufficiently distinguish between adversarial and inquisitorial systems.[97] Before the inquisitorial process is discussed in more detail, it is important to separate modern inquisitorial criminal justice systems from the Spanish Inquisition, which notoriously used torture to compel the cooperation of the suspect.[98] The only element it had in common with today's inquisitorial process was the prominent role given to judges. The judge is at the center of the fact-gathering process, but torture or even the expectation of a defendant's cooperation is not.[99] This is why some argue that "magisterial" is a more adequate term than "inquisitorial."[100]

Ever since the development of the Reichsstrafprozessordnung (the code of criminal procedure for the German Empire), the characteristic feature of the German criminal procedure is the so-called Inquisitionsmaxime (the obligation of the court to discover and consider all the evidence and all the facts that are of importance for the decision). Three distinguishing features of the (German) inquisitorial system can be identified: impartial investigation, judge-centeredness, and defendants' rights. All of them are crucial for an understanding of similarities and differences to the American system, and all affect narrativization.

The Impartial Investigation

From a legal perspective, an inquisitorial system can be understood as one in which a neutral magistrate, rather than the parties themselves, undertakes the task of managing the investigation and developing and presenting the evidence, motivated solely by an interest in finding the truth. The parties play a less direct role in the process, although the prosecutor is often cast in the role of a neutral inquisitor, whose task is defined as much by the duty to acquit the innocent as to convict the guilty.[101] There is significant variation among European systems in how these paradigms are applied. Some are closer to the inquisitorial ideal than others.[102] Although they all share the reliance on a neutral and transparent investigation and search for the truth in the *pretrial phase*, systems employ different inquisitorial frameworks. France, for instance, relies on an examining magistrate, who, after a decision from the prosecutor,[103] carries out the *instruction* to establish the truth (*manifestation de la vérité*).[104] This examining magistrate has broad discretion in how to conduct the investigation. The feature of an examining magistrate has been retained in other European countries including Spain, the Netherlands, and Belgium but was abolished in Germany in 1974 and Italy in 1988.[105] In Germany, the investigative stage is dominated by the prosecutor and the police (operating as the investigative arm of the prosecutor).[106] In Germany, the prosecutor is institutionally independent from the court and is less driven by winning.[107]

At this stage, judges become involved only when a search or an arrest is necessary. In this situation, an impartial judge (Ermittlungsrichter, or "investigative judge") must issue the warrant. The Netherlands also employs a prosecutor who conducts the investigation. Should that lead to sufficient evidence, an examining judge can be asked to initiate a preliminary judicial inquiry.[108] While in the past only the examining judge could apply "means of coercion" (search and seizure, wiretapping, etc.), now these measures are "autonomous" and the examining judge mainly examines witnesses.[109]

Another characteristic of the German prosecutor is a compara-bly limited amount of discretion.[110] The German prosecutor is largely bound by the principle of legality: the concept that a prosecutor must commence investigations if there is evidence that an offense has been committed.[111] The general idea is that cases are supposed to be disposed of (in whatever way) by a judge and not dropped when prosecutors see fit (which would be following a principle of opportunity). The master narrative must (in theory) always be developed by a neutral organ of the system and not left to the effects of adversarial stress. Dutch investiga-tion and prosecution, however, are "not matters of duty but of authority," meaning that, for instance, "prosecution may be abandoned 'for reasons of public interest.'"[112] European systems are diverse in this regard, and there is no noticeable trend to strengthen either the principle of legality or the principle of opportunity.[113]

European systems do have one feature in common: prosecutors are not elected officials and therefore do not have to consider public ac-countability when pursuing cases. That again influences how narratives are formed. In France and in Germany, for example, candidates for posi-tions in both the judiciary and in the prosecutorial service are recruited in the same way, have to take the same exams, and are not elected.[114] They do not have to answer to constituents, and they recognize this as an important foundation for an independent judiciary.[115] When a legal entity is independent in that way, it influences, at least in theory, the way cases are approached and what narrative agenda is followed: Is it one of truth? Or is it one that caters to constituents, one's own career agenda, criminologically sound principles, or popular ideas of punishment?

For the purpose of investigating and prosecuting criminal offenses, German prosecutors maintain broad investigatory authority. They can summon witnesses and suspects, guide the police in their investigation, and, under exigent circumstances, order searches and seizures.[116] In most criminal matters (except homicides and economic/white-collar crimes), the police usually conduct investigations without much over-sight from prosecutors.[117] And even in more serious cases, prosecutors often trust the expertise and experience of law enforcement. In general, the German system is seen as "marked by a high degree of cooperation and of mutual trust and confidence between police and prosecutors."[118] Observers described the relationship between both agencies as strikingly harmonious.[119] The prosecutor is expected to investigate in an impartial manner, looking into all elements of innocence and guilt. Such a high degree of cooperation affects how case stories are developed, so that, for instance, the statement of facts in a criminal charge often resembles the report the police submitted at the completion of the investigation. That can, of course, cut both ways, as chapter 5 will demonstrate.

Chronicling the Investigation: The Dossier

While not necessarily an expression of the inquisitorial idea per se, but important in light of narrative, the so-called Ermittlungsakte (investigatory file, dossier) can be considered a chronicle of the inquisitorial process. The dossier contains the evidentiary and procedural elements out of which the case narrative is constructed. It is a comprehensive collection of witness statements, memoranda from the police, photos, videos, results from scientific examinations, evidence found during searches, statements from suspects, court orders, warrants, and so on. The dossier must be complete (Grundsatz der Aktenvollständigkeit), meaning that all documentation relevant for a suspect's guilt or sentence must be included in the file. During an ongoing investigation, the dossier, which is initially held by the police, need not be shared with the defense if "this may endanger the purpose of the investigation" (Sec. 147 (2) StPO).[120] Since this is not typically the case, the defense can ask to access (and copy) the file while the investigation is ongoing so it can evaluate potential charges and the evidence and perhaps even influence the direction of the investigation by, for example, raising legal points and suggesting the collection of evidence as to the suspect's innocence to the prosecutor, who may potentially incorporate those documents into the file.

As long as the dossier retains its status as the investigatory file (before it becomes the court file), it does not include an (explicit) legal analysis; neither does it present evidence in a technical, legally relevant order. It often reflects the chronology of an investigation, including parts that are deemed irrelevant later on. If the dossier is a chronicle in Hayden White's sense, it is a chronicle of the process of the investigation of an imagined but already concrete crime and how that crime came about; the two primary categories of data (incriminating and exculpatory) are tied to a potential crime narrative. Like the chronicle, the dossier "seems to wish to tell a story, aspires to narrative,"[121] but it might remain just a chronicle should an investigation be terminated because no further leads can be found and the crime remains unresolved. The status of the dossier begins to change, however, when police consider their investigation completed and the prosecutor evaluates whether charges can be filed. Once the conclusion of the investigation is noted in the file,[122] and because there is now the potential of a story (the crime) imagined by the state, the defense has a legal right to review the entire dossier.[123] It has been argued that "in practice . . . German pretrial procedure closely resembles the American model,"[124] in that prosecutors follow "the twofold aim of which is that guilt shall not escape or innocence suffer."[125] But the dossier levels the procedural playing field significantly for German defense attorneys because they know more and much earlier what the state's case maintains.

Apart from being a collection of data, the dossier has significance as a physical entity. The very first page of a dossier is the last in the actual file, so the top page is always the most recent document added to the file. In a system that stresses the importance of the written form for laws and files (Akten), there is a "performative, factifying [faktifizierend] quality to the action of filing"[126] because through that act legal reality is created ("*quod non est in actis non est in mundo*"—what is not in the records does not exist [is not in the world]).[127] That is true not only for the dossier but also for the trial record, which develops its own (narrative) reality. The record establishes what happened (even if it didn't), and what is missing did not happen (even if it did). "Facts recorded in the record form the basis of the procedure regardless of what actual occurred in the trial."[128] So files, in themselves, have an amorphous existence—they "are means of work and annoyance, rampant beings which must be conquered and domesticated."[129] Much of how a file, or the whole dossier, is organized is driven by bureaucratic customs or state laws (so-called Aktenordnungen, or "filing/file regulations") that cover recordkeeping (system of file numbers, how deadlines are noted and handled, etc.).

Judicial Dominance of the Trial

The second distinguishing feature of the German inquisitorial system is judge-centeredness. The German criminal trial fuses narrator and narratee of the master narrative together in one entity: the judge (or sometimes a panel of judges). In trial, they pose questions to a witness, ask for clarification, and can expand the scope of their investigation if the search for truth requires it. Attorneys are not passive. Not only can they ask questions; they can also request the court take more evidence. Nevertheless, judges enjoy considerably more autonomy and discretion in this process. The master narrative is then written out in the verdict, with each supporting piece of evidence listed and contextualized.

Almost every aspect of German legal culture, proceedings, and thinking has some reference to the role of the judge within the system. "Judicial power is exercised by independent courts subject to the law only" (Sec. 1 GVG). Thus, judges are more than referees; they steer the course of the proceedings. And it is their objective to discover and reproduce the truth by examining all sources of relevant information listed in the dossier so as to leave no room for reasonable doubt.[130] In a verdict, judges first lay out what has actually happened based on the result of the discovery phase of the trial. Second, they then decide how the events are to be classified legally (legal subsumption). And third, they decide on the legal consequence.[131] The image of a civil law judge is that of a civil servant with high social prestige who performs important but essentially uncreative functions.[132] Trained in legal methodology, judges are required to consider every possible legal angle of a case; they eschew rhetoric and are taught to formulate their outcomes with a maximum of objectivity.[133] German criminal trials are conducted by the presiding judge.[134] Lay elements in decision-making exist but are not as dominant as in the United States.[135] The German system trusts in an independent and professionally trained decision maker. In a criminal trial, judges use the dossier as a basis for their own reconstruction of the case. The principle of instruction allows the court to expand its view beyond the facts that are included in the dossier or the story presented by the prosecutor or the defense.[136] The attorneys in a German trial have a right to examine witnesses (after the judge has finished questioning), and they can also make specific requests to acquire further evidence (Beweisantrag).

Courts usually comply with such requests[137] and have limited options for refusal.[138] Since it is the court's objective to determine the truth, the role of the attorneys is not fully comparable to those in the United States, where their involvement is essential. In Germany, parties could "sit back and let the court do the work of fact-finding."[139]

Just as in the American system, a complex set of rules regulate evidence introduced at trial. It would go beyond the scope of this chapter to explain them in detail, but most are driven by the court's duty to hear all evidence that pertains to finding the truth. Hearsay evidence, for instance, is generally admissible, as it might lead to a fuller image of the case.[140] It is not considered problematic because, in a verdict, judges must justify and evaluate the use of hearsay. Other regulations are particular to the concept of transparent trial proceedings, like the principle of immediacy (Unmittelbarkeitsprinzip).[141] But in other regards, German criminal procedure recognizes many testimonial privileges (rights not to testify)—including for spouses or medical professionals, for example; these privileges limit what evidence is available.

The involvement and dominance of judges are still regarded as the major truth-promoting elements in the German system. Truth itself is constitutionally significant[142] and must permeate every step in the process of developing guilt, including the plea bargaining process.[143] Judges establish a defendant's guilt solely on the evidence introduced at trial and develop what is commonly referred to as "forensic truth."[144] The judicial decision-making process has a high degree of transparency and allows for review of fact and law. Judges must write out their verdicts and must explain which fact is used for which element of the crime. Though not all inquisitorial systems require judges to give their opinion in writing, many do, as in Germany and, for certain cases, France.[145] The inquisitorial judges in Germany must invariably and meticulously explain in writing how they arrived at their verdict and how the evidence gathered in the trial relates to their verdict. They must answer why a specific witness was considered as credible and why they trusted an expert. Whether or not the judge followed the truth-finding objective can be reviewed upon appeal as a question of law.

Apart from the rules that establish and protect the standards of the judiciary, there is also a culture of trust in career judges and their impartiality. In contrast to the United States, German legal education focuses on the judge as the ideal-typical lawyer. Especially during their first year at university, law students are trained to see both or many sides of a legal question and a case. Until the first state examination (usually after four years), law students write "expert opinions" (Gutachten) on legal questions that address all potential aspects of a case (facts are usually an undisputed given). Afterward, in the second part of their education, students learn to argue within a procedural setting, taking the side of a plaintiff, defendant, or the state, but the default angle is still that of a judge.

Defendants' Rights Within Inquisitorial Systems

Defendant's rights and privileges can be rendered in narrative terms in two ways: they establish how much narrative agency a defendant has, as well as what means are available to the state to tell its story. Narrative agency, as addressed in chapter 2, is closely related to the question of how much a suspect or defendant must or can participate in whatever form in an investigation and how far the state can go in collecting evidence. The more that suspects become the object of investigation, the less (narrative) agency they enjoy. The belief that inquisitorial systems do not protect suspects against self-incrimination seems to be ineradicable and rooted in an outdated understanding of the inquisitorial. Scholars believe that inquisitorial systems permit governments to obtain evidence through the "simple expedient of compelling it," and during trial judges "may compel the defendant to be a witness against himself."[146] Sometimes the inquisitorial paradigm is falsely equated with a willingness to sacrifice defendants' rights,[147] assuming that inquisitorial systems reduce "truth obstructing" features (as Findley calls defendants' rights) like the privilege against self-incrimination.[148] As much as developing a true narrative is at the core of German criminal procedure, the Federal Court of Justice has held that there "does not exist a principle in criminal procedure which requires that the truth be won at any price."[149] The extent to which suspects and defendants are expected to cooperate varies across Europe.[150] But in Germany, procedural and constitutional protections that are comparable to or broader than protections in the United States limit how the state can construct its narrative.[151] When European defendants offer information voluntarily, they often do so for purposes other than the investigation.[152]

Defendants' privileges extend to all stages of a case. In the pretrial phase, the prosecutor is the "primary guarantor" of the integrity of the investigative stage and must safeguard the rights of the suspect.[153] Law affords defendants (and specified others) broad testimonial privileges. Every suspect has the right against self-incrimination, including the right to remain silent. An individual who becomes a suspect (regardless of whether this person is in custody or formally interrogated) must receive Germany's version of Miranda warnings.[154] The protection of individuals' autonomy in making decisions about the extent to which they wish to participate limits police and/or prosecutorial interventions. Any interrogation must be free of "ill-treatment, induced fatigue, physical interference, administration of drugs, torment, deception or hypnosis."[155] Telling suspects, for instance, they were incriminated by another suspect/person would count as illegal deception if that statement were not true.[156] Evidence acquired this way is inadmissible. Since defendants are not considered witnesses, they cannot perjure themselves—meaning that they can lie without penalty or consequences at any stage of the proceedings, including at the trial.[157] In this regard, a suspect's agency is more broadly protected in Germany, and many of the legitimate interrogation techniques still used in the United States would be unconstitutional, or at least questionable, under German law.[158] Beyond the suspect, spouses, fiancés, civil partners, and other (specifically listed) individuals can refuse to testify, even if the relationship no longer exists.[159]

When it comes to the exclusionary rule for evidence, Germany presents a similarly complex maze of regulations and exceptions as the American system. The main rationale behind the exclusionary rule is not police deterrence or guiding the narrative a jury hears; rather, it is upholding constitutional rights and values. Criminal procedure regulates how police and prosecutors are supposed to acquire evidence and how judges must handle evidence that violates a procedural norm or might violate an individual's constitutional rights. Judges (in contrast to the American jury) are usually familiar with most of the evidence, regardless of whether or not it was obtained legally.

A specific feature of German evidence law is the distinction between the legality of collecting evidence (Beweiserhebung) and its admissibility and use in court (Beweisverwertung). Not all illegally obtained evidence will necessarily be excluded, and even lawfully collected evidence can be inadmissible.

As mentioned above, Sec. 136a StPO explicitly prohibits certain methods for obtaining incriminatory statements. Violations of this prohibition (and a few similar norms) result in mandatory exclusion. But in cases where other procedural regulations are violated, fruits might still be inadmissible. Most notable in terms of narrative agency: exclusionary rules that are independent of the violation of a procedural norm. For instance, the contents of a lawfully seized diary might still fall under the exclusionary rule. Admissibility would depend on how private and intimate the incriminatory content is.[160] German courts distinguish between certain spheres of privacy,[161] which are then afforded more or less protection. The inner, most intimate sphere of privacy is considered untouchable and can never be used (for instance, intimate entries in a diary even when these entries are criminally relevant).[162] Evidence that stems from the less protected (but not intimate) sphere can be used only if community interests in crime control or prevention prevail over its exclusion. Courts must balance the kind and type and seriousness of a crime, the probative value of the information, and the level of intrusion into an individual's rights; even undeniably relevant, reliable, and legally obtained evidence might be excluded.[163] Courts must consider and balance public safety interests and individual rights—and they must do that in their verdicts. A way to understand German (and other European) evidentiary systems is to consider them as driven by the rights inherent to defendants and additional values, like privacy and dignity, that might supersede typical agendas of parties involved in criminal proceedings. A broader view of Continental justice may see greater justice not only in trial procedures but also in the context of a more humane and less degrading penal system.[164]

Conviction and Post-conviction

When American jurors return with a verdict, they do not need, or even have an opportunity, to provide a narrative for their verdict. What the jury thought had happened, or if something is even relevant to their decision, is not explained and is therefore unreviewable.[165] It is quite the contrary in Germany.

Reason and Narrative in the Verdict

According to Sec. 267 (1) StPO, "the reasons for the judgment must specify the facts deemed to be proven and establishing the statutory elements of the criminal offence." The verdict requires a self-contained (self-sufficient) presentation of all external and internal facts (geschlossene Sachverhaltsdarstellung), which fulfill the elements of the crime in question. The verdict then must subsume the established facts under the law. The obligation to give reasons is considered "a strong incentive toward rationality and toward basing the judgment on a plausible version of the facts."[166] Using just the trial verdict, an appellate court must be able to determine a court's evidentiary and legal basis so that it can retrace the factual narrative and how the law was applied. Even when, as discussed earlier, subsuming the law is never a linear and rational process (in the sense that first the facts are determined in a neutral manner and then the law is applied), the great advantage of a written verdict lies in its transparency and reviewability. It makes the master narrative visible and reviewable, and it holds the trial court accountable.

Appeal

American appellate courts are not supposed to second-guess the facts as they are developed by trial courts. Judges cannot go outside the record in search of additional facts, and an attorney must not encourage appellate judges to do so.[167] The opposite is true in the German system, which provides two kinds of appeals that significantly reduce a trial verdict's degree of factual finality.

The so-called Berufung is an appeal that is by and large a new trial in which new evidence can be introduced. The second type of appeal is the Revision, which is similar to the American appeal system allowing the review of legal issues—both procedural and substantive. The kind of appeal available depends on the type of court that has original jurisdiction over the trial. If a prosecutor in the charging decision determines that the defendant, if found guilty, would face a sentence of up to four years, then a municipal court (one judge or a panel of one judge and two lay judges) has jurisdiction. If the prosecutor expects the sentence to exceed four years, then charges must be filed at the circuit level (the große Strafkammer, generally consisting of three professional judges and two lay judges). In Germany, the majority of all cases will enter the judicial system at the municipal level. Only 20% see a Strafkammer. The Berufung proceeding can be filed against a judgment of a municipal court (Amtsgericht) to have the facts and law reviewed (or just the law). That decision influences which court has jurisdiction of the appeal. Crimes that are tried before a Strafkammer cannot be appealed on factual grounds, meaning that only a Revision is possible.[168] This kind of appeal is limited to indirectly addressing factual issues (mainly violations of the trial court's procedural duty to investigate the factual truth). Defendants who appeal the facts (and law) in the municipal court, but have their conviction upheld, can then (in a second appeal) question the application of law and ask the state supreme court for review. This means that, for most criminal cases, two appeals are available. A case that enters the system on the circuit level can be appealed only once and only for potential legal errors to the highest court, Germany's Federal Supreme Court (which consists of five professional judges).

There are now multiple post-conviction remedies available. One would be a constitutional complaint (Verfassungsbeschwerde) based on the argument that a decision violates a defendant's their constitutional rights—for example due process, equality before the law (Art. 3 GG [Grundgesetz, Germany's Basic Law/Constitution]), personal freedom (Art. 2, Sec. 2 GG), freedom of expression (Art. 5, Sec. 1 GG), or the general right to "unfold one's personality" (Art. 2, Sec. 1 GG).[169] Such complaints are rarely successful. A second independent path for post-conviction relief exists when verdicts are inconsistent with fundamental concepts of material justice.[170] Section 359 StPO (Wiederaufnahme des Verfahrens) expresses that idea by allowing a reopening of criminal proceedings at any time for reasons that affect fundamental tenets of a conviction like truth and justice that are seen as the ultimate goals of any criminal process.[171] Maintaining and upholding a factually false conviction is considered "unbearable" in light of such values.[172] Material justice can exist only on the basis of a factually true conviction and takes precedent over finality.[173] In the context of narrative and preventing wrongful convictions, Sec. 359 Nr. 5 StPO is most relevant because it stipulates that finality can be overcome if "new facts or evidence" arose that would support the defendant's acquittal, lead to a lesser sentence, and/or result in a substantively correct decision.[174] As an expression of the belief that a factually untrue verdict could never be just, a case can be reopened if new facts are discovered that would either reduce or completely diminish the convicted's guilt. The concept of new "facts" is understood broadly to include actions, events, circumstances, properties, and relations that are new. A fact is "new" when it occurred after the verdict or if it existed but was unknown to the trial court at the time of trial.[175] (An already existing fact is considered new as well if the trial court knew about it but decided not to consider it.) In narrative terms, then, every element of a narrative (as the representation of an event or series of events) can be reestablished; the Wiederaufnahme then functions as an instrument to correct a false narrative.

Despite its rare use and many practical difficulties, this section of German criminal law expresses the high rank that factual truth holds in the culture. Procedural justice always finds its limits when a new narrative can be established. What has been criticized about the American system (that "the most important issue at trial doesn't get reviewed; namely, did the jury get it right and is the defendant really guilty—or not guilty—of the offense with which he was charged")[176] is, at least in theory, not an issue in the inquisitorial system.

An Inquisitorial Narratology?

The previous sections show the difficulty to clearly delineate the features of an inquisitorial or German narratology. The path on which a case narrative develops and moves through the system is set in a multidimensional legal landscape, influenced by substantive and procedural laws, the culture that exists within the profession, the ultimate purpose of criminal justice, and many more factors. I pointed out two prerogatives that influence the approach toward narrativization: the inquisitorial aim of truth-finding, and a concept of rationality as it has existed since the so-called reception, the reconstitution of Germany's legal system through Roman law. The acts of interpretation and representation are seen as methods to "break open the shell of the word and to carve out the kernel of meaning" and then bring facts and law into congruence.[177] This concept of rationality is not open for the recognition of narrative as a method that is always at play—it would go "against the grain of the civil law ideology."[178] But legal narrativization as the individualized selection of one out of many possibilities[179] is always present. Suspects tell their stories to their attorneys, and attorneys convey them to the court, and then courts inquire into the narrative and retell it. Retelling happens at many stages in the judicial process, including the appellate. In light of the strong objective to find the truth, new evidence can be considered, even after a case has become final.

Narrative structures are as inherent in the inquisitorial system as they are in the adversarial system, and there are probably more similarities than differences between the two. However, differences in the procedural layout and the objective of finding factual truth affect the way a case is narrativized. While there are fewer differences as to adversarial storytelling in the investigative stages, much changes once a case is prepared for trial and then actually tried in a courtroom. Whether or not a specific event is a criminal case will first be imagined by police (anticipating substantive criminal law), and then it will be reimagined and narrativized in a dossier by the prosecutor before the case is tried. Copies of this dossier are handed to the defense and the judge. In a trial, the judge (or a panel of judges) is central and charged with finding the factual truth of a case. Truth is thought to arise through an inquiry into the facts that have been collected. A judge uses the dossier as a basis to develop the court's own narrative, so cases develop from the top down because the court has the overriding responsibility for determining the truth; due to that responsibility, the judge/court dominates the narrative. In other words, judges pull elements of the story from the evidence that is noted in the dossier.

In court, structural differences become more pronounced: judges are actively involved in developing the master narrative.[180] They are not dependent on what is presented by the adversaries, who, despite being on opposite sides, participate in the development of the master narrative.[181] The entire process hinges on judges as impartial inquisitors, and one can argue that makes the process less "dramatic"[182] (in Dershowitz's sense). But to say that there is no narrativization or subjective interpretation would be inaccurate. Judges "indisputably incessantly and necessarily interpret" and produce the very facts that form the basis of their verdicts.[183] Verdicts and facts are not logically deduced; they are created.[184] The laws and texts that are interpreted must be considered as products of the imagination, and the legal endeavor must always be seen as fictional.[185] The (partial) ignorance of the story dimension is therefore not justified. While for most cases trust in a technical procedural setup, the transparency of a written verdict, the principle of instruction, or (in theory) an unlimited factual appeal might prevent, it is possible that wrongful convictions may be even harder to remedy than in the United States because of the reality of court-affirmed master narratives. Not everything that influences a narrative will be in the verdict. It has been argued that, when the author and the recipient of a narrative share similar experiences and expectations, the likelihood of a wrongful conviction is lower because both sides know what is important and can anticipate narratives from the other side.[186] German judges, prosecutors, and defense attorneys share a similar world, but that factor might also contribute to wrongful convictions. The (comparatively) weak defense is confronted with a court that has already approved a prosecutor's charge as being valid. That potential alliance (and the mutual narrative that made it to court) is potentially more likely to persevere than a narrative that gets a fresh look from the jury. Although the German system seems to come with many (possibly even more) safeguards against wrongful convictions than the American system, wrongful convictions are still possible. If the system fails, what are the reasons? And what role does narrative play? In chapter 5, I will review and discuss one well-known wrongful conviction and apply the lessons from this chapter to an actual case.

5

Anatomy of a German Wrongful Conviction

Failing Truth?

They are looking in the wrong spot.[1]
—Laura Baker, the teenage daughter of Hans Baker, from
the Case of the Missing Farmer (Baker Transcript, 34)

On the night of October 13, 2001, Hans Baker, a farmer in a small town in Bavaria, Germany, stepped into his Mercedes and drove to the local sports club, where he sat down at his table and started drinking.[2] Baker was not very popular. He rarely changed clothes when he came from the farm and was considered a brawler, especially when he was drunk. At around one o'clock in the morning, after having consumed four liters of beer, he left the bar with an estimated blood alcohol level of around 0.25%. He never returned home, and this is the last time he was seen alive by anyone. The next day, Helen Baker, his wife, reported him missing. Over the next few days, police conducted a thorough albeit unsuccessful search for Hans.

In May 2005, the circuit court in Ingolstadt sentenced Baker's wife, Helen, and Michael Smith, who was the former fiancé of one of the Bakers' daughters, Kim Baker, to eight-and-a-half-years in prison for the manslaughter of Hans. The two daughters (Kim and Laura), who were 15 and 16 years old at the time of Hans's disappearance, were sentenced to two and a half years and three and a half years of juvenile imprisonment for aiding and abetting the homicide. The verdict was based on confessions in which the defendants admitted to slaughtering and dismembering Hans at his house and then feeding the remains to the pigs and dogs. Nothing of Hans's body was left. The defendants also stated that they had brought the car to a scrap metal dealer who disposed of it. All defendants recanted their confessions before the trial. Despite the lack of even a single piece of physical evidence, the court was certain about the conviction.

On the night in question, according to the verdict, Helen waited for Hans to return home from the bar and, when he had entered the house, hit him with a piece of construction wood. According to the prosecutor, the daughters are said to have kicked their father when he lay on the ground. Michael Smith also hit the defenseless, drunken victim while being cheered on by Helen and the two daughters. Baker was then moved to the basement, where Michael and his fiancée are said to have smashed Hans's head with a hammer while he was still alive. The next morning, they dismembered the dead farmer with a knife, a saw, and an ax. Michael had described in his confession how he cut off Hans's arms and legs, cut open the body, took out the organs, drained the blood with a margarine cup into a bucket, and then fed the pieces to the dogs. What remained was thrown on the dung heap. The victim's car was brought to a salvage yard, where it was scrapped with the help of the owner of the yard. All appeals of the verdict were unsuccessful.

Then, in March 2009, during a routine cleaning of a lock at the River Danube, firefighters pulled a car out of the water. It was Hans's Mercedes. Behind the wheel was Hans's partly skeletonized but otherwise undamaged corpse. That fact alone was proof that the details of the crime and its gruesome aftermath were not true. "At that time," the prosecutor stated, "we knew the story with the dogs was false." Even though large parts of the trial court's narrative could not have been correct, judges rejected a motion to reopen the case. Attorneys appealed, and the Bavarian Supreme Court issued an order to reopen. In 2011 (by then all the defendants had been released from prison after serving more than two-thirds of their time), a second trial took place, and a different court acquitted the defendants. In an unusual statement, the trial judges expressed their belief in the defendants' guilt; it simply had not been possible to determine which of them had caused the death. The owner of the junkyard, who in separate proceedings had been charged with a form of obstruction of justice, denied any involvement in the scrapping of the Mercedes and claimed the police officers had threatened him with a gun to admit to having helped Helen and Michael. The obstruction charges were dropped, but he was then prosecuted for slander for alleging he was threatened by police.

The Case of the Missing Farmer received some of the greatest media attention during the time, partly because of the dramatic circumstances, but also because it shattered the belief that the German legal system does not produce wrongful convictions. Well-documented reports of wrongful convictions have existed for a long time and have been covered in the journalistic and academic discourse. Thomas Darnstädt, a trained lawyer and journalist, in his book *Der Richter und sein Opfer* (The judge and his victim; 2013), and Sabine Rückert, who wrote *Unrecht im Namen des Volkes* (Injustice in the name of the people; 2007), provide detailed accounts of multiple cases and the factors that contributed to these wrongful convictions. Both authors argue that pressure on the police, systemic tunnel vision, and inadequate oversight over the judiciary are factors (among many others) that lead to wrongful convictions. On the doctrinal/scholarly side, Karl Peters published a three-volume analysis titled *Fehlerquellen im Strafprozess* (Sources of error in criminal proceedings; 1970–1974), which still is the leading analysis of potential errors (legal and factual) in criminal proceedings. Despite this awareness, false convictions have come under closer scholarly scrutiny only recently, but there is no consensus as to what is a wrongful conviction and what might count as potential contributing factors. There is also resistance to the general debate. One author, for instance, argues that by invoking the "ghost of the wrongful conviction"[3] a "climate of distrust" of the judiciary is created.[4] Journalists in their effort to reveal miscarriages of justice are dismissed by, for instance, Thomas Fischer, a former presiding judge at the Federal Court of Justice: "The likelihood that journalists of all people know what the truth and a false conviction are is similar to that of a social worker knowing the best method of cancer therapy in an individual case."[5] Klaus Tolksdorf, a former president of the German Federal Court of Justice, said that there will always be wrongful convictions but that they remain an "absolute exception."

Wrongful Convictions in an Inquisitorial System

In Germany, typical wrongful conviction cases are not documented as often as they are in the United States. Although specific convictions have been acknowledged as problematic, an ideal-typical understanding of the wrongful conviction phenomenon has not yet materialized. That has little to do with an ignorance toward the fallibility of the criminal process—rather, it is related to how "wrongfulness" is conceptualized.

In the American adversarial system, factual finality is reached when a jury renders its verdict, whereas in Germany (see chapter 4), finality is a more fluent concept in the sense that for most cases there are multiple points in the proceedings (including post-conviction) where review of the factual foundation of a case may occur. Moreover, a system that arguably already has laws in place that safeguard factual truth throughout all stages of a case—safeguards that the innocence movement as a social and reformatory movement is petitioning for—may be less likely to accept that wrongful convictions are a systemic issue.

The Scope of Wrongful Convictions in Germany

Opinions on what counts as a wrongful conviction run a broad gamut without settling on a specific definition. It is argued that a conviction can only be considered wrongful if sufficient incriminatory evidence existed at the time of the trial, and despite that evidence the court intentionally acquitted anyway, and vice versa. The question of whether the defendant is in fact innocent is seen as a "non-epistemic, metaphysical question, which moves in circles."[6] Only a legal layperson could be of the opinion that facts per se existed; they exist only when they are procedurally substantiated.

DEFINING "WRONGFUL CONVICTION"

For some, the term "wrongful conviction" appears to have no reasonable purpose in German law.[7] Most scholars, however, do accept the concept of a wrongful conviction, but they differ in what it entails and requires. A few focus on whether the verdict is the result of judicial negligence (i.e., by incorrectly weighing the evidence or applying the law), leading to an undesirable outcome,[8] and some distinguish between wrongful convictions in the broader sense (no procedural mistakes were made but historical truth is misrepresented) and the narrow sense (the false conviction is a result of purely procedural errors).[9] Others argue that a procedural rather than substantive paradigm of truth is necessary for defining wrongful convictions.[10] Closer to the American understanding are concepts that work with the idea of actual innocence.[11] As of now, there is only one study that analyzes the case files (which are typically sealed and not publicly accessible) of known cases of actual innocence. The study, which was undertaken by the Center for Criminology, included only cases in which the proceedings had been reopened because of newly discovered evidence and the convicted person(s) had been acquitted by another court[12]—the ideal-typical wrongful conviction scenario.

The variation in definitions—including those that deem wrongful convictions conceptually impossible—is surprising given the role factual truth plays in German criminal procedure. The whole criminal process stresses fact-finding and (at least in theory, as most definitory scholarship is theoretical and not based on case studies) allows for the introduction of new facts and the revision of verdicts on factual grounds as a procedural matter. Since judges and courts—legal professionals—are responsible for the verdicts, and not juries as in the American system, one could argue that decisions are more transparent and open to discourse than they are in the United States. This might merely be reflecting a system that practically does not rely on factual decision-making by an entity untrained in law and evidence. These reasons, when taken together, in combination with the comparatively low number of known cases of actual innocence,[13] may well explain why the body of German innocence research is comparatively small.

For the sake of clarity, I will use the term "wrongful conviction" for stereotypical cases in which a defendant did not commit the crime they were convicted for.[14] These cases must have become final, that is to say, with no further appeal possible except for post-conviction relief through Sec. 359 StPO.[15] As long as an appeal is still possible, a case cannot be considered a typical wrongful conviction. It might be a *false* or *erroneous* decision, but it is not *wrongful* in the ideal-typical sense.

THE PREVALENCE OF WRONGFUL CONVICTIONS

Evidence of wrongful convictions existed long before a more generalized innocence awareness began to develop, but until recently legal scholarship has not taken up wrongful convictions as an issue in its own right. Despite the lack of official data, there are many documented cases—online or published in case collections—in which courts erred and convicted wrongfully,[16] yet the discussion is still at a point where it addresses the question of whether wrongful convictions are a systematic problem at all. Likewise unclear is their prevalence.[17] Existing studies on the prevalence of wrongful convictions are limited in scale, looking only at small data sets that do not provide enough detail to infer a reliable wrongful conviction rate. There are also issues that relate to the accessibility of data.[18] Only the study by the Center , a federal research and documentation institute, provided some insights because it could access the files of cases that were reopened according to Sec. 359 StPO followed by an acquittal after retrial by a different court. For the period between 1990 and 2015, the Center for Criminology identified a total of 35 cases, 29 of which had the actual files available.[19] Most of these wrongful convictions were covered in the media and are listed in unofficial case registries. This study's goal was not to estimate a wrongful conviction rate but to look for common or typical issues in these cases and then compare them to the typologies known from American scholarship.

A Typology of Errors

Because of the low number of known wrongful convictions, it is difficult to infer a typology of errors in Germany. Superimposing the paradigmatic causes as they were developed in the United States on top of German data is difficult because of the differences in the procedural schemas in the two countries.

MISTAKEN WITNESS IDENTIFICATION

Eyewitness misidentification, which is relevant in 29% cases in the United States, does not play a pronounced role in Germany. However, the study by the Center for Criminology, sees eyewitness misidentification as a leading source for wrongful convictions in Germany (17 cases, or 45.8% of all cases) because they included false accusation cases (12 of the 17) as "special case[s] of eyewitness error."[20] That skews the image, since deliberate false accusations in cases where no crime has been committed are not comparable to a mistaken identity; in fact, the identity of the alleged perpetrator in these cases was undisputed. Only two out of these 17 cases (7% total) were actual misidentifications, and in each there was an "exceptional resemblance" between the alleged and actual perpetrator of a robbery.[21] One could surmise that potential reasons for the comparatively low number of misidentifications lie in fewer cross-racial identification issues, better-trained judges, and a different police culture.

PERJURY OR FALSE ACCUSATION

False accusation cases, which account for 59% in the United States, appear to be the most prominent subgroup of wrongful convictions noted in the German literature. However, most of the findings are based on individual case studies by defense attorneys or forensic psychiatrists.[22] The Center for Criminology counted 12 false accusations (34% of the total).[23] In 11 cases, girls or women accused a relative or acquaintance of sexual misconduct that did not happen. Although sometimes physical evidence was introduced (in some instances, accusers fabricated evidence like emails, text messages, and self-inflicted wounds, but there was also medical and psychological evidence attesting to the opposite), the narrative component was particularly strong. Most cases had a similar masterplot: a young, vulnerable victim claims to have been harmed by an adult (often with a previous criminal record). Prosecutors and judges seem to adhere to that archetypical framing narrative and disregard exculpatory evidence. Schwenn reported cases in which judges dismissed medical evidence stating that the alleged victim was still a virgin, when she claimed to have been raped by multiple perpetrators with multiple large items.[24] If there are discrepancies and contradictions in the accuser's testimony, they were often explained as the result of psychological conditions such as PTSD. Schwenn, who works as a defense attorney specializing in these types of cases, points out that one indicator of a wrongful conviction is the participation of victim support agencies and their staff. When the alleged victim visits such an agency at the "birth hour of the accusation," they aid in the development of powerful victim narratives.[25]

FALSE CONFESSION

The study by the Center for Criminology counts five defendants who falsely confessed to homicides they did not commit.[26] These were probably only two individual cases, one of them with four defendants. In light of such limited data—not just in this study but in general—no general conclusions can be drawn. It is worth noting that German criminal procedure prohibits interrogation methods that limit a suspect's intellectual freedom, including torture and any kind of deception, induced fatigue, and the like. Another aspect is that the German system is not based on "pleas"—whether guilty or innocent—and plea bargaining (or its equivalent) is much more regulated than in the United States. Since judges must be actively involved in such negotiations, defendants are not as easily overwhelmed as they can be in the United States, meaning that they are less incentivized to accept responsibility.

FALSE OR MISLEADING FORENSIC EVIDENCE

Experts play a prominent role in criminal proceedings. Trials have become technically complex, and judges must often rely on the experts. In 12 instances studied by the Center for Criminology, expert testimony was a contributing factor in the conviction (it is relevant in 24% of U.S. wrongful convictions). Most often (in 6 cases), experts evaluated victim witnesses in false accusation cases.[27] In other cases, experts falsely assumed criminal liability ("sanity") when the defendants were not mentally fit to be tried.

Judges usually rely on and trust experts, especially when they have worked with certain experts in the past or are acquainted with them.[28] Although defendants can request the court to hear a different expert or look beyond the existing evidence, truth-finding is the prerogative of the courts, which makes it difficult to introduce counternarratives and evidence in support. But experts are not always beyond the reach of a wrongfully convicted defendant. The expert in Donald Stellwag's case was later held liable to pay DM 150,000 in damages to Stellwag for providing the flawed identification analysis.

OFFICIAL MISCONDUCT

Official misconduct, which impacts 54% of all wrongful convictions in the United States, is a factor more difficult to observe in Germany because there is less room for Brady violations (the willful or inadvertent withholding of evidence favorable to the defendant), since all evidence is collected in the dossier and made available to the defense and the court. Although it is possible that prosecutors intentionally leave exculpatory facts out of the dossier, known wrongful convictions do not flag this as a particular problem. It is more likely that prosecutors and judges develop tunnel vision and are biased against the defendant. Although judicial independence and discretionary decision-making are typically thoroughly checked, the evaluation of evidence and deciphering and constructing what it signifies remain the original tasks of a judge. "[F]actual conclusions need not be undeniable; it is generally sufficient that they are possible and that he is convinced of their correctness."[29] A verdict "must show that the assessment of evidence is based on a sound factual basis and that the conclusion drawn by the court is not just an assumption or proves to be a mere presumption."[30] As much as this sounds like considerable freedom in evaluating the weight of evidence, few (if any) cases show signs of judges intentionally ignoring exculpatory facts or framing defendants despite their better knowledge. However, if tunnel vision sets in early, a framing narrative can move through the case with little interference.[31]

Tunnel vision as a "human tendency"[32] must be seen as a distinctive factor in wrongful convictions in Germany. For example, during the so-called Zwischenverfahren (intermediate proceedings), the court that has jurisdiction over a trial must "decide whether main proceedings (i.e., the trial) are to be opened or whether proceedings are to be provisionally terminated" (Sec. 199 (1) StPO). In other words, the judges who are potentially presiding over the case consider the indictment based on whether there is sufficient evidence. This step was introduced as a safeguard when the prosecutor and judge became two separate and independent entities. But judges might bias themselves when they allow the case to proceed based on their finding of sufficient evidence (Hinreichender Tatverdacht, or "probable cause"). Critics argue that, in the ensuing trial, judges avoid cognitive dissonances by looking more favorably at evidence that supports their initial understanding of the case.[33] This has been described as the "inertia" or "perseverance" effect.[34] That can lead to "cognitive distortion,"[35] a typical risk of judge-dominated fact-finding.

The authority given to courts and judges can lead to a harmful overconfidence.[36] In addition to a lack of adversarial checks in a trial atmosphere dominated by judges, there is also the issue that prosecutors and judges usually have strong institutional ties. Although all lawyers go through the same legal education, judges and prosecutors are picked from the top of their university class, which puts them inside a specific legal subculture. This closeness of prosecutors and judges has kindled criticism as to how one-sided a trial might (but not necessarily must) become. These strong ties between prosecutors and judges (Schulterschlusseffekt, or the "locking-of-shoulders" effect) make it even easier for preconceived framing narratives to prevail.[37] This and unchecked tunnel vision were arguably the main issues in the Case of the Missing Farmer, discussed in the next section.

The Case of the Missing Farmer

None of the existing studies on wrongful convictions focused even remotely on processes of narrativization within the German criminal justice system. The reading of the following case establishes that narrative is—or can be—an overriding factor in a system that puts into place many safeguards to promote factually truthful convictions. It also shows in detail how, once prosecutors and judges are convinced of a narrative, signs of innocence or guilt become interchangeable. "Evidence" is context-dependent, and the creation of that context resides in the hands of judges.

It was a singular moment: a witness called the police offering a hypothesis as to what might have happened to Hans Baker, thereby creating a framing narrative so strong that it was channeled throughout all the stages of this case. Narrative "channeling," as it is used in this context, stands for *a process of narrativization that is influenced by psychological effects inhibiting the consideration of an alternative story*. Inertia, perseverance, and anchor effects contribute to such channeling. Once an officer, prosecutor, or judge is confident of a certain story, inertia can set in, making it more difficult to "consider alternative hypotheses impartially."[38] The initial story becomes perpetuated because factually exculpatory scenarios are not considered.[39] Especially in circumstantial cases (like the Case of the Missing Farmer) judgments made under conditions of uncertainty are often affected by the starting point—the "anchor" from which they are reached.[40] Although inertia, perseverance, and anchoring affect the shape of legal narratives in all systems, I posit that channeling is a risk typical to inquisitorial systems because of the comparatively limited instances of narrative review. Ideally, a jury hears a case with little narrative prejudice—all potential stories are new; but an inquisitorial judge is familiar with the whole case narrative and its development when the trial is opened. During the investigation phase, it is possible for defense attorneys to intervene and proffer debiasing "consider-the-opposite" strategies,[41] though Hans Baker's case file does not show any attorney involvement until the trial, when the case narrative had already coagulated.

It is impossible to decompress the factual and legal narrative to an extent that would still be accessible. There are many micro-narratives, nuances in how the main events are represented, and slight changes in argument that if they were retold in full would do little to enhance our understanding of the narrative. I will only occasionally address these micronarratives when they play a role in how narrators develop their beliefs.

The Investigation—Creating Suspicion

The disappearance of Hans Baker created a narrative gap that needed filling, what Bruner calls in narrative terms, a "tantalizing mystery."[42] Neighbors, acquaintances, and the police wondered about the circumstances of his disappearance, creating, when no efforts of finding him were successful, lingering cognitive dissonance. What the early moments of the investigation in this case show is that any kind of speculation can inspire an investigator to imagine the events of a crime. The alleged conflict between Hans and the rest of his family made the story tellable, filling the void of what yet needs an explanation.[43] Narrative "thrives on conflict" but also requires the desires, intentions, and beliefs of an agent, a character.[44] All of that came together early: Michael Smith in his rebellion against the father of his fiancée is joined by wife and daughters who wanted more financial freedom in a plot that ends tragically.

CREATING SUSPICION

The legal narrative begins on page one of the dossier in the criminal investigation of Hans Baker's death. This first page is the missing person report filed by his wife on October 14, 2001—two days after Hans's trip to the bar. Multiple steps were taken to locate him, including sending police to nearby parks, distributing flyers, and later the use of helicopters. In December 2001, wife Helen Baker applied for legal guardianship of Hans's property since she had no legal authority to make executive decisions. In April 2002, police still treated the case as a missing person case and suggested another search be conducted given that it is likely Hans Baker ended up in either a lake or the nearby river. When this did not produce any leads, police wrote a preliminary summary of the case in July 2002, suggesting suicide as a potential explanation because Baker's health has been declining and his financial situation was difficult.[45]

For almost a year, no further entries were made in the file. Then, on April 28, 2003, a detective filed a report of an interview with a witness. The witness, an acquaintance of Helen's who had previously contacted the police in support of Helen, said she "would like to state something of importance." She recalls meeting Helen and her daughter Laura at her home for coffee. When they heard a helicopter outside, the witness mentioned to Helen and Laura: "They are looking for your husband, Hans," whereupon Helen and Laura laughed and Laura asserted, "They are looking in the wrong spot [lit. "corner"]."[46] The witness suggested to the officer that the whole family is not very smart and that they made comments without thinking. However, on the last page of the transcript, the officer noted that the witness wanted said, " I don't want to express any suspicion, I just have a vague assumption for myself." The witness then points out that there are many dangerous dogs living on the farm, and one of the daughters (Kim Baker) is "aggressive" and so is her boyfriend, Michael Smith, who is unemployed and lives with Kim. Hans does not approve of that and wanted Michael gone. The witness "could imagine that the dogs may have eaten Hans for some incomprehensible reason. Moreover, the family has a large dung heap on the farm. Some time last year, the courtyard had been paved."[47] No support for these speculations was offered, and the officer did not press for any. It was all speculation. But from a narrative perspective, the witness's assertion was now a possible story that police could follow up on.

THE LOGIC OF STORY TIME AND RECONSTRUCTION TIME

The continuing investigation exemplifies what has been discussed in narrative theory as the difference between "story time" and time as it is represented in the narrative. Reading the case in retrospect (knowing that Baker's body and car were not disposed of by the defendants) clarifies how police read certain clues and gave them (in hindsight) false relevance. While the time structure of the story (the events) is always chronological, the time structure of the narrative discourse can take many shapes.[48] In a criminal case, the temporal relevance of when "evidence" is discovered is rarely considered but can be important for the development of the story plot because evidentiary signposts are

(unconsciously) read on a timeline. For example, a Mercedes sales catalogue with Michael Smith's phone number scribbled on it was found in
the office of the salvage yard owner. This became a clue because it created a connection between Hans's missing car (a Mercedes), the owner
of the salvage yard (who might have helped in disposing it), and Michael
smith (potentially being involved in the crime). Had Baker been found
in the river in his car a few hours or days and not years after he had
disappeared, police would probably not have pursued the case the same
way because they knew the car was not salvaged. The catalogue would
be meaningless. But with the car missing, it became a clue not only for
the alleged murder but also for the salvage yard owner's involvement in
it.[49] A legal narrative, like the one that developed in Baker's case, will be
judged by its plausibility for a specific legal mold (the crime) and what
certain signs can potentially mean. There is little consciousness of the
multiple ways in which signs may be read. The judges who later acquitted the defendants on retrial argued that, even if they had known about
the car in the river, they would have pursued the case in a similar way.
But how could they be sure? Knowing the case file and crime narrative
influenced their reading of the case. It once again shows that narratives
have a long reach.

CONFIRMATION NARRATIVES

After initial interviews of potential witnesses, police had enough suspicion for a framing narrative despite the lack of anything concrete. They
worked from an alleged statement Laura Baker had made to a witness
after police searched the farm for the missing Hans. Laura mentioned
that police had looked everywhere ("they even looked in the freezer
and the washing machine").[50] According to that witness, Laura laughed
"daftly" and added: "We're not so stupid as to put the father in the
freezer."[51] She also added that police did not search the pile of manure.
It is unclear in which context and why that comment was made, but it
contributed to the developing narrative that was in line with the initial
suspicion.

Based on these statements, police acquired a search warrant for the
farm. Although the affidavit for the warrant refers to the suspects as
"unknown," it is clear that police investigated the members of the family and Michael Smith. Two witnesses "incriminate"[52] Laura, Kim, and

Helen Baker with the remarks about the helicopter, the freezer, and the dung heap. It was also "commonly known" that Hans argued with his daughters and the fiancé, Michael. These statements gained even more weight in light of some construction work (leveling and paving) done on the farm, which could be seen as a way to cover up evidence. It was also found suspicious that "[a]lready 4 weeks after the disappearance, the wife, Helen Baker, tried to have her husband declared dead. This is likely to be due to two life insurance policies, which were not paid out despite the dire financial situation."[53] Outside the framing narrative, one could argue that Helen was running out of money (which she was) to support the farm and family, but it was probably read as a motive for the crime. The search did not turn up any evidence.

Signs that would cast doubt on the suspects' involvement in the crime were not read or seen. When, for instance, the barkeeper stated that he saw Hans leaving on a route that does not directly lead back to his home, police were surprised. Instead of following up, they continued pursuing the murder story they were already convinced of. In retrospect, to reach the place where Hans's car and body were found years later, one would have to drive how the barkeeper described. Other aspects of the investigation that did not quite fit the main narrative were explained away or ignored: How can a body be vanished without a trace? Why would the wife of the missing person speak with a barkeeper when in fact she had just participated in killing him and therefore had seen him last? Narrative has the power to filter out logical interferences. The transcripts are full of these micro-inconsistencies that were later smoothed out. But these ignored, missed, or dismissed micro-narratives might contain clues to the truth or at least question the veracity of the main narrative.[54]

One procedurally permissible way to steer witness testimony and confirm one's own narrative is what is called a Vorhalt (lit. "hold/put before"). It is a presentation of facts that has the function of jogging a witness's or suspect's memory or confronting them with contradictions. This gives an interrogator the opportunity to proffer facts to the witness. These presentations appear to have played a significant role in the construction of the narrative. For instance, the tenant who lived in the Baker home had maintained that she did not hear any arguments or a fight in Helen and Hans's bedroom on the night he disappeared. The officer then states: "In the night . . . there was a serious argument in the bedroom of the Baker family, which you must have heard."[55] Note that the detective uses the indicative: Police had no evidence that would confirm a fight; nor was there evidence that confirmed that Hans Baker had returned home at all. The officer then stressed (without having expressed any doubts as to the witness's credibility) that the witness must testify truthfully and that she could be arrested and charged as an accomplice if she did not. The witness repeated that she had not noticed Hans coming home or heard anything that sounded like a fight—a statement her daughters confirmed in subsequent interviews. The tenant's testimony did not line up with the police narrative, and the mother was later charged first as an accomplice to the homicide and then with obstruction of justice. Police were so convinced of their story that they seemed to know better than the witness herself what she "must" have heard. Even when a Vorhalt is not specifically noted in the transcript, it can be inferred when, for instance, the transcript states, "When I am asked whom I told that Mr. Baker drove straight ahead, I can say that I very likely spoke with my daughters about that."[56] This kind of phrasing interrupts the typical question-and-answer rhythm of the interview. It is simultaneously question and answer in one, spoken by the witness, probably as a result of a Vorhalt.

The proximity (time and place) of all the interviews suggests that information gained in one interview might have been used in others, especially in light of the number of Vorhalte that were made during the various interrogations. The transcripts, although written in the first person, are not verbatim representations. Witnesses appeared to be speaking in full sentences, mostly in High German, which they probably didn't during the interviews because many of the witnesses grew up in the region of Bavaria where Hans disappeared and probably spoke some form of dialect (later transcripts include dialect, and in the video footage of the reenactment all suspects spoke with so much dialect that it was subtitled). When the earlier transcripts include words in dialect, they are put in quotation marks and used when witnesses or officers directly referred to the crime and how it was conducted, as if the brutality of the act is related to the uneducated, simple existence of the suspects. Moreover, the transcript does not include slips, breaks, stammers, fillers, or anything else that could provide a more authentic image of the interrogation. These transcripts are a prefiltered version of the content, but, by signing them, witnesses and suspects submitted them as their own. In some instances, it is obvious that a detective intervened during a statement and a witness continues with "if I come to think of it" or "if I now think precisely about it," without a note that there had been an interruption or prompt. In one interview, for instance, the witness is asked about a sweater that Michael Smith found at the bar and brought back home. The witness states:

> I had asked Helen Baker at the time whether she had shown [the sweater] to the police. Helen then answered the police said they would not need it.
> It really seemed to me as if she was mourning for her husband.[57]

The shift from the sweater to mourning without any transition might simply have reflected the witness's train of thought; it could also have been a response to a question that was thrown in without being recorded. Peter Brooks uses the term "rhetorical improprieties"[58] to describe issues that can arise when narrated monologue is constructed to fulfill a purpose within the larger discourse. Such transformations and translations of an answer rarely raise doubts on the prosecutorial or judicial levels. Since they occur in the early stages of an investigation and are re-narrativized multiple times before they reach the court, they are visible to readers only if they are trained in or otherwise sensitized to this kind of rhetoric.[59] Narrative discourse in a police environment is always guided and rarely develops freely; it is the result of questions and an overall preconceived conception—a schema—of what the officers expect or want to hear.

In the subsequent interviews, more rhetorical improprieties can be observed, but they also exemplify how a reader's perception of time is affected by narrativization. When one reads to discern the facts, it is easy to miss temporal gaps. The main suspects were all first interrogated on the same day but in different rooms or places at different times so that it might have been possible to use statements made by one as a Vorhalt in another interrogation.

Helen Baker's interrogation on January 13, 2004, began at 8:30 AM and lasted until 12:40 PM, when a break was taken. The record of what has been said in those four hours is very brief and can be read within a minute. It is also noted that during the "informal conversation" suspicion arose that Helen was involved in the crime and that at 11:20 AM she was Mirandized. It is unclear at what point and how Helen became a suspect because the record is silent in that regard; it only notes that she admitted to pushing Hans, who fell and hit is head.

Quite similarly, the record of Michael Smith's interrogation contains large temporal gaps. Right at the beginning, at 11:30 AM, the detective notes:

> Before the recording of the following statements, an in-depth conversation is held between 8.00 AM and 11.15 AM. After initially denying certain facts, the witness makes the following statements.[60]

There had been more than three hours of "conversation" off the record before the official interrogation began. Starting at 1 PM, Michael is interrogated as a suspect. In that interrogation, multiple presentations remind him of statements he had made during the preliminary conversation. Sometimes, Michael confirms such a presentation only "by a clear nod and 'hm.'"[61] Kim Baker's interview followed. Just like the others, she was treated as a suspect. The officers asked her about potential sexual abuse through her father (potentially looking for motive), but they did that without preface or warning or offering to have a psychologist or social worker present.

That the officers were looking for a confirmation of their framing narrative came out in Laura Baker's interrogations as well. The transcript notes that the officers took 11 minutes to explain the necessity of Laura's "unrestricted cooperation."[62] At the end of the interrogation, one of the officers confronted her with testimony that allegedly confirms her father's return. That confused Laura. She requests the interview to be stopped. Less than an hour later it continued. At the beginning, but recorded only in a note, the officers confronted Laura with partial confessions made by her mother and Michael, which devastated Laura, who now needed another break. During that break, Laura met her (otherwise not involved) boyfriend in the staircase. "In a whispering voice but for the two detectives that were with her, Laura admits to her friend that she had killed her father because he had sexually abused her";[63] in the ensuing interrogation, the officer told Laura that her version of the events "cannot be correct."[64] Laura admits to lying and confirmed that Hans had come home on that night and continued with a version of the events that fit the imagined crime, but not without contradictions. The last question asked by the officer: "Are you mentally and physically normal?" Laura answered: "Yes."[65]

A confession alone is typically not sufficient as evidence for a conviction. It requires further corroboration or at least very strong coherence and detail. On February 3, 2004, all suspects were brought to their home for a reenactment of the crime. The weekly newspaper *Der Spiegel* published parts of the police video that shows the reenactment.[66] In that video, one officer interrupted the suspects when they did not seem to "get it right." Officers appeared to be comforting one of the suspects by hugging her and consistently addressed the daughters in an informal way by using the German second singular ("Du"). The officer also referred to the victim as "daddy" (instead of "your father") and called Helen Baker "Mam," short for "Mama," a term used by Kim and Laura. While this behavior may not reach the level of undue influence, another did: at a crucial point in the reenactment, the official video recording is paused, and when it resumed, the officer stated "short addition: after a short conversation with Kim Baker in which it was explained to her that the events couldn't have happened the way she had explained, she agrees to, again, show what happened." The transcript includes multiple instances of suggestive questions that resulted in answers that appeared close to what the officer suggested.

HOW DETAILS MATTER

Michael Smith's confession was a central pillar of the case. To confirm the veracity of a confession, courts rely on certain markers developed by forensic psychologists.[67] But these markers, like any other evidence, are embedded in narrative. Michael Smith's confession is exemplary in how it apparently presents many signposts of truthful narration when, in fact, all these details are made up and a result of narrative imagination. According to Friedrich Arntzen, who developed credibility markers in his *Psychology of Witness Statements*, criteria that speak for a truthful statement include:

- Detail and distinctive features that include original presentations, psychological and emotional processes, negative complications, presentations of interactions, etc.

- Homogeneity of testimony
- Relative consistency and inconsistency of testimony
- Testimony can be fleshed out and amended upon questioning
- Relived emotional involvement
- Uncontrolled testimony[68]

Smith's statements are richly detailed. The part in which he described what he did with Hans's body stretches over 18 pages in the transcript. He mentions the different tools he used for various body parts, explained how he had to reheat the kettle that he used to boil and soften the severed head because the fire went out, lists the number of trash bags he needed to wrap and transport the body parts, that he washed his hands in the rain barrel, where he drank beer, and the lengths of the breaks he needed. Many almost insignificant objects are mentioned—like the empty margarine container used as a scoop. He also includes vignettes like playing with the dogs or feeding the animals before he went back to the basement.

Michael appears emotionally involved, occasionally being in tears, especially when he described how he had planned the crime and the process of dismembering Hans's body in the basement:[69] "The accused has a hard time making this statement. In this statement, he looks down and it takes him about 10 minutes to express it."[70] This relived emotional involvement was seen as another fact that speaks to the truthfulness of the confession.

Memory lapses (forgetting, for instance, the smell of the body), like minor inconsistencies, were seen as supporting the authenticity of his confession.[71] Later, the verdict will emphasize that Michael's emotional responses and the details he provided in this interrogation add to the credibility of the testimony. When the case was reopened and retried, the apparent problem of how much weight this confession was given was not brought up again; neither was an explanation provided of how the confessions came about. Only Helen Baker said that she was put under pressure by the police.

The dossier, which has now accumulated more than 1,650 pages, concludes with a "summary report" (Schlussbericht) written by the police. It spans over 10 pages and provides a chronological narrative of how suspicion arose. It stresses that Helen, her daughters, and Michael "became increasingly entangled in contradictions,"[72] which led to their confessions. Although not legally required, the report goes over potential motives for the crime and explains what the accused are "accused" of (only prosecutors can technically accuse): murder. There is no discussion of the potential motives for the initial incriminating remarks, no word on why they were thought to be suspicious—just the claim that, "in the fall of 2003, clues that Hans Baker died of non-natural causes intensified."[73]

The Indictment

The so-called Anklageschrift (charge, bill of indictment) is the next central piece of narrative created in the German criminal process. It informs a defendant about the factual and legal bases of an accusation and substantiates the particulars of the crime. The indictment includes the main results of the criminal investigation and provides a coherent narrative of the case. This narrative is based on "the relevant results of the investigation" (Sec. 200 (2) StPO) as they are evaluated and filtered by the prosecutor.[74] The guiding principle is that every element of a crime for which the prosecution seeks a conviction must be positively addressed, but what prosecutors think is irrelevant, inconsistent, or might invite a different reading does not need clarification.

An indictment does not necessarily lead to a trial because, in an intermediate step, judges must decide whether there is sufficient cause for a trial. If a case proceeds, it is presided over by the same judges that were involved in this step. In Hans Baker's case, one indictment against all four defendants was filed on June 14, 2004 (almost three years after Hans had gone missing), accusing the four defendants of murder.

The statement of fact is written in chronological order, providing a summary of the case on four pages. It does not only condense and summarize the historical events; it also narrativizes them "as if" they happened that way. What might appear as contradictions, doubts, or even conjecture in the original documents is now smoothed out and reduced to a coherent narrative. For instance, the conflicting statements as to the relationship between Hans Baker and Michael Smith that were visible throughout the investigation are now resolved into "strong tensions." In just a few lines, the prosecutor connected these tensions to Michael Smith's motive and the plan among all defendants to kill Hans Baker.[75]

The smoothing of evidentiary ripple can be observed throughout the indictment, especially when no physical evidence was available at all. A defendant's specific state of mind (*mens rea*) became "apparent," and crucial elements of the plot (for instance, where Hans had entered the house) were surmised because Hans entered the home through a side entrance "as usual." The murder weapon that was never found was described as a "70x5cm rectangular piece of wood."[76] Statements allegedly made by the defendants are reported in free indirect discourse to make them appear genuine, and there is great detail when the harrowing specifics of how Baker was killed are laid out.[77] The indictment does not offer any direct physical evidence in support of the narrative of the homicide or its aftermath. The indictment notes, for instance, that Hans's car was "prepared for scrapping and then disposed of in the following days."[78]

In a circumstantial case, the narrative in the indictment is more than the representation and combination of evidence—it develops evidentiary force itself. Just as in the police report, inconsistencies and gaps in the confessions had to be smoothed out so that one streamlined account of the crime was presented. Since all defendants changed or modified their narratives, the indictment had to decide on one version and pick elements that fit the imagined story. Initially, all defendants stated that both car and body were disposed of in a nearby pond (and not the river, where it was later found); later the story was changed to the version in which Smith dismembered the body. None of the contradictions were ever addressed in the indictment. It is written as if there was no doubt.

In the next section of the indictment, prosecutors expanded on the main results of the investigation and provided factual support for their narrative. Particular attention is given to statements the suspects made. For instance, the indictment notes that Helen Baker mentioned to neighbors to report Hans Baker missing "already" soon after he had gone missing. The subtle "already" (bereits) makes it appear as if such a behavior is somewhat suspicious, as if she was following through with a plan. But wouldn't—in the eyes of a prosecutor—a report filed later have been even more suspicious? When it came to reconstructing the night Hans Baker went missing, the indictment noted that he did not "behave in any way conspicuous, neither depressed nor sad, and in particular did not express thoughts of suicide."[79] The reason the prosecutor mentioned what Hans Baker did *not* talk about? The prosecutor had to address the theory that Hans Baker considered suicide. However, one witness at the bar mentioned that, when patrons tried to stop Hans from taking his car, he appeared adamant about driving himself. These statements, which could point toward suicide, were not discussed in the indictment. An indictment is not a critical reading; it is a construction. So it is not surprising that some minutia (like the "already") become amplified. The police file consists of multiple instances in which the suspects "conceded" or "confirmed" the police's version after breaks or certain presentations. Comments like "the helicopter searches in the wrong place (lit. "wrong corner")," "the police did not look through the dunghill during the search," and "we are not so stupid as to put the father in the freezer"[80] were used to anchor suspicion, even though all witnesses who reported these remarks provided more context. The witnesses noted that "Helen and her daughter always made stupid remarks" and that "the whole family is not very intelligent, they are, in my opinion, very dumb."[81] The suspect's statements could be read differently, meaning, for example, that "If we had killed father [conditional], we wouldn't be that stupid to put the father in the freezer." In light of the unsuccessful helicopter search, the statement could have been read as "they have not found him here before, and looking in the same area again will not lead to anything." This is not to suggest that that the suspects meant it that way but rather that it would have been possible. Later, all the defendants were found to be severely intellectually challenged, with IQs not exceeding 70.

This section of the indictment concluded with a coherent narrative of the alleged events based on Michael Smith's confession, which was "confirmed by the statements of the other defendants."[82] "Other possibilities, which could explain the 'disappearance' of the [victim], must be excluded." As with similar tunnel vision cases, the search for truth ended and was replaced by efforts to corroborate the crime story. This goes so far as to seeing credibility in even the most contradictory statements from intellectually challenged defendants:

> Also, the way the accused testified speaks for a planned and agreed upon crime. The initially extremely contradictory and differing statements of the accused can easily be explained in hindsight by the agreements made among the accused following the bloodshed.[83]

Contradictions are proof of premeditation. What must have appeared as uncoordinated is interpreted as plausible and meaningful. The conviction of a certain truth somewhere hidden in these statements became the leading force behind everything that followed, establishing a momentum so strong that the state, even after the car had been found, held on to it. A once-established narrative of a story will be upheld even when its factual foundation is shattered.

The context-dependent nature of narrative is apparent throughout the case file, and there are instances that exemplify how even common sense or logic succumb to the momentum of story. In one version of the confessions, the defendants mentioned the possibility of an accidental death as a result of a quarrel when Baker came home. The prosecutor argues: "Against the alleged 'accident' speaks the later dissecting of the corpse and feeding to the dogs. Such behavior is not conceivable in the case of negligent behavior."[84] What is not conceivable for one might be somebody else's desperate attempt to deal with a situation that had escalated. This is not to say that such an accident was likely to have happened, but these very facts show that what the prosecutor presumed was conceivable was in fact wrong.

The Trial

One of the specifics of the German criminal trial is that prior to opening the main hearing (i.e., the trial) the "court which is competent for the main hearing shall decide whether main proceedings are to be opened or whether proceedings are to be provisionally terminated" (Sec. 199 (1) StPO). The court "shall decide to open main proceedings if in the light of the results of the preparatory proceedings there appear to be sufficient grounds to suspect that the indicted accused has committed a criminal offence" (Sec. 203 StPO). At this point, the court can decide whether more evidence is needed or if the case can be tried. If the case moves to trial, it will be the same judges presiding over the case that conducted this interlocutory process. This process has been criticized as allowing the judges to develop an opinion as to the defendant's guilt prior to the trial. In narrative terms, judges agree to a certain framing narrative that they will be in charge of proving or disproving.

In the Case of the Missing Farmer, the trial took 24 days spanning across five months. All defendants were tried at the same time before the same court, a juvenile court (große Jugendkammer), as three defendants were juveniles at the time of the alleged crime. Because of the severity of the alleged crime, the bench consisted of one presiding judge, two associate judges, and two lay judges. The court had to function as a juvenile court to have jurisdiction over juveniles and adults and could apply juvenile criminal law to the juveniles and adult criminal law to the adults. German criminal law does not contain the concept of a waiver to adult court. For young adults (between 18 and 21), usually the opposite happens in that they are treated as juveniles. That was the case for Smith. The main difference between juvenile and adult law is that juvenile criminal law provides a much more individualized set of interventions that considers the developmental differences among juveniles. Also, maximum prison sentences are lower (for juveniles that limit is 15 years).

Reconstructing a German criminal trial is difficult because there are no verbatim records of the statements made in court. A new law (the DokHVG) has been created to change that. The record mainly summarizes procedural aspects: for example, that a specific witness is called and that the witness made statements on the matter, if objections are raised, or if certain statement should be recorded verbatim. A typical entry would look like this:

> The witness Peter Fahrer was interrogated as follows:
> Personal Information:
> Fahrer, Peter
> 56 years, farmer, address: Külbstr. 13, 53131 Mainz
> - not personally or by marriage related to the defendants -
> As to the matter:
> The witness Peter Fahrer testifies to the matter.
> The witness is not put under oath and was with consent of all parties
>   released at 12:45pm.

Verbatim statements into the record are possible, but there are not any in the transcript of this trial. In contrast to the actual verdict, a trial is based on the principle of orality, which requires that only what is spoken openly in court can be the basis of the decision.[85] The record, however, does not trace how the court investigates, what questions are asked in what sequence, how they are answered and interpreted, and so on. Here, the judges did not go beyond the scope of the indictment in their investigation of the underlying facts and followed the evidence proffered in the indictment. On the last day of trial, the verdicts were read. Michael Smith and Helen Baker were sentenced to eight years and six months, Kim Baker to three years and six months, and Laura Baker to two years and six months. Under German law, a detailed written verdict is required to explain how facts were found and how they fit under the law.

The Verdict

Each trial ends with an oral verdict issued by the judges. If the defendant is convicted, "the reasons for the judgment must specify the facts deemed to be proven and establishing the statutory elements of the criminal offence" (Sec. 267 (1) StPO). German trial and appellate courts must issue a written verdict that expands on the apposite factual and legal reasons. In less complex cases, the verdict can be read into the record. In others, like this one, "it shall be placed on file without delay" (Sec. 275 (1) StPO). While the transcript of the trial is comparatively laconic, the written verdict in this case was detailed and almost 230 pages long. Typically, a verdict must cover the personal background of the defendants, the statement of facts, consideration of evidence, legal consideration, reasons for the sentence, and how costs are distributed.

The trial verdict closely follows the allegations made in the indictment but goes into much more detail to support them. As with the indictment, the verdict begins with a preface that provides background on the defendants, including prior convictions, alcohol consumption, school, jobs, and family. The judges paint a picture of a dysfunctional and abusive family. Hans is peaceful only when sober and potentially sexually abusive toward his daughters, Helen Baker is described as the "boss of the family,"[86] and Michael Smith quarreled and maintained sexual relationships with both sisters and his former girlfriend. Out of these tensions, motive developed.

The court had no "doubt as to the credibility of the statements"[87] of the defendants and was convinced that Baker had come home the night in question, since there were no other explanations for Baker's disap-

pearance.[88] Alternative scenarios were dismissed. Had it been a car accident, the car would have been found. A suicide would not have been in
line with Baker's character. Witnesses described him as a coward and too
sniveling to conduct such an act. Like the prosecutor, the judges thought
it was very unlikely that someone who wanted to commit suicide would
farm his field in the morning and behave normally in a bar at night. The
court assumed it was qualified enough to exclude a suicide based on witness statements and the simple assumption that, in the case of a suicide,
his body or at least his car would have been found.[89] Since they cannot
imagine the improbable—that a car vanishes without trace just a few
miles away from where it was last seen—that narrative gap is filled with
the murder plot. The court supports this with the confessions:

> None of the other potential explanations would explain why the defen-
> dants indicated Hans Baker had come home that night. There is no mo-
> tive for why the defendants should make such statements and thus expose
> themselves to the risk of prosecution if Hans Baker had not come home.
> One would just have to say so to the officers. Nor can it be argued that
> the defendants were surprised or thrown off guard because they were
> consistent throughout the interrogations, which, for the most part, were
> attended by their attorneys. Both interrogating officers are known to the
> court as reliable; there is no reason to doubt their testimony.[90]

The court followed the narrative as it was laid out in the indictment,
not seeing or considering the many inconsistencies in the suspects'
statements, how they denied that Hans Baker had come home, and
how police may have been guided by their narrative desire to elicit the
statements they needed. They did not acknowledge that the whole case
began with Helen Baker's missing person report. German procedural
law allows judges to arrive at their verdicts "according to its free conviction gained from the hearing as a whole" (Sec. 261 StPO). Judges can
but need not trust a statement or witness as being credible. They must
reconstruct the events exhaustively but can follow their own conviction, as simplistic and biased as it might be. Only the exclusionary rule,
logic (meaning that the arguments of the court must be clear, coherent, and without contradiction), and the laws of natural sciences limit
this evaluation. Judges are free to apply their own take on, for instance,

the circumstances under which someone would commit suicide, which sometimes leads to simplifications. One might argue that, given the circumstantial nature of the case and the absence of (at least) a claim of police misconduct from the defense, it was fair for the judges to rely on the confessions; however, it is then problematic how little the court scrutinized how the confessions came about. The verdict does not address the sometimes hours of preparatory conversations before official interrogations took place. Neither does it address how vulnerable the suspects were because of their intellectual challenges.

Judging the court's reasoning without hindsight bias is difficult. The judges looked in detail and meticulously at the substantive side of the confessions and asked experts to evaluate whether Smith's descriptions of how Baker was killed and dismembered were accurate. The expert confirmed that "twitching" or "shaking" are not unlikely; neither are the noises that Smith said Hans Baker had made.[91] When Laura Baker testified that she got her old teddy bear from the attic after the crime, the judges, guided by an expert, saw it as a "cry for help" so she could deal with the stress of the crime. Such behavior was considered understandable and age appropriate,[92] speaking "for the truthfulness of the confession"[93] because Laura could have simply denied the assault on her father. At times it would have been difficult not to read statements as incriminatory. While in jail, Laura said in a mediation meeting that she had to think of "how the boyfriend of my sister struck my father dead."[94] Had she accepted and internalized the label and the false narrative?

Especially in cases with circumstantial or no evidence other than an accusation from a victim, experts are highly influential. This case was no exception. The court often followed the expert's evaluation because he "presented his statements in a detailed and comprehensible manner. The expert has been known to the court for many years and his professional competence is beyond doubt."[95] Michael Smith's made-up story received the seal of approval from the expert, and the expert also helped the court to put less weight on the absence of blood in the basement. Smith stated he had put Baker's body on a tarp. The medical expert explained that neither the strike with the piece of wood nor the use of the hammer would have led to large amounts of blood—not more than "a spot the size of two large hands."[96] The judges concluded: "According to all this, the absence of further trails of blood does not contradict the course of events described by the defendants." Inconsistencies—like the thickness of the tarp being used—signified the credibility of these statements.[97] Thus, once the main narrative is established, smaller elements that don't seem to fit are absorbed easily. In other instances, judges apply a reasonable person standard to ambiguous situations that would invite multiple interpretations. For instance, when Helen Baker drove to the bar after Hans had not come home, she paid her husband's tab, something she had never done before.[98] The court found it striking that

> when Helen Baker visited the bar, she did not inquire about the particulars of her husband's visit. If her husband had not actually come home, it would have been expected that she would inquire whether he had actually been there, whether something was conspicuous, something he said or something like that. The fact that she did not do this and at the same time settled her husband's debts shows that the accused at that time knew what had happened to her husband.[99]

This is speculation based on what the judges thought they or a "reasonable" person would have done in that situation. But the court admits openly that "[a]ll these occurrences after the crime are, of course, not sufficient evidence, but they are indices which fit into the image which the defendants . . . themselves have described in their statements."[100] In the opinion of the court, there was no discernable, recognizable motive that would explain why the accused should incriminate himself so heavily if the described procedure did not correspond to the facts.

Probably the strongest element of the state's case was the detailed description of how Michael Smith dismembered the body. The court found it rich in detail and therefore credible. It was observed how Michael Smith changed saws (first wood then metal) to cut off the foot. "[S]omeone who imagines such complex events would not incorporate additional complications."[101] The court found these particulars especially important.[102] Given the mental challenges of the defendants, "it cannot be presumed they made these facts up."[103] When the medical examiner noted a few inconsistencies relating to the anatomy of the body and that the testimony lacked detail, the court found no fault, because neither the suspect nor the officer had any background in anatomy and therefore couldn't ask the right questions.[104]

The verdict does not (and by law need not) explain why sometimes details and sometimes the lack of them are seen as signs of credibility. The court can evaluate evidence freely and has discretion in how the logic of a case is put together. The lack of biological evidence was "understandable" given that Smith used a tarp. There also was a spot on the floor in the basement where there might have been blood, but it was painted over.[105] If parts from the investigation or indictment do not fit the evidence, they were explained away. For instance, the theory that Baker's remains were thrown on a dung heap and later brought out to a field could not be supported. The fact that no bone fragments were ever found was, according to the verdict, irrelevant, since Smith could have lied about that part; it would be horrible for him if a piece of Hans's body was ever found. The court also thinks that Smith could have fed the bones to the pigs, which ("as the court knows") are omnivores and eat everything. Confessing to that would be psychologically very hard. By not admitting to this part, Smith protected the family from knowing that the pigs (which were later consumed) contained Baker's body parts, which entered the food chain again.[106] Another possibility was that Smith brought the remains in plastic bags to a refuse incineration plant. Residential refuse is not screened for unusual content, and it is therefore possible that Smith disposed of the body that way.[107] The court acknowledged that it was not possible to fully clear up what had happened to the body, but that eventually carries little relevance, since the chamber was convinced that all elements of the crime were fulfilled.

The point here is not to argue that the court's conclusions were impossible; rather, it is to unmask the narrative logic at play here. Credibility, the congruence of facts, the role of details, and contradictions are all subject to narrative construction. The initial narrative as it developed throughout the investigation solidified during the trial.

Appeal

All four defendants filed appeals based on procedural errors. Since finding the truth is also a procedural issue, the defendants argued that the court should have taken and analyzed a sample of the concrete floor in the basement of the farm (the area that was painted over). This error was dismissed as being harmless, as were the others.

Reopening Procedures

On March 10, 2009, two cars were found at a lock on the River Danube. Divers reported the license plates of both cars. One of the cars was the missing Mercedes, and behind the wheel was Hans Baker's body—fully intact. According to the medical examination, death by blunt trauma against the skull could be excluded because the skull bone and all vertebrae were intact, and the brain did not show any indication of hemorrhages. This led to reinvestigation of the case—by the same officers and prosecutors that were involved before.

The defendants considered the body and the car as new evidence that would allow for the reopening of a final verdict. Not only did these findings contradict the murder narrative in significant parts; they also put into question the credibility of the confessions, which was based on how detailed and emotional the defendants described what they did to Baker's body. Given the new evidence, the argument went, the emotional reaction and all the details should not be considered as relevant anymore. In addition, the theory that the Mercedes had been salvaged was now wrong as well. However, the state held on to the main narrative, though it conceded that the verdict erred regarding how the corpse and the car were disposed of. But these new facts had no bearing on the crime itself—that is, the act of killing. The state now argued that finding the car in the river was in line with the defendants' testimony from the first interrogations. At that time, Michael Smith and Helen Baker claimed they had driven the car into a pond. "Only when during the investigation no corpse could be found in any body of water, the convicted Smith claimed he had dissected the body and fed the dogs with it."[108] In the verdict, the pond narrative was considered false because Smith felt ashamed to admit that something even worse happened (feeding the body parts to the pigs). Now, the pond narrative was no longer a lie; it had been the truth all along. Again, narratives are easily exchangeable without the need to evaluate overall coherence. That the car was found in the river and not the pond was not seen as problematic, as both places were in close proximity. Furthermore, although Hans Baker's skull was intact, Smith might still have thrown a strike at him, knocking him nearly unconscious but not killing him. It is possible that Hans Baker died in the water and not when he came home. "Under these circumstances, in particular due to the knowledge of the 'disposal site' of the corpse in the River Danube, suicide, a traffic accident, or a crime by others can also be excluded."[109]

Two things became very clear at the time of the filing of the motions to reopen: Hans Baker's body was not fed to the dogs or the pigs, and the car did not get scrapped. And yet the prosecutor still maintained a murder narrative (albeit a completely different one) because the defendants made statements that describe a scenario that shows at best vague similarities to the one of the multiple original narratives. But why would the defendants say "pond" when they mean "river"? If it was meant to distract the police or prosecutor, then one can wonder why Smith confessed at all.

The district court denied the motions to reopen based on the lack of relevance of the new evidence. First, it only showed that neither Smith nor any other person caused injuries to the bone structure (skull and vertebrae) of the victim directly leading to the farmer's death.[110] Second, the new facts related only to events that followed the crime. Therefore, the new elements had no bearing on the facts the conviction was based on.[111] The court still saw "various conceivable possibilities" for how Smith could have caused Baker's death.[112] His throat could have been cut, or he could have been strangled. The court also sided with the prosecutor regarding the similarity between a pond and a river. According to the court, the initial story aligned well with the new facts,[113] suggesting that the initial verdict would not have been different had the car and the body been found earlier. So the judges maintained the original framing narrative by recompiling fragments of the multiple, often contradictory narratives the defendants provided throughout the process. In the ruling, little attention is given to the process of how the crime narrative was constructed.

The defense then appealed the dismissal of the motions to reopen to the highest court of the state. The attorneys argued that the court had replaced one fact pattern with another and stressed (next to procedural issues) that the way Hans Baker was killed was not just a peripheral aspect; rather it was a part of the initial accusation and the foundation for the guilty verdict. It must be considered within the whole case narrative. The supreme court, which decided on the motions to reopen, agreed with the lower court in that the disposal of the body and the car had no relevance to the facts that provided the basis for the initial guilty verdict. However, it dismissed the lower court's argument that the way Hans Baker was killed was irrelevant. Generally speaking, how a crime was executed is relevant in many ways, especially in homicides where the specific conduct can change the nature of the crime from manslaughter to murder and vice versa.[114] As a result, the supreme court allowed for the case to be reopened.

The new trial spanned four months. It ended with a verdict that acquitted all defendants but did not free them of all accusations. The new trial court assumed that the defendants (with varying degrees of involvement) caused the death of the victim; there simply had not been sufficient evidence to prove it. In the verdict, the court held:

> The defendants had to be acquitted for factual reasons. Based on the discovery, the chamber is convinced that Hans Baker came home on the night in question and that the defendants initiated the events that led to his death, but the chamber could not determine with certainty sufficient for a conviction which of the defendants took part in these events and how Baker's death was caused.[115]

The court argued that the newly found evidence would not exclude the possibility of a crime because an accidental death by, for instance, driving the car into the river would be unlikely given the location where the car was found and its condition.[116] The verdict did not suggest how the car got into the river and simply maintained that a homicide was still conceivable. A suicide was ruled out as well because of the position in which the corpse was found and the fact there was no key in the ignition. The engine did not show signs of internal damage, which would be difficult to explain had Hans Baker driven himself (whether intentionally or not) into the river. The court then repeated that the farmer showed no signs of depression or suicidal thoughts, at least not to the knowledge of people who knew him or met him before he went missing. Other reasons for Hans Baker's death, such as a crime by a third party, were considered unlikely. How the crime had happened, and who took part in what way, could not be resolved. Although the court trusted the defendants' confessions, there was not sufficient evidence to support them. So while on paper the court followed what the higher court suggested, in the new verdict the judges' narrative sided with the initial story as it was imagined by the officers who started the investigation.

Conclusion

Existing data on the prevalence and causes of wrongful convictions in Germany is scarce. There are too few documented and analyzed cases to draw conclusions as to how often they happen and what the main contributing factors are. The concept of a wrongful conviction as such is heavily debated and its existence disputed. Procedural differences to the American system further complicate any comparison. Even if a concept of wrongfulness based on actual innocence proven after a final verdict is applied to German cases, there still is no clear image. There are few known cases of misidentification, and most of the cases discussed in that category involve situations in which no crime was committed because an alleged victim falsely incriminated someone or the police, prosecutors, and judges misinterpreted facts. That moves the focus to institutional tunnel vision as a typical (albeit not often observed) problem within the German criminal justice system. What distinguishes the German from the American system is that the narrative discourse is more closed: a narrative, once developed, can be channeled without much interference from one stage and entity to the next, each entity amplifying the narrative in turn.

The Case of the Missing Farmer illuminates how effectively police, prosecutors, and judges can select and omit from the narrative archive what serves their narrative. Certain facts can first be interpreted as contradictions and later as supportive of a changed narrative. Emotional testimony or detailed confessions under tears support the credibility of a confession for a guilty verdict, but when it turns out that all these same details were false, courts do not dismiss the confession as not credible; instead, they re-narrativize. A narrative, once established, is hard to change, especially when narrator and narratee stand on the same narrative plane. A trial rarely provides space for a contest of narratives. It is not constructed that way. And while that appears to eliminate the downfalls of the adversarial trial, as discussed earlier in chapter 4, the lack of open-mindedness to different versions of a story can cause its own set of problems. Any narrative in the inquisitorial system is susceptible to confirmation bias. Although we cannot be sure precisely how Hans Baker died and how he ended up in the river, it is obvious that the police, the prosecutors, and the judges all erred and that any alternative narratives were deflected.

The German criminal justice system has been described as "proactive" or "interventionist." In contrast to a reactive system that lets citizens decide over the criminal conflict, the proactive system is regulatory and involved.[117] Here the state establishes specific values and objectives of procedure, and all branches of power help to promote these values. Laws based on that model are not only a means to regulate procedure; they also protect and incorporate rights and values. The goal of criminal proceedings is not conflict resolution alone—it is also the execution and enforcement of substantive law. Criminal procedure is inquiry, not contest.[118] Even a confession should not render the inquiry into the facts obsolete because the courts impose legal guilt. As we have seen from the Case of the Missing Farmer, there is no perfectly truthful and fair criminal justice system. Storytelling and the "narrative desire" go deeper than procedural rules. Yet developing an awareness of the narrative dynamics of a trial and the "silent claims that stories make,"[119] and allowing criminal review to be open for questions of narrativization, can be crucial elements for creating procedures that value accurate storytelling and truthful verdicts.

6

Conclusion

The Ultimate Dystopia or Toward a Narrative of Legal Truth?

Wrongful convictions are the worst possible outcomes of criminal justice proceedings. They represent the system's failure and the failure of those who have in one way or another sworn to put their personal convictions aside for the greater good of a fair and unbiased criminal justice process. Before the late 1980s, when the innocence movement began to gain momentum, wrongful convictions had already been known in the United States and other countries. But they were not considered an issue that needed addressing, and even their existence was sometimes denied by prosecutors and judges alike. "Innocent men are never convicted. Don't worry about it, it never happens in the world. It is a physical impossibility."[1] These established beliefs in a functioning justice system were impervious to criticism. Only through the argumentative force of DNA were wrongful convictions pushed out of the realm of the anecdotal and speculative into the forensic realm, revealing many larger systemic issues. As I have contended throughout this book, factual truth as a value and pursuit does not rank highly in American criminal justice proceedings. It may in theory, but not in the adversarial, prosecution-dominated, plea-bargained reality. The rigid structure of a justice system that has not updated its methods of truth-finding and does not allow for factual review made it difficult for attorneys to even present proof of innocence. Reform, it seems, would not be initiated from within the system. Thus, it was not surprising that help for the wrongfully convicted came from outside the system, from entities that were much less entangled in the fabric of a typical trial and the processes leading up to it. Organizations like Centurion Ministries, investigative journalists, and innocence projects across the United States took on the cause of those who claimed innocence.[2] DNA was important, and innocence projects, like the one founded by Barry Scheck and Peter Neufeld in New

York, took cases only when biological evidence was available. -DNA based exonerations have been the minority and will even decline further because more pretrial testing is undertaken and existing cases will have been resolved.[3] As we have seen, even with exculpatory DNA available during the trial, wrongful convictions still occur. So the solution to the problem of wrongful convictions is not and cannot be DNA alone (or other kinds of evidence, for that matter); it must be linked to the underlying factors that lead to such outcomes. The scholarly side of the innocence movement revealed universal truths about the failings of the system including suggestive eyewitness identification methods, unreliable forensics, incentivized witnesses, false confessions, tunnel vision, and so on. Knowing these factors helped reform police policies, and legislatures across the United States addressed some of the most visible (and addressable) concerns such as interrogation methods, identification procedures, and the like; however, as Brandon Garrett notes, even today "much of the law and procedures remain the same."[4] Wrongful convictions must be seen within the context of the slow-moving colossus that is the American criminal justice system. That system remains highly punitive, retains one of the highest incarceration rates of the world, affords a comparatively high degree of unreviewable discretion to police and prosecutors, and settles most criminal conflicts through plea negotiations and other means. Even though all systems produce wrongful convictions, each system has its own type of error clusters.

American Exceptionalism?

As much as we have learned about individual factors that cause miscarriages of justice, they are pieces of a larger picture that demands further explaining. Another way of looking at this is to ask: If the established deficiencies like tunnel vision, eyewitness misidentifications, misconduct, and similar factors are universal, would they not exist in other criminal justice systems as well? I have refrained from expanding my comparison of wrongful convictions to other countries (besides Germany) because of the methodological difficulties of such comparisons. Whether a system is part of the common law or civil law model affects how criminal codes (procedural and substantive) are applied, and the narrativization of facts works differently in adversarial and inquisitorial systems. It is understandable that most systems in the Innocence Network are from the common law/adversarial tradition, and only a few (like Italy and the Netherlands) fall into the other category. Each system deserves consideration in its own right,[5] and it would be problematic to rely on just one cluster of factors explaining wrongful convictions universally.

Why does the United States lead in the numbers of wrongful convictions among Western criminal justice systems? Other countries, like Germany, present comparatively fewer exonerations. While absolute and relative numbers are difficult to assess (and would not be meaningful given the differences between the justice systems), there is not much of an innocence movement to speak of in Germany. A strong academic debate about wrongful convictions exists, but not to the extent known in the United States. Does that mean that other systems are less prone to producing false convictions? Is America the exception among Western criminal justice systems? Brandon Garrett doubts that premise and argues that lower numbers reported from other countries might simply mean "that the countries need to examine their convictions far more carefully."[6] This suggests that other systems must suffer from the same problem but are not as advanced as the United States is in recognizing them. The claim that America's criminal justice system is exceptionally functional (in protecting suspects and discovering systematic failures) is not new, but at least in this context such a viewpoint distorts the image.

First, American exceptionalism in criminal justice is more easily found in the high degree of punitive and assembly line–style processes that often favor finality over accuracy. Second, there is an unwillingness to look for solutions outside one's own system. And while no other system's approach to a certain problem can or should control one's own system, in comparison to European countries the United States stands alone in its approach to dealing with and reflecting on crime and justice writ large.[7] "Outside of the United States, it is a fairly usual practice more generally to consider laws in other countries, whereas learning from foreign legal systems is less common in the United States."[8] This means that, without knowing how a particular system works, any suggestions as to why its data on the prevalence of wrongful convictions is different from the United States is a mere guess. The robust wrongful conviction scholarship as it developed in the United States is not easily transferable to other systems (and vice versa). Tunnel vision as an effect of confirmation bias is universal in psychological terms but presents itself differently in the adversarial and inquisitorial systems. The same is true for other known factors. The fact that eyewitness misidentifications are a main problem in the United States, but do not seem to be an issue at all in Germany, tells us how difficult comparisons are. In addition, wrongful convictions must be read within the context of an existing criminal justice system. The United States follows a tough-on-crime protocol that results in incarceration rates that are seven times higher than in Europe. It is not that countries like Germany do not see egregious crimes that evoke strong feelings and require a political response—crime is just as present an issue there as it is in the United States. The difference is that public fear and outrage may not have the same feedback on Continental politics and legislation than they have in the United States.[9] A typical high-profile case might gain media attention and an emotional response from the public; however, since prosecutors and judges do not answer to the public (or anyone for that matter), the judicial and the political and public discourse are much more decoupled than they are in the United States. I would also argue that this at least partly explains overcriminalization in the United States.

Just as in the United States, Continental criminal processes rely on zealous representation of clients, but they are always geared toward truth as a value that rises above partisan advocacy. Truth is a constitutional mandate that must not succumb to trial strategies. In Germany, the entire investigatory file is shared among the participants; such open discovery in criminal proceedings does not exist in the United States, but Germany has always retained this feature. Another difference is that prosecutors and judges are vetted and selected from the best-performing graduates among any given cohort. Once appointed, these prosecutors and judges only serve the law and their conscience and (except for the highest court) are not elected and are not bound by constituent feedback. The most central difference is the role of the court. Judges are legally charged with finding factual truth and must explain their reasoning in writing so that an appellate court can review how evidence and law were brought into concordance. This is a form of built-in inter-rater reliability (albeit within the context of a still subjective undertaking) that does not exist in the United States. ("Inter-rater reliability" is a measure of consistency used to evaluate the extent to which different judges agree in their assessment decisions.)

That being said, throughout the chapters I have demonstrated that no systems can prevent wrongful convictions. Legal guilt is not simply the product of legal processes and investigative procedures. There is a stronger force at play, present in all systems, that influences how facts are created and a case is constructed: narrative. "Narrative," as understood here, distinguishes between the *events* as they happened and their *representations*. Wrongful convictions are, in the end, a factual misrepresentation sanctioned by the law. Representations are not only the complete, written statements of facts, indictments, charges, or appellate verdicts; they are ubiquitous in the sense that a case and its myriad facets exist only as an accurate image (more or less) drawn by the participants involved who imagine a certain scenario to be true or likely true. Evidence is likewise dependent on such imaginations. As such, narratives have quasi-evidentiary power, often so strong that they can overcome exculpatory evidence like DNA. Only through narrative is meaning created. Crime stories (and the evidence that supports them) depend on a regulated form of legal imagination and are influenced by the dynamics of storytelling—that is to say, who has what kind of narrative agency and who must listen in a certain way. Narrativization is a universal and necessary process in the United States and other countries, but systems differ in how much of a narrative advantage is given to, for instance, the prosecutor. Who can present a first framing narrative? Whose narratives are more scrutinized and whose are less scrutinized? In the United States, prosecutors enjoy a narrative advantage that is inherent to the adversarial system. In the American adversarial system, the first narrative (the prosecutor's opening statement) primes the jurors, who construct a socially coherent narrative out of what they hear from the prosecutor. Or they will make one up, attributing good and bad intentions to actors, filling in gaps through schemas.[10] The master narrative that jurors form is what they base their verdict on, and that version of events becomes the basis for all subsequent proceedings. A narrative, once it is embedded, becomes so strong that it even affects the jurors' postverdict memories of the evidence.[11] Narrative is always at work and often unconsciously drives an investigation and a case.

That is also true for Germany's narrative blueprint, which is influenced by Roman civil law and an inquisitorial impetus to truth-finding. That approach might effectively buffer inaccurate narrativization through a high degree of reviewability on all levels and a constitutionally mandated commitment to truth, but it cannot prevent them altogether. Against the common belief that legal hermeneutics are precise and accurate, narrative affects how laws are interpreted and applied. The interpretation and application of law are always narrative in nature. Interpreters have a particular case in mind—whether in the form of an already concrete image of a scenario or in the form of a schema. Von Arnauld calls this process "the lawyer's alchemical art,"[12] that requires, as Bruner notes, "legal ingenuity."[13] In that sense, we must acknowledge that the (civil law) lawyer's conviction that fact-finding and legal argumentation are decoupled and independent of narrative is problematic. Both systems—common law/adversarial and civil law/inquisitorial—struggle with narrative awareness. While narrativization is more openly at play in adversarial proceedings, it is not critically enough reflected upon. As long as the trial is paramount in finding the truth, the master narrative lies in the hands of the jury, whose decision-making and narrativization processes are immune to appellate review. An inquisitorial system tries to reduce the narrative noise by concentrating fact-finding in a neutral, trained entity, but it lacks narrative awareness in the sense that judges do not think it plays any role at all given the technical setup of a trial.

Narrativizing Truth

Narratives as a force influence and potentially contribute to wrongful convictions. Narrativization is present even before an officer arrives at the crime scene, and it is at play after a verdict becomes final and unreviewable. Legal guilt, as has been argued, does not require an actual crime; it requires a procedurally acceptable crime *narrative*. This is not unlike the concept of labeling, which assumes that the nature of crime is an attribution process aimed at the creation of meaning.[14] This represents a bridge to another emerging field: narrative criminology, the discipline based on the idea that stories have "the potential . . . to theorize the etiology of crime," situating stories as antecedents to crime.[15] Narrative is seen as a "factor in the motivation for and accomplishment of crime and criminalization."[16] Crimes are considered as an acting-out of certain narrative scripts, and thus actions in general are shaped by their storytelling potential.[17] Narrative criminology (as with conventional criminology) has a focus on etiological approaches to crime and less so on questions of criminalization,[18] but the points made throughout this book could be read as supporting the argument of narrative criminology because of the similar goal of revealing "power structures and hegemonies of consensus" that determine legal reality.[19] The nexus between legal narratology and narrative criminology deserves adequate space for a more detailed exposition, and there is a lot that can be gained by pursuing this approach.

At this point, I need to clarify what might be the elephant in the room: Given the constrictive power of narrative, is there still an opposition between fictional and (as Doležel calls them) cognitive (or referential) texts? Because if not, and if all language use is poetic and nonreferential, then

> we have to accept the logical, ethical, and existential consequences of this position. We land in the ultimate dystopia, a world where we cannot make a distinction between what is false and what is true, what happened and what did not happen, who is honest and who is a liar, who is guilty and who is innocent, what is genuine and what is fake.[20]

To accept the constitutive perspective of narrative in wrongful convictions it is not necessary to agree with such a strong dystopian conclusion or with historical relativism in general. However, for convicted defendants who spent decades in prison, this dystopia had become reality. And there remains a difference between factual and fictitious narratives. Nonfiction narratives are ultimately falsifiable by testing the accuracy of what happened through corroboration and inquisition.[21] Fiction is not falsifiable.[22] As we have seen, wrongful conviction narratives oscillate between these two areas of falsifiable facts and unreviewable fiction. These oscillations do not happen automatically; they are—consciously or not—controlled by narrators. Here, then, lies what is so specific to legal narratives in contrast to historical narratives: the role and function of the author. Whereas it is clear in the historical discourse that (ideally) the narrator of a history "is not a device wielded by the author, it is the author,"[23] such clarity as to who is speaking for whom does not exist in law. False confessions exemplify that dichotomy as much as any statement of facts does. What is presented as fact in a closing argument are elements that are part of an attorney's narrative. The reason why it is easy to be unaware of narrativity is because of what Abbott calls the "scalar" nature of narrative.[24] Not everything presented in court is narrative. A photo, blood analysis, cell-phone records, or other facts are not narrative in themselves; rather, they are elements of larger, authored narratives. It requires narrative sensitivity in the reader of these narratives to understand that these details are mere signposts used to create a plausible story. After all, as the German case analysis showed, the level of detail of a narrative is seen as corresponding with its veracity because of the so-called reality effect.[25] Prosecutors never claim to be mind readers, but they leave the impression as if they know what someone was thinking, what motivated them, or that it was plausible to think that way, thereby appealing to the principle of minimal departure. They also have on their side the presumption that their audiences expect them to tell the truth, that their intent is to be a reliable narrator, and that their accusations are not scurrilous. We are much more aware of fictionalizations when we read fiction than when we read history.[26] In the legal discourse, literariness and truth-functionality often come together[27] because of the underlying communicative aims. But these aims must always be second to an open-mindedness and an ability to refine the factual picture.

In this book I have shown that narrative is universal and always present in law and that it has the ability to create the legal reality that places innocent defendants in prison for a long time, or perhaps even on death row. There is no simple solution to the narrative problem in wrongful convictions. Less discretion in individual narrators like police and prosecutors, and a commitment to truth as the ultimate value within the criminal justice system, must be part of such a solution. Many safeguards are employed in other systems, as in Germany. But even in that country, more checkpoints must be installed to control and review a developing narrative. The innocence movement has shown how imperfect and fallible the justice process can be. As much as we strive for scientific clarity in that process, DNA and other methods are not the solution. There will always be wrongful convictions for as long as justice systems remain impermeable to narrative considerations. At their core, wrongful convictions are a problem of false narrative representation. If everyone involved in such processes becomes aware of how these processes work, or at least that they exist, only then can we hope for more truth and a more humane form of justice.

NOTES

INTRODUCTION

1 Doctorow 1983, 26.
2 Warden 2022b.
3 Syed, November 13, 2015.
4 Bandes 2008, 9.
5 Dwyer, Neufeld, and Scheck 2001, xix.
6 Between 2000 and 2021, exonerations based on DNA ranged from 13 (lowest) to 30 (highest) per year, while exonerations due to other factors ranged between 45 and 166 per year. National Registry of Exonerations.
7 People v. Rivera, 2011 IL App. (2d), 091060 ¶ 13.
8 See People v. Rivera, 2011 IL App. (2d), 091060 ¶ 34. The defense qualified this proposition as "sickening" and "irrelevant." State of Illinois v. Juan Rivera, Trans. (5/5/2009), 18080.
9 State of Illinois v. Juan Rivera, Trans. (5/5/2009), 18101.
10 State of Illinois v. Juan Rivera, Trans. (5/5/2009), 18163.
11 State of Illinois v. Juan Rivera, Trans. (5/5/2009), 18166.
12 See Harmon-Jones 2019, 6.
13 State of Illinois v. Juan Rivera, Trans. (5/5/2009), 18180.
14 State of Illinois v. Juan Rivera, Trans. (5/5/2009), 18180.
15 State of Illinois v. Juan Rivera, Trans. (4/29/2009), 16952.
16 State of Illinois v. Juan Rivera, Trans. (5/5/2009), 18176.
17 People v. Rivera, 2011 IL App. (2d), 091060 ¶ 3.
18 National Registry of Exonerations.
19 This is also expressed in the Latin phrase *ex factis jus oritur*, meaning "the law arises from the facts"—a principle of international law.
20 Bruner 1986, 11.
21 "Every story, we have said, in principle explains itself. In other words, narrative answers the question 'Why?' at the same time that it answers the question 'What?' To tell what has happened is to tell why it happened." Ricœur 1984, 152; or more succinctly: "to narrate is already to explain" (178).
22 Brooks 2006, 5.
23 Brooks 2006, 2.
24 See Barton 2016, 21–22.
25 Abbott 2021, 12. Leo (2009, 333) uses the term "ground truth" to refer to "what really happened" in wrongful conviction cases. That term is used in other fields to

refer to a fundamental truth that is directly observed and known (as opposed to information arrived at by inference). This is how "story" is understood here, and "story" will be used throughout this book because legal scholarship does not use "story" and "narrative" consistently with similar meanings.

26 See Abbott 2021, 17.

27 See Culler 2002, 169–70: "Narrative theory requires a distinction between 'story,' a sequence of actions or events conceived as independent of their manifestation in discourse, and 'discourse,' the discursive presentation or narration of events." The distinction between a story and its representation as narrative goes back to Russian Formalists, who understood *fabula* as story and *syuzet* as the rendering of the story in narrative. See Abbott 2021, 17–18.

28 Other examples include Jeffrey Deskovic and Juan Rivera. Rivera's coerced confession was used in three trials to gain a conviction. DNA from semen found on the victim did not match Rivera's genetic profile. The state argued that the sample was either contaminated or stemmed from a source unrelated to the crime. See Warden 2022b.

29 Brooks 1984, 316. He sees that desire as the motor of plot and "the need to tell one's own story as a primary human drive that seeks to seduce and to subjugate the listener" (326).

30 Van Hoecke 2015.

31 Crime narratives are always rich and can be looked at from many angles, and there is not just one approach to describing narratives of wrongful convictions. The analyses in this book focus on how factual narratives were misconstrued, but such an analysis is open to other approaches.

1. DISCOURSES OF GUILT AND INNOCENCE

1 Dwyer, Neufeld, and Scheck 2001, xx.

2 State of Texas v. Michael Morton, Trans. (2/10/1987), 229–230.

3 U.S. v. Garsson, 291 F. 646 (649), S.D.N.Y 1923.

4 See Gross 2008, 186.

5 MacFarlane 2006, 435 ff.

6 See www.innocenceproject.org.

7 Leverick, Campbell, and Callander 2017, 81.

8 Leverick, Campbell, and Callander 2017, 64. They note North Carolina as a state that employs an independent body for review.

9 Bennett 1997, 1.

10 Kaiser and Brown 2015, 233.

11 That guilt is now disjointed from the underlying facts. Even if, on the day after the verdict, new evidence was discovered that clearly exonerated the convicted, they would still be guilty under the law for as long as the original verdict stands.

12 Bennett 1997, 20.

13 Bennett 1997, 20: "In this sense, a story is a reconstruction of an event in light of the teller's initial perception and immediate judgments about the audience, the

interests that appear to be at stake, and, perhaps most importantly, what has gone before in the situation in which the story is presented."

14 See Bennett 1997, 21. Bennett lays out a story-model of the adjudicatory process and argues that "at every stage of the storytelling-interpretation process, both storytellers and interpreters make choices about how to symbolize a story element" (20). That means that what is true can be "disbelieved due to improper symbolization or structurally inadequate presentations" and "false accounts may be believed due to the skillful juxtaposition of internally consistent symbols" (16–17).

15 See Olson 2018, 19.

16 Abbott 2021, 8.

17 LinkedIn 2022.

18 Photographs, of course, are powerful. Crime scene photographs have a particularly strong effect on jurors and can be tied into the larger framing narrative a prosecutor develops. For the argument that the court is a theater of proof, "in which the power of sight may be . . . the most effective rhetorical mode of persuasion and an especially fragile basis for conviction," see Mnookin and West (2008, 6).

19 Olson 2018, 23.

20 Fludernik 2010, 5.

21 Fludernik 2010, 6.

22 Barthes 1977a, 79.

23 Bruner 1990, 45: "Rather, I mean a readiness or predisposition to organize experience into a narrative form, into plot structures and the rest. . . . It seems to me that such a view is irresistible."

24 See A. Nünning and V. Nünning 2002a, 1.

25 Fludernik 2010, 5 ff.

26 See Goyal 2014, Paragraph 2, [view date:12 Feb 2019].

27 See Martinez and Scheffel 2009, 26. This table provides an overview of six typical narrative properties and how they are used by 19 authors.

28 Abbott's introduction focuses more on the construction, transmission, and reception of narratives than on the field of narratology.

29 Abbott 2021, 13 f.

30 Abbott 2021, 13.

31 Olson 2018, 19.

32 Stern 2018, 4.

33 Abbott (2021) sees this as the building block for longer narrative structures. It also allows the recognition of "other definitions as definable narrative subsets and useful in their own right" (13). That is close to Genette (1982), whose definition of narrative is "the representation of an event or sequence of events, real or fictitious, by means of language and more particularly, by means of written language" (127).

34 Other, larger narrative subsets, like a photograph, cannot fall under this definition of narrative but they could be integrated, for instance, when describing someone's character or a crime scene.

35 Abbott 2010, 10.
36 Abbott 2021, 14. The terms "fabula" and "sjuzet" are also used for story and narrative discourse. See Abbott 2021, 17–18.
37 See Abbott 2010, 10.
38 Abbott 2021, 16.
39 Genette 1982, 133.
40 Genette 1982, 133.
41 Genette 1982, 134.
42 Genette 1982, 134.
43 Courts recognize the effect the appearance of a defendant can have when, for instance, they allow a defendant to wear regular clothing or hire a cosmetologist to use makeup on tattoos. See, for instance, the case of John Ditullio, who was granted a cosmetologist to help covering tattoos, including a swastika, so the jury would not be unduly influenced. Schwartz, December 5, 2010.
44 Abbott 2021, 13.
45 Olson 2010, 348.
46 This term was coined by Hans-Georg Gadamer, who was crucial in the development of twentieth-century hermeneutics. Fore-understanding (German: Vorverständnis) of a text is "not something to be attained through the process of understanding but is already presupposed" (Gadamer 2011, 327). Josef Esser adapted the concept of fore-understanding to legal hermeneutics. He argued that the process of interpretation is a process of selective evaluation of facts, which again works with a selective fore-understanding of rules and norms. This understanding is driven by extralegal concepts of justice or simple pragmatics (Esser 1972, 134), which, because of the "total autonomy of the legal system," are excluded from critical reflection (Esser 1972, 141). Although Esser's and Gadamer's approaches are focused on the process of the interpretation of laws, they can be applied to the stages of proceedings when signs of the real are interpreted. The "identification of a 'legal problem' is always the result of a judgment process outside of positive law" (Esser 1972, 82). That, however, is an assessment that depends on the task—on whatever level.
47 Sebold 1999, 103.
48 Sebold 1999, 149.
49 Sebold 1999, 198.
50 Sebold 1999, 173.
51 Sebold publicly apologized and said she was struggling with the role she played "within a system that sent an innocent man to jail." Matthews 2021.
52 Fleischhut, Meder, and Gigerenzer 2017, 110.
53 Norris 2017, 52.
54 Norris 2017, 53.
55 Dershowitz 1996a, 101.
56 Bandes 2008, 9.
57 Zalman 2011, 106; Findley 2011b, 1159.

58 Literary representations often address the ambiguity of guilt and innocence when the deed itself is clear but not how it should be qualified legally or morally. In the law and literature discourse, the most prominent example is probably Herman Melville's *Billy Budd*, in which the protagonist struck dead a superior after being provoked. Billy's natural innocence is contrasted with the law of the mutiny act as it is executed on a ship at war.

59 This book assumes that, despite the high number of known wrongful convictions, the vast majority of police, forensic experts, prosecutors, attorneys, and judges pursue their cases with honesty and accuracy.

60 For example, David Lee Gavitt spent 26 years in a Michigan prison for the 1985 killing of his wife and baby girls in a blaze that was erroneously labeled arson. Decades later, the fire was ruled an accident. Gavitt was exonerated in 2014. See Henry 2016.

61 Findley 2011b, 1159.

62 Narrative terminology is inconsistent. Some use "masterplot" and "master narrative" synonymously. When possible, Abbott's use of narrative terminology is followed. The importance of masterplots in wrongful convictions will be addressed below; master narrative is a different concept. It refers to finalized narrative that underlies a jury verdict.

63 See Bandes 2008, 15.

64 See Medwed 2017, 3.

65 Medwed 2017, 3.

66 Wisconsin Innocence Project 2022. See also Graham Burnett 2001. Burnett describes the difficulty for a jury to reconstruct a situation of self-defense when no witnesses are present.

67 A google Ngram of "wrongful conviction" shows a steady increase of that term beginning in the early 1980s—when the innocence movement gained momentum.

68 See Findley 2011b, 1186.

69 Herrera v. Collins, 506 US 390 (1993).

70 Herrera v. Collins, 506 US 390 (1993). Chapters 4 and 5 discuss details of German reopening proceedings.

71 Findley 2011b, 1208.

72 Herrera v. Collins, 506 US 390, 399 (1993).

73 Herrera v. Collins, 506 US 390, 402, emphasis added.

74 See Cohn 1999, 109–31.

75 Del Mar and Gordon 2013, 331.

76 Del Mar and Gordon 2013, 333.

77 Zalman 2013, 332.

78 United States v. Garsson, 291 F. 646, 649 (1923).

79 See Zalman 2013, 332.

80 Weber 1949 [1904], 90.

81 Warden 2022a.

82 On March 26, 1887, the *Omaha Daily Bee* reported that Jack Marion had been hanged for the murder of his friend John Cameron. At his trial, the jury found that the evidence "left but little doubt" as to Marion's guilt. Four years after Marion's execution, the alleged dead friend reappeared. Similarly, on August 28, 1844, the *Bombay Times and Journal of Commerce* reported about a case of a false confession to a murder that never took place. Here again, the alleged victim returned (555).

83 There are a few exceptions. One is the case mentioned in the *Bombay Times*. It resulted in abolition of "torture as a means of procuring evidence or confessions of guilt" in the Turkish Empire. A better-known case from 1660 is that of the alleged murder of William Harrison in Campden, England, in 1660. John Perry and his family were convicted of the murder and then hanged, although Williamson's body had not been found. When Harrison returned to England, a new law established the "no body, no crime" rule that lasted for 294 years. See Watson, January 4, 2017.

84 See Acker et al. 2014, 4.

85 Borchard 1913, 684.

86 A lively debate among scholars in Germany at the end of the nineteenth century addressed whether claims against the state are heritable as far as pecuniary damage is concerned. See Borchard 1913, 700.

87 Sello 2001. Title is my translation, as this work has not appeared in English. The book discusses 150 wrongful conviction cases from Germany, Austria-Hungary, Switzerland, Luxemburg, England, the United States, France, Belgium, and Italy.

88 Borchard 1913, 606 n 48.

89 Most notably Barbara and Jerome Frank's *Not Guilty* in 1957 (including 34 cases) and Hugo Bedau and Michael Radelet's article in the *Stanford Law Review* in 1987, addressing 350 capital and potentially capital cases.

90 Acker et al. 2014, 5.

91 Norris 2017, 3.

92 Dwyer, Neufeld, and Scheck 2001, xx.

93 Norris 2017, 121.

94 Scholars are divided as to whether the first case was Gary Dotson's or David Vasquez's. See Medwed 2017, 2.

95 Norris 2017, 123.

96 United States v. Garsson, 291 F. 646, 649 (1923).

97 United States v. Garsson, 291 F. 646, 649 (1923).

98 Herrera v. Collins, 506 U.S. 390, 399 (1993).

99 Herrera v. Collins, 506 U.S. 390, 420. In 2001, Justice O'Connor appeared more critical of constitutional safeguards: "If statistics are any indication, the system may well be allowing some innocent defendants to be executed." Associated Press, July 4, 2001.

100 Herrera v. Collins, 506 U.S. 390, 399 (1993).

101 Herrera v. Collins, 506 U.S. 390, 399 (1993).

102 See Grunewald 2014, 1174 ff.

103 For instance, under American law, hearsay evidence is not admissible because a defense attorney cannot interrogate the initial source of the testimony in court. That is typically seen as a truth-promoting feature because it prohibits the use of potentially unreliable evidence. In a German court, however, such evidence can (within limits) be admissible because judges in their search for truth are charged to consider all evidence under a totality of circumstances and later must simply explain the weight they attach to such evidence.

104 National Registry of Exonerations.

105 Acker et al. 2014, 6.

106 Laporte 2018, 2.

107 Gould et al. 2013, ii.

108 Gould et al. 2013, ii.

109 Gould et al. 2013, iii.

110 The case summary is taken from Bazelon, July 4, 2021.

111 Bazelon, July 4, 2021, 30.

112 National Registry of Exonerations (28% as of June 2021).

113 See Andrew M. Smith and Cutler 2013, 6. The case of Larry Davis and Alan Northrop is a compelling and paradigmatic example of how mistaken identification can lead to conviction of the innocent. After the rape of a housekeeper in La Center, Washington, in January 1993, Davis and Northrop were arrested as suspects. During the attack, the victim was blindfolded and could provide only a vague description of the assailants, stating that one had dark and the other blond hair. A sketch and a description were released to the public, and someone called the police suggesting that Davis and Northrop fit the general description. Police put together photo arrays containing the two men, but the victim could only tentatively identify Davis. She was later presented with a live lineup that contained both men, whom she identified. Davis and Northrop were the only two men that had also been in the photo array. Immediately before the identification procedure, a friend of the witness described the two men who were questioned by the police. Although no other evidence connected the men to the crime, they were convicted. They spent more than 16 years in prison before being exonerated. DNA from the rape kit revealed consistent profiles of two unknown men, excluding Northrop and Davis.

114 By the time of Bazelon's article, a vast amount of scholarship had been published on how to conduct more reliable identification procedures. And yet. "many investigations and prosecutions grind on, impervious to the latest studies." Bazelon, July 4, 2021, 31.

115 Loftus 1979, 19.

116 Andrew M. Smith and Cutler 2013, 4.

117 O'Brian and Findley 2014, 45.

118 O'Brian and Findley 2014, 42. In fact, a witness can even replace their image of the actual perpetrator with the one they picked. The victim in Ronald Cotton's

case saw the perpetrator in court and asked herself: "How could I have been in the same room as my rapist and not recoil? I didn't even recognize him." Thompson-Cannino, Cotton, and Torneo 2009, 213.

119 Thompson-Cannino, Cotton, and Torneo 2009, 269. The witness appeared to be charged with a certain job she had to do, like an exam: "When I finished, I could tell I passed" (47).

120 Bazelon, July 4, 2021, 31.

121 Manson v. Brathwaite, 432 U.S. 98 (1977).

122 Garrett 2011, 168.

123 Garrett 2011, 168.

124 See Garrett 2011, 170.

125 Greenbaum 2019, v.

126 Greenbaum 2019, v.

127 See Gross et al. 2005, 544.

128 Chapter 2 discusses the cases of Chris Ochoa and Jeffrey Deskovic. Chris Ochoa confessed to a rape and murder he and his codefendant did not commit because they might otherwise have faced the death penalty.

129 According to Appleby and Kassin (2016, 128), there are two reasons why confessions are trusted by jurors. One is that a self-report tends to exhibit a "truth bias" independent of the actual veracity of a statement. That can be attributed to the fact that people trust statements made against self-interest. The second reason why confessions are trusted is that they often contain "content cues" like accurate details about the crime that are commonly associated with truth-telling.

130 Laporte 2018, 5.

131 Laporte 2018, 9.

132 National Research Council 2009, 100.

133 Laporte 2018, 6.

134 Laporte 2018, 6.

135 Gross and K. Jackson 2015.

136 United States v. Dennis, 183 F.2d 201, at 224, quoting Judge Learned Hand.

137 Hoffa v. United States, 385 U.S. 293, 311 (1966).

138 Garrett 2011, 124.

139 Garrett 2011, 127.

140 Findley and Scott 2006, 292.

141 Findley and Scott 2006, 293.

142 Findley and Scott 2006, 307.

143 Findley and Scott 2006, 325.

144 See for a detailed discussion see Findley and Scott 2006, 342 ff.

145 Bazelon, July 4, 2021.

146 In 2021, 80% of respondents in a survey stated they had little or no confidence in the criminal justice system. Gallup 2021.

147 Weinberg 2012, 177. Punnett (2018) questions, however, that texts like *Actual Innocence* are true crime because "they are not written in a narrative style and they

make no attempt to tell a story that is true in the manner of one that is not" (104). "Narrative style" refers to Punnett's definition of true crime in that "true crime seeks to create emotional sensations regarding criminal events and transport moral messages and social truths through entertaining narratives rich in detail and color" (93). True crime allows for a certain quantifiable amount of "free play" to enhance the transportive qualities of a fictional narrative, as long as the text's teleology is striving toward nonfictional pedagogy.

148 Martelle, May 2, 2010.

149 Weinberg (2012, 177) calls it "literatures of wrongful convictions."

150 Norris 2017, 130.

151 For instance, Dwyer, Neufeld, and Scheck (2001, 16) write about how the "curtains skip along the breeze" in the apartment of a suspect when it is unlikely that this detail made it into the official record.

152 See Cruz, June 11, 2015.

153 Dwyer, Neufeld, and Scheck 2001, xiii. In his author's note, Rachlin (2017, 3) begins by saying that his book "is a work of nonfiction," but just like in *Actual Innocence*, the author works with gap-filling, making remarks on how easy or not a sound could be heard at a place he wasn't present at that time.

154 Thompson-Cannino, Cotton, and Torneo 2009, 92.

155 Thompson-Cannino, Cotton, and Torneo 2009, 98.

156 Thompson-Cannino, Cotton, and Torneo 2009, 265. One point to note is that it is the end—the exoneration—that makes these narratives successful. No one would want to read a book from someone who just claims to be innocent.

157 See Cruz, June 11, 2015.

158 Golob 2018, 138.

159 Golob 2018, 146.

160 Banks-Anderson, March 15, 2016.

161 Golob (2018, 148) works with cultivation theory to make this point.

2. SPEAKING OF THE TRUTH

1 J. B. White 1985b, 247.

2 State of Texas v. Richard Danziger, Trans. (10/21/1990), 1304.

3 State of Texas v. Richard Danziger, Trans. (10/21/1990), 530.

4 National Registry of Exonerations.

5 Just like in Lemert's model of the concept of secondary deviance, Ochoa's "life and identity are organized around the facts of deviance" (Lemert 1967, 41). All that without primary deviance.

6 Olson 2014, paragraph 16.

7 This term is borrowed from H. V. White (1978, 122–23), who argues that historiography involves forms of "fiction-making." The adequate representation of the truth must involve "[t]he imagination no less than the reason . . . and this meant that the techniques of fiction-making were as necessary to the composition of a historical discourse as erudition might be" (123).

8　As discussed in chapter 1, I mainly follow the formalist convention and distinguish between events (the story) and their representation in narrative. I use "story" and "series of events" synonymously, and "storytelling" is similar to "narrativization."

9　Ricoeur 2016, 239: "So rather than being predictable, a conclusion [of a story] must be acceptable."

10　Brooks 1996, 19.

11　Abbott 2021, 115.

12　Olson 2014, paragraph 10.

13　United States v. Havens, 446 U.S. 620, 626 (1980); also Tehan v. United States, 382 U.S. 406, 416 (1966) ("The basic purpose of a trial is the determination of truth.").

14　See Dershowitz 1996b, 43: "That's how we try to achieve justice in this country—by each side seeking to win. It's called the adversary system."

15　Herrera v. Collins, 506 U.S. 390, 417 (1993).

16　Laudan 2006, 3.

17　Laudan 2006.

18　See Brooks 1984, 326, describing "the nature of narration as a form of human desire."

19　Brooks 2006, 8.

20　State of Texas v. Richard Danziger, Trans. (10/21/1990), 984.

21　State of Texas v. Richard Danziger, Trans. (10/21/1990), 1032.

22　In this section, Ochoa was asked if he ever denied the crime, and he answered that he had even lied to his family: "You know, you don't want, I didn't want them to think I was, I could have done such things like that, plus I was scared that if I did admit to them they just shun me aside, which is understandable." State of Texas v. Richard Danziger, Trans. (10/21/1990), 1033. He later mentioned that he still "didn't want to admit to myself, I guess, you know, something like that, somebody has a conscious [sic], you know, you don't want to admit it, you know, unless you're proud of the thing and you're going to come right out and say it." State of Texas v. Richard Danziger, Trans. (10/21/1990), 1065. Here his personal truth about his innocence conflicts with the official truth, and Ochoa had to, once again, deny his innocence contrary to his own conviction. His confession and his regrets that he cannot "ever bring her back, but I can at least try that much" are the actual lies that violate his oath to speak the truth, but they are part of the state sanctioned narrative, whose actual veracity has become irrelevant.

23　State of Texas v. Richard Danziger, Trans. (10/21/1990), 1068.

24　State of Texas v. Richard Danziger, Trans. (10/21/1990), 1033.

25　State of Texas v. Richard Danziger, Trans. (10/21/1990), 1315.

26　Brooks 2006, 26.

27　See Miller 1995, 67.

28　See Miller 1995, 68.

29　Grunewald 2021.

30　Olson 2018, 20.

31 Hanne and Weisberg 2018a, 15.

32 For instance, L. L. Edwards and J. Stanley Edwards (2002, xxiv), in their *Introduction to Paralegal Studies and the Law*, organize the content around the story line of a case. The story-telling approach to conveying legal information by using a case that "dramatic[ally] unfold[s]" is considered as being more effective in conveying legal information than other methods.

33 Amsterdam and Bruner 2000, 110.

34 Amsterdam and Bruner 2000, 110.

35 Levit 2009, 261–62.

36 Champagne 2015. This stands out to the Continental lawyer, who is trained to open in a unified, formalized manner. In Germany, the "accusatory sentence" (Anklagesatz) summarizes the facts of the alleged crime and the underlying elements of the crime. Introducing a theme or adding rhetorical hooks and flourishes would be culturally inappropriate.

37 This can involve the listener on a deep emotional level that is measurable as an increase of the neurochemical oxytocin. Zak 2015.

38 Gilbert, Gilfarb, and Talpins 2005, 3.

39 Olson 2018, 27. Judges in the United States are expected to be dispassionate as well and held to be changed by the robes they wear (Public Utilities Comm'n v. Pollak, 343 U.S. 451, 466 (1952)). But as much as they should submerge private feelings (Maroney 2011, 632), they play too little of a role in the process of narrativization that it would be relevant.

40 According to A. Nünning and V. Nünning (2002a, 13), narrative theory has been shaped in three broadly defined phases: the pre-structuralist beginnings (until the mid-1960s), the structuralist main phase (until the end of the 1980s), and revision and interdisciplinary refinement of narrative theory. In each phase, the understanding of the concept of narrative changed.

41 Hanne and Weisberg 2018b, 3.

42 Stone Peters 2005, 444. "Humanism" and "hermeneutics" are the other two. A. Nünning and V. Nünning (2002b, 12) count "legal narratology" as part of the group of "other interdisciplinary" narratologies among the "most important" newer narratologies.

43 See Brooks and Gewirtz 1996.

44 Posner (1997a, 741), for instance, misses the absence of "any sustained consideration of the methodological issue—by what means is one to study the story element in law," meaning the absence of literary theorists and philosophers who traditionally occupy the field of narrative. Posner's criticism of the book is symptomatic for the still-prevailing heterogeneity of the field. See Sternberg 2008, 30.

45 Brooks 2006, 5.

46 Fish 1994, 141.

47 Brooks 2006, 3.

48 Olson 2014, n 27.

49 See Hanne and Weisberg 2018b, 3.

50 See Fish 1994, 141. Brooks (2006) explains that the "legal discourse wishes to see itself as complete and hermetic"; expertise foreign to itself must "pass through the narrow gate watched over by the judge—at trial, and then at the appellate level—who is supposed to know the judicial from the extra-judicial" (20).

51 Luhmann 1983, 59.

52 Luhmann has an inquisitorial judge in mind who is very active throughout the criminal process. German judges are seen as the main representatives of the criminal justice system, of truth, and of due process.

53 Simon-Shoshan 2013, 9.

54 Wetlaufer (1990, 1548) makes a similar point when discussing epistemological and ontological consequences of rhetorical conventions. He references Mark Twain's complaint that his training as a riverboat pilot deprived him of the ability to see and appreciate the river for what it is to laypeople. The romance and grace of the river were lost to evaluations of usefulness. To the untrained jury or public, the trial and the multiple narratives it entails are spectacle, whereas to the litigator they are tools to steer the case into their desired direction, that is, one in which one is always right and the adversary is always wrong. Wetlaufer 1990, 1558.

55 Wetlaufer 1990, 1546.

56 Wetlaufer 1990, 1548.

57 Wetlaufer 1990, 1555.

58 Viehweg 1974, 20. Court decisions are too a large extent the result of subjective reasoning and therefore can hardly be falsified. Viehweg 1974, 111.

59 Wetlaufer 1990, 1588.

60 Wetlaufer 1990, 1595.

61 Wetlaufer 1990, 1959.

62 Wetlaufer 1990, 1560.

63 Posner 1997a, 744, quoting Catharine MacKinnon.

64 Posner 1997a, 743.

65 Posner 1997a, 744.

66 Posner 1997a, 747.

67 Stone Peters 2005, 443. See also von Arnold 2008, 44; Posner (1997a) criticizes that "much of the best scholarship on the story element in law owes little to these or any other fields outside of law itself" (740).

68 Hanne and Weisberg 2018b, 3.

69 J. B. White 1985b, 112–113.

70 J. B. White 1985b, 111.

71 J. B. White 1995, 1369.

72 Procedure projects and pursues a specific type of justice. For instance, the procedural requirements of impartiality and due process demand a defendant be granted a cosmetologist to cover up a swastika tattoo (see Schwartz, December 5, 2010). However, such protections do not exist in cases where a hate crime is tried, and the swastika becomes a piece of (admissible) character evidence.

73 United States v. Jackson, 405 F. Supp. 938, 946 (1975).

74 To establish a guilty mind (*mens rea*), the law merely requires "that the defendant know the facts that make his conduct fit the definition of the offense." Staples v. United States (92-1441), 511 U.S. 600 (1994).

75 United States v. Jackson, 405 F. Supp. 938, 946 (1975).

76 Ricoeur 2016, 255.

77 An explicit expression of this idea can be found in the French Civil Code from 1804 (the Code Civil des Français, or Code Napoléon): "A judge who refuses to decide a case, on the pretext that the law is silent, obscure or insufficient, may be prosecuted as being guilty of denial of justice." See Rabello 1974, 63.

78 United States v. Jackson, 405 F. Supp. 938, 946 (1975).

79 Stone Peters 2005, 447.

80 Stern 2018, 124. In his critical review of *Law's Stories*, Richard Posner (1997a, 737) is uncritical in regard to how he himself uses terms like "story" and "narrative"— story being a short narrative.

81 Olson 2018, 23.

82 Stern 2018, 123.

83 See Stern 2018, 127.

84 Brooks 2006, 25.

85 Olson 2018, 24.

86 Martinez and Scheffel 2009, 10.

87 Martinez and Scheffel 2009, 10.

88 Bruner 1991, 6.

89 Brooks 2003, 95.

90 United States v. Jackson, 405 F. Supp. 938, 945–46 (1975).

91 Dworkin 1986, 229.

92 Wisconsin 943.13(1m)(b).

93 Cover 1983, 4–5. Chapter 4 will provide more background on the narrative function of the process of subsuming facts under a law by judges in the civil law system. That process is at least as narrative as it is analytical.

94 Von Arnold 2008, 14.

95 Simon-Kerr 2020, 3; Miller v. Fenton, 474 U.S. 104, 114 (1985): "When . . . the issue involves the credibility of witnesses" a court "therefore turns largely on an evaluation of demeanor, . . . there are compelling and familiar justifications for leaving the process of applying law to fact to the trial court and according its determinations presumptive weight."

96 One of the most famous examples for causal narrative reasoning is Benjamin Judge Cardozo's fact pattern in *Palsgraf v. Long Island Railroad Co.* In evaluating the degree of negligence, it matters, for instance, if the plaintiff is just a person standing on a platform or also a customer who is entitled to a high degree of care by the railroad. It matters how the size and appearance of a package are described and the distance between the falling scales and the plaintiff. See Little 2007, 80.

97 Fischer 2015.

98 A legal narrative is much more like a literary work because "[h]istory is full of accidents, and literature is not." Horowitz 2011, 69.

99 Brooks 2017, 14.

100 Currie 2006, 309 [quotation] and 310.

101 Currie 2006, 312. But see Bruner (1991), who argues that narrative accounts cannot provide causal explanations; they supply "the basis for *interpreting* why a character acted as he or she did. Interpretation is concerned with 'reasons' for things happening, rather than strictly with their 'causes'" (7).

102 Currie 2006, 312.

103 See Hamilton 2007, 19.

104 Currie 2006, 309.

105 It literary translates to: "After this, therefore because of this." Abbott 2021, 49.

106 See Fagan and Geller 2015.

107 Abelson 1981, 33.

108 Abelson 1981, 717.

109 Abelson 1981, 717.

110 Currie 2006, 314.

111 Currie 2006, 313–14.

112 Hand 2015, 203.

113 Abbott 2010, 10.

114 Abbott 2010, 11.

115 Abbott 2010, 12.

116 Abbott 2010, 12.

117 Abbott 2010, 12: "The sun rose. The wind blew. The dog barked."

118 The best-known study is Bennet and Feldmann, *Reconstructing Reality in the Courtroom*. See Olson 2014, paragraph 10.

119 Goodpaster 1987, 122. In chapter 4, a closer look will be taken at inquisitorial trials, where impartial and independent judges are charged with finding the truth.

120 Polk County v. Dodson, 454 U.S. 312, 318 (1981).

121 Parklane Hosiery Co. v. Shore, 439 U.S. 322, 355 (1979).

122 For a comparison between the legal relevance of factual truth in Germany and the United States, see Grunewald 2014 and chapter 4 in this book.

123 Goodpaster 1987, 120. Abbott (2021) defines the criminal trial "as a huge, unpolished narrative compendium featuring the contest of two sets of authors, each trying to make their central narrative of events prevail by spinning narrative segments for their rhetorical impact" (187). Given the multitude of narratives at play, with each witness and expert adding another nuance to an ever-growing compendium, it is hard to speak of two sets of authors. The jury must be seen as an author in its own right. It decides which parts of the "narrative compendium" make it into the master narrative; they fill narrative gaps, speculate, create alternative masterplots, and so on.

124 United States v. Cronic, 466 U.S. 648, 655 (1984).

125 Griffin 2012, 285. It is not clear what the author means by "inquisitorialism," but inquisitorial systems certainly work with stories as well; they are just developed and regulated differently—and in many regards more accurately and reliably.

126 Abbott 2021, 186.

127 J. B. White 1985a, 174. See also Goodpaster 1987, 120; United States v. Cronic, 466 U.S. 648 (1984).

128 Herring v. New York, 422 U.S. 853, 862 (1975).

129 J. D. Jackson 1990, 85.

130 Garrett (2011, 155) found that storytelling powers are not distributed equally. On average, the defense offered six witnesses, the prosecution 14.

131 Bennett 1997, 72.

132 State of Texas v. Richard Danziger, Trans. (10/21/1990), 530.

133 "It's a given that criminals such as arsonists and serial murderers often return to the scene of the crime—sometimes to relive the crime. But not only criminals do so." Foster, July 27, 2010.

134 See Abbott 2021, 191.

135 Nunn 1995, 798.

136 Ricoeur 2016, 239.

137 Olson 2014, paragraph 16, referring to James Boyd White.

138 For example, David Lee Gavitt spent 26 years in a Michigan prison for the 1985 killing of his wife and baby girls in a blaze that was erroneously labeled arson. Decades later, the fire was ruled an accident. Gavitt was exonerated in 2014. See Henry 2016.

139 Arthur C. Danto (2007) explains that narrative sentences and descriptions have, as truth-conditions, "events which occur later than the events primarily referred to" (20). That means that a narrative description derives its truth after the event has already passed. Historical narratives are a "redescription of an event which was presumably hidden from the man of whom it is true, and it may be argued that it was not true of that man at that time, but became true only when the last truth-condition was met, some time after the acceptance" (Danto 2007, 20). This, of course, is true for all narratives within the larger narrative of a case, including wrongful conviction narratives.

140 Brooks 2003, 88. For instance, see Dwyer, Neufeld, and Scheck 2001. In the intro-duction to *Actual Innocence*, the authors narrate the case of Dennis Fritz, who was wrongfully convicted of a rape and murder. At the night of the arrest, "[h]e left his mother's home in handcuffs on that spring night in 1987. He would not return until the spring of 1999" (xvii). Although the authors do not predict the outcome (exoneration), they write their narratives with the outcome in mind. That can have multiple effects on how events and facts are represented in narrative and wrongful conviction narratives in particular.

141 Abbott 2021, 154.

142 Bruner 1990, 45.

143 H. V. White 1978, 122; in a similar way, Griffin (2012, 302) points out that stories (better: narratives) are "indifferent" to the truth (in the sense of historical facts). However, Griffin's argument that the "most successful stories—with the greatest utility to litigants—also comport with facts in the world" is problematic (303). Apart from not making clear what "successful" means (successful in artistic terms or having the potential to win a case?), all narratives that led to wrongful convictions were successful in the sense that they convinced a jury, but they did not comport with the facts in the world. Bennett and Feldman (1984) also doubt that "completely undocumented stories will be believed in many instances" but presume that a "well-constructed story may sway judgments even when evidence is in short supply" (67–68).

144 Bruner 1991, 4. Narratives, as Bruner concludes, "are a version of reality whose acceptability is governed by convention and 'narrative necessity' rather than by empirical verification and logical requiredness."

145 See Weisberg 1996, 77.

146 Ginzburg 1991, 84–85.

147 H. V. White 1978, 121. And both are just as likely to fail. As Rosenberg (2018) argues, there are no facts of the matter, no belief-desire pairings, that allow us to anticipate, confirm, or disconfirm narrative explanations.

148 H. V. White 1973, 5.

149 H. V. White 1973, 5.

150 H. V. White 1973, 7. A similar structure exists in the criminal trial; see Griffin 2012, 288.

151 H. V. White 1973, 7. White acknowledges the existence of other "archetypical" kinds of stories and explicitly names the detective story. Sherwin (1994, 40) refers to the idea of emplotment when he argues that "recurring storylines, familiar genres and plots, and typical characters, conflicts and resolutions" are a way to keep "the mess out" of storytelling. Rideout (2013, 71) uses the term "external coherence" to refer to the stock of social knowledge that provides narratives with broader cultural content. The same concept is probably addressed by the term "masterplot," representing stories that are told over and over again and that are linked to our culture and identity. Some masterplots appear to be universal, like stories of revenge. Abbott 2021, 53. Kurt Vonnegut (2005) developed yet another conceptualization by diagramming stories as a function of good and ill fortune (y axis) and beginning and end (x axis). He describes typical stories (boy meets girl, Cinderella) as following the same plot development and argues that a successful story is one that pleases the audience. Although Vonnegut refers to anthropologically primitive people, his point can easily be related to a trial when he says that "[p]rimitive people deserve to lose with their lousy stories."

152 Cohn 1999, 114.

153 Danto 2007, 26. Danto points to narrative integrity when he speaks about the exploitation of narrative expectations "by narrators who put in false clues and

dead ends, to thwart the narrative imagination: probably the best place to study the structure of narrative is the mystery novel, where narration is a duel fought between writer and reader."

154 Danto 2007, 27.

155 For an insightful analysis of the role of culture in narrative techniques, see Williams (2009, 49). How much lawyers can make use of these techniques depends on the narrative blueprint of the system. Griffin (2012) argues that the competing narrative paradigms in an adversarial trial may "exclude salient facts of what happened" (309).

156 Gilbert, Gilfarb, and Talpins 2005, 3.

157 See Abbott 2021, 53.

158 "I expect Chris Ochoa will testify, how once the robbery had been completed, they proceeded to 'have a little fun' with Nancy DePriest." State of Texas v. Richard Danziger, Trans. (10/21/1990), 10. In the closing, the prosecutor summarized: "The robbery changed into something about having a little fun."

159 State of Texas v. Richard Danziger, Trans. (10/21/1990), 1280.

160 This theme was further stressed during the trial when Danziger was asked about whether his sex life depended on rape: "So you can have a great sex life and that wouldn't fulfill what you needed for rape." State of Texas v. Richard Danziger, Trans. (10/21/1990), 1242.

161 Danto 2007, 18.

162 H. V. White 1999, 28: "[O]ne narrative account may represent a set of events as having the form and meaning of an epic or tragic story, while another may represent the same set of events—with equal plausibility and without doing any violence to the factual record—as describing a farce."

163 H. V. White 1999, 28.

164 Bennett and Feldman 1984, 93. Abbott (2021, 50) uses the term "normalization" to describe the desire to bring events into narrative coherence.

165 Bennett and Feldman 1984, 93.

166 J. B. White 1985b, 263.

167 Danto 2007, 27. With this, Danto moves away from an understanding of historical narratives based mainly on reason. He quotes Hegel, who argued that the "sole thought which philosophy brings to the treatment of history is the simple concept of Reason: that Reason is the Law of the world and that therefore, in world history, things have come about rationally." Danto says that "the action derives its relevant description from events subsequent to their occurrence, whether these were meant or not to happen by that agent." Danto 2007, 20.

168 Sewell 2005, 199.

169 Bennett and Feldman 1984, 96.

170 Bennett and Feldman 1984, 96.

171 Bennett and Feldman 1984, 60.

172 Bennett and Feldman 1984, 93, consider the assumption "misguided" that trials involve the straightforward presentation and testing of facts.

173 Ferguson-Gilbert 2011, 284: "Prosecutors' idea of justice is a guilty verdict for the people of the city, county, state, or territory the prosecutor represents. The prosecutor aims for the sole end of achieving convictions against each defendant." Prosecutors are legally and ethically required to "seek justice, not merely to convict," but practically that is hardly ever enforced, neither during a trial nor on appeal.

174 Danto 2007, 27.

175 For example, every year about three dozen children die of heat strokes because their guardians forgot them in their cars. Prosecutors vary in how they respond. Some charge manslaughter or child endangerment; others do not charge at all. Their decisions are influenced by legal factors like proof but also the desire among some prosecutors to extend mercy to parents who made tragic mistakes. The public opinion and the media influence the narrative that prosecutors develop. See Otterman, August 1, 2019.

176 "To recognize the present as historical is to perceive both it and one's consciousness of it as something the meaning of which will only be given in the future, and in historical retrospection. For it is recognized as having the structure of what will be a past historical moment, namely as one the meaning of which is available to historians, but not necessarily to those to whom it was present, that meaning having been concealed from them for whatever reason it is that the future is hidden." Danto 2007, 17, 20.

177 O'Hara 1980, 113. In the same section, O'Hara refers to chance as an element that cannot be omitted from consideration. This point deserves further discussion, because in many wrongful convictions it was mere chance that an individual became a suspect.

178 Leo and Drizin 2010, 15.

179 Leo and Drizin 2010, 15.

180 Terry v. Ohio, 392 U.S. 1, 5 (1968).

181 Terry v. Ohio, 392 U.S. 27.

182 Danto 2007, 27.

183 Cohn 1999, 15.

184 Cohn 1999, 15.

185 H. V. White 1978, 123.

186 H. V. White 1978, 123.

187 The early twentieth-century philosopher Hans Vaihinger argues that jurisprudence has "an easier task in dealing with its fictions than has mathematics, for its cases are covered by arbitrary ordinances and a transference is easily made. We have only to think of the case *as if it were so*." Vaihinger 1935, 51. That allows for a degree of imagination not typical in other truth-seeking disciplines. Vahinger's claim has become interwoven into the newly kindled debate on the concept of legal fictions (like corporate personhood, etc.). The false stories that underly wrongful convictions are not legal fiction in the sense this concept is used by

Fuller (1967) because in contrast to, for instance, corporate personhood, there is no acknowledgement of the falsehood of the false story. See also Knauer 2010, 91.

188 "[N]ovels present us with a semblance or illusion (Schein) of reality that we don't take in a conditional sense, but what we accept as a reality so long as we remain absorbed in it." Käte Hamburger in Cohn 1999, 6.

189 In a similar vein, von Arnauld and Martini (2015) argue that literary stories are not integrated with the same "radicalism" into an institutional practice that, like law, is "not concerned with the narratological aspects of storytelling" (350). To the contrary, law is and must be concerned with storytelling; that concern is (and that is what the authors probably meant) simply not normative.

190 State of Texas v. Richard Danziger, Trans. (10/21/1990), 1290.

191 Grunewald 2021.

192 H. V. White 1978, 85.

193 H. V. White 1978, 125.

194 H. V. White 1978, 122.

195 Von Arnold (2008, 44) contends that the law and literature movement is not held together by a closed theoretical concept; rather the concern to expose the classical positivist methodical understanding of jurisprudence as an illusion through confrontation with literature or literary studies.

196 Dershowitz 1996a, 102.

197 Klein and Martínez 2008, 3.

198 American Bar Association 2017.

199 Brandt (2017, 95), in her analysis of narratives in the sciences, describes the purpose of narrative as providing a pattern of organization and the production and communication of knowledge.

200 See H. V. White 1978, 123: "History came to be set over against fiction, and especially the novel, as the representation of the 'actual' to the representation of the 'possible' or only 'imaginable.' And thus was born the dream of a historical discourse that would consist of nothing but factually accurate statements about a realm of events which were (or had been) observable in principle, the arrangement of which in the order of their original occurrence would permit them to figure forth their true meaning or significance."

201 See H. V. White 1973, 6–7. See Fludernik (2010, 7) for a discussion of the relationship between narrative as a subject of investigation and narrative as a method.

202 Authorship as understood here is not the same as in intellectual property law and other areas where it is used technically or somewhat metaphorically. See Ashworth and Horder 2013, 86.

203 Barthes 1977b, 146.

204 Copy on file with the author.

205 "Richard then put the money in a white cloth sack (coin bag) along with some money in a zippered vinyl bank bag."

206 Berlow 2000.

207 A written confession is the polished product of hours of interrogation. It has no traces of how it came about; it does and cannot represent dialect or accent, grammar, interruptions, prompts, or diction that were part of the oral narrative. These elements are lost in the process of transcribing what was allegedly said. Only rarely do courts wonder about authenticity if they read the words of a suspect, a witness, or the attorneys. Brooks (2006, 7) uses *Bumper v. North Carolina*, 391 U.S. 543, 546–47 (1968), as an example where a judge (Justice Stewart) questioned the validity of a transcript as being an original representation of what a witness said for narratological reasons.

208 In narrative terms, he "underread" the plea agreement.

209 Innocence Project 2019.

210 "But Richard Danziger is the victim of a conspiracy, the victim of a framing. We're all lying but he's telling the truth." State of Texas v. Richard Danziger, Trans. (10/21/1990), 1314.

211 Grunewald 2021.

212 Garrett 2011.

213 Gadamer 2016, 23.

214 Gadamer 2016, 23.

215 On file with author.

216 Brooks (2006, 9) argues that such scrutiny would undermine the authority of too many narratives that the law relies upon, like transcripts from lower courts. Only occasionally—and Brooks discusses one example—do courts see how, for instance, free indirect discourse can mask the actual story and as a result original authorship.

217 Brooks 2006, 2.

218 Herrera v. Collins, 506 U.S. 390, 416 (1993).

219 Brooks 2006, 21.

220 Brooks 2006, 9.

221 Gudjonsson 2003, 55.

3. THE EVIDENTIARY POWER OF STORIES

1 State of Texas v. Michael Morton, Trans. (2/10/1987), 231.

2 According to a Study by the University Münster, only 50% of all homicides are discovered because doctors who are often called and fill out death certificates lack training in death investigation. See Przybilla 2016; Merten 2003, 2558.

3 Roach 2010, 388.

4 Roach 2010, 388.

5 Zalman 2008, 71–72, 75.

6 Rossmo and Pollock (2019, 798), describe wrongful convictions as a "form of investigative failure."

7 White 1985a, 175.

8 White 1985a, 175.

9 Williams (2009, 49) is critical of law's narrative requirements because they "lock" the lawyer into the internal logic of doctrine and through that "invoke[s] a subtle process of anaesthesia." Through the "objective" narrative voice of the law, "real life drama, trauma or tragedy of the accused is recorded or trapped within the bricolage of doctrine, like a fly in amber."

10 Williams 2009, 49

11 State of Texas v. Michael Morton, Trans. (2/9/1987), 44.

12 B. S. Jackson 1988.

13 943.20(1)(a) Wisconsin.

14 Bennett and Feldman 1984, 95.

15 Motive, however, is a powerful narrative device. Often, without a clear motive a convincing story cannot be told. Sonia Sotomayor (2013, 210) stresses the importance of explaining the "why" of a crime in a prosecutor's narrative.

16 See Weigend 2011, 395.

17 Lisska 1996, 93.

18 See Weigend 2011, 395.

19 Marian 2016.

20 Damaška 1998, 294.

21 Damaška 1998, 294.

22 See Grunewald (2014) for a discussion of the role of truth in the inquisitorial and adversarial system.

23 Griffin (2012, 285) is correct in correlating adversarialism with storytelling but misunderstands that inquisitorialism does not "prohibit" stories—inquisitorial systems simply regulate them differently.

24 Sometimes, the two systems are referred to as "inquisitorial" and "accusatorial." Pérez-Perdomo 2007, 127. As inquisitorial systems also have accusatorial elements, this distinction seems less characteristic than the first. Merryman and Pérez-Perdomo 2007, 127–29.

25 This is in contrast to inquisitorial systems, where cases develop from the top down when an impartial judge or panel of judges inquires into the facts and creates his or her own narrative; discussed further below.

26 Abbott 2021, 190.

27 "For every crime there is a story. Good lawyers find the story." Abbe Smith 2010, 324.

28 See Ferguson-Gilbert 2011.

29 Goodpaster 1987, 120.

30 For example, if a story is told in sequence, it is more likely to be believed by a jury. Lempert 1991, 561–62. Abbott (2021, 49) argues that seeing causation in sequence is a human desire and an ancient fallacy.

31 Garrett 2010, 8; Goodpaster 1987, 122.

32 Bennett and Feldman 1984.

33 See Langbein 1977, 1; Damaška 1973, 512–54; Frase and Weigend 1995, 318; Mack 1996, 71–85; van Kessel 1992, 409–87.

34 Goodpaster 1987, 118.
35 Landsman 1983, 714.
36 Goodpaster 1987, 120.
37 J. B. White 1985a, 174.
38 Machura and Robson 2001.
39 United States v. Cronic, 466 U.S. 655 (1984). Experienced trial lawyers may be less optimistic about the truth. Holbrook (2015), who also uses the theater metaphor, says that each side "presents a different play to the audience, and the audience picks the play it prefers" (45).
40 Herring v. New York, 422 U.S. 853, 862 (1975).
41 Landsman 1983, 716.
42 See ibid., 715.
43 United States v. Cronic, 466 U.S. 648, 655 (1984). The belief in the truth-finding capabilities of the adversarial trial is still widespread. See, for example, Freedman 1998, 78: "Our constitutional adversary system is based . . . on the premise that the adversary system is more effective [than the inquisitorial] in the search for truth."
44 Gordon 2013, 341.
45 Mark Cohen, a criminal defense lawyer from Manhattan, quoted in Eligon (May 15, 2011).
46 Nunn 1995, 798.
47 Packer 1968, 160. Packer's presumption of guilt is a working hypothesis that institutions apply. It does not interfere with the presumption of innocence, which is normative and means that "until there has been an adjudication of guilt by an authority . . . the suspect is to be treated, for reasons that have nothing whatever to do with the probable outcome of the case, as if his guilt is an open question." Packer 1968, 161. Both models are complementary. See Findley 2008, 2.
48 Gilbert, Gilfarb, and Talpins 2005, 7. Sotomayor (2013) notes how she learned to make jurors feel the "moral responsibility to convict" and that appealing to emotions is "perfectly valid in the art of persuasion" (209). She would put jurors in the "shoes of the accused or victim, as needed to make them feel the cold blade against their necks." (211).
49 See Abbott 2021, 196.
50 Whren v. United States, 517 U.S. 806, 813 (1996).
51 Arguably the best-known literary example of a racial narrative superseding a factual and legal is the trial of Tom Robinson in Harper Lee's *To Kill a Mockingbird*.
52 Findley and Scott 2006, 292.
53 Ferguson 1996, 86.
54 Nunn 1995, 791.
55 Rideout (2013, 71) uses the term "narrative coherence" to describe the function of plausibility in a different way. Through narrative coherence an action is presented as complete both in its larger meaning and its parts, its elements are unified and connected; that coherence will increase the likelihood that a judge or jury will

accept one party's underlying story, independent of the quality of the evidence presented as information or facts.

56 Griffin 2012, 285.

57 B. S. Jackson 1988.

58 Heller (2006, 252) argues that jurors consistently overvalue direct evidence and undervalue circumstantial evidence.

59 Bruner 1991, 4.

60 In a trial, storytelling begins with the voir dire process (questioning potential jurors for trial). Here, lawyers seek to determine the kinds of stories a juror is willing to accept. Lempert 1991, 561–62.

61 Bandes 1996, 383.

62 State of Texas v. Richard Danziger, Trans. (10/21/1990), 8.

63 Lempert 1991, 564; see also Pennington and Hastie 2003, 543.

64 A detective matches—brings into congruence—what they find at the scene with a script they have in mind. That script is legally and cognitively predetermined. The developing narrative is matched with requirements of the process, prosecutors match it more closely with the law, jurors match the narrative with the scripts and masterplots they bring to the jury bench, and so on.

65 Nunn 1995, 792.

66 Zak 2015.

67 Zak 2015.

68 See Levit 2009, 277.

69 Gerrig and Egidi 2003, 34.

70 Gerrig and Egidi 2003, 34.

71 Gerrig and Egidi 2003, 40.

72 Gerrig and Egidi 2003, 37. Resonance can be described as a fast, passive, and easy process by which cues in working memory interact in parallel with, and allow access to, information in long-term memory.

73 See Zak 2015.

74 Grice 1989.

75 "I expect a partner's contribution to be appropriate to the immediate needs at each stage of the transaction. If I am mixing ingredients for a cake, I do not expect to be handed a good book, or even an oven cloth." Grice 1989, 28.

76 Brooks 2006, 10.

77 Blume, Johnson, and Paavola 2007, 1088.

78 Blume, Johnson, and Paavola 2007, 1088.

79 Blume, Johnson, and Paavola 2007, 1089; see also Gordon 2013, 340.

80 This identification process is "at least partially subjective, idiosyncratic, and experience based." Gordon 2013, 340.

81 B. S. Jackson 1988.

82 J. B. White 1985a, 174.

83 Estes v. Texas, 381 U.S. 532 (1965): "Court proceedings are held for the solemn purpose of endeavoring to ascertain the truth which is the sine qua non of a fair trial."

84 Brooks 2006, 9.

85 Abbott 2021, 188.

86 Parklane Hosiery Co., Inc. v. Shore, 439 U.S. 322, 344, 349, (1979), quoting Kalven and Zeisel.

87 Hans 2007, 581.

88 See Hühn 1987, 457. He introduces the detective as a reader, based on the assumption that "the story of the crime is mediated in the discourse of the detective's investigation" (452).

89 State of Texas v. Michael Morton, Trans. (2/9/1987), 11. By "focusing" on Morton, the prosecutor meant that certain investigative interventions (like a search, an arrest, etc.) require probable cause, which must be based on information the officers gathered (constructed) when investigating the crime scene.

90 See State of Texas v. Michael Morton, Trans. (2/9/1987), 32.

91 Morton 2014, 21.

92 Abbott 2021, 52. The Cinderella story would be one example, but masterplots are much more universal.

93 State of Texas v. Michael Morton, Trans. (2/10/1987), 316.

94 State of Texas v. Michael Morton, Trans. (2/12/1987), 724.

95 A neighbor saw Morton's red and watery eyes, expecting him to "break down or be dumfounded or shocked." State of Texas v. Michael Morton, Trans. (2/12/1987), 786.

96 State of Texas v. Michael Morton, Trans. (2/17/1987), 1158.

97 Bornstein and Greene 2011, 65. There often is a double standard at work when it comes to normalizing behavior. What is considered not normal might just be a reflection of a social norm that appears to be violated but not what is empirically normal behavior. For instance, the neighbor who found the victim inside the home considered it unusual "anytime a mother leaves her child out of their eyesight." State of Texas v. Michael Morton, Trans. (2/9/1987), 15. The neighbor had children herself but left her house three times while looking for Chris. She was asked, "Where were your children at this time?" And she said: "In the house." State of Texas v. Michael Morton, Trans. (2/9/1987), 21. The standard she used to judge Chris's behavior is not the one she applies to herself. And that might be justifiable given the circumstances, but it shows how easily external and internal normalcy can be switched.

98 Riggins v. Nevada (90–8466), 504 U.S. 127 (1992) (Kennedy concurring).

99 See Feldman Barrett, March 12, 2017.

100 Morton 2014, 85.

101 State of Texas v. Michael Morton, Trans. (2/12/1987), 725. See also Morton 2014, 21.

102 Morton 2014, 22.

103 Innocence Project 2018.

104 State of Texas v. Michael Morton, Trans. (2/9/1987), 135–36.

105 Bennett and Feldman (1984) use yet another concept of story: "A story is simply a communicational form that provides for the development, climax, and denouement of action in the context of a defined collection of actors, means motives, and

scenes" (7). Thus their understanding of story differs from the one used in this book.

106 Bennett and Feldman 1984, 5.

107 Bennett and Feldman 1984, 98.

108 Bennett and Feldman 1984, 98.

109 State of Texas v. Michael Morton, Trans. (2/17/1987), 1127.

110 State of Texas v. Michael Morton, Trans. (2/10/1987), 228.

111 State of Texas v. Michael Morton, Trans. (2/10/1987), 230.

112 State of Texas v. Michael Morton, Trans. (2/10/1987), 230.

113 State of Texas v. Michael Morton, Trans. (2/10/1987), 231.

114 A video recording of a crime (direct evidence) requires much less inference than a fingerprint on a door (circumstantial evidence), since the fingerprint must be contextualized and by itself connects a person only with an object but not an event, like theft.

115 See People v. Ford, 66 N.Y.2d 428, 441 (N.Y. 1985).

116 People v. Sanchez, 61 NY2d 1022, 1024 (1984). Some states, like New York, do not require "moral certainty" anymore.

117 Jolly 1993, 83.

118 See Jolly 1993, 81.

119 State of Texas v. Michael Morton, Trans. (2/12/1987), 676.

120 State of Texas v. Michael Morton, Trans. (2/16/1987), 1018.

121 State of Texas v. Michael Morton, Trans. (2/13/1987), 835.

122 Abbott 2021, 186.

123 Drizin 2014.

124 Goode, November 15, 2011.

125 Goode, November 15, 2011.

126 Appleby and Kassin 2016: "As to why the accompaniment of a prosecutorial theory proved so important, research shows that storytelling in particular presents a potentially important contextual influence on the inferences that people draw from evidence. Successful trial lawyers often stress the value of a causal narrative to help jurors understand complicated trial information."

127 State of Texas v. Michael Morton, Trans. (2/17/1987), 1121.

128 Abbott 2021, 190.

129 State of Texas v. Michael Morton, Trans. (2/17/1987), 1099.

130 State of Texas v. Michael Morton, Trans. (2/17/1987), 1098.

131 State of Texas v. Michael Morton, Trans. (2/17/1987), 1100.

132 State of Texas v. Michael Morton, Trans. (2/17/1987), 1147.

133 State of Texas v. Michael Morton, Trans. (2/17/1987), 1148–49.

134 See Stamm 2019, 88.

135 See Cooper 2016; Colloff 2012.

136 State of Texas v. Michael Morton, Trans. (2/12/1987), 734.

137 State of Texas v. Michael Morton, Trans. (2/10/1987), 243.

138 State of Texas v. Michael Morton, Trans. (2/10/1987), 247.

139 State of Texas v. Michael Morton, Trans. (2/10/1987), 248.

140 State of Texas v. Michael Morton, Trans. (2/16/1987), 952. In his memoir, Morton (2014) stresses that they used that phrase because it was "*so* ignorant and *so* awful" (82).

141 State of Texas v. Michael Morton, Trans. (2/12/1987), 776.

142 State of Texas v. Michael Morton, Trans. (2/10/1987), 284.

143 Colloff 2012.

144 State of Texas v. Michael Morton, Trans. (2/17/1987), 1152–53.

145 See Posner 1997b, 296.

146 Posner 1997b, 295.

147 State of Texas v. Michael Morton, Trans. (2/16/1987), 1020.

148 State of Texas v. Michael Morton, Trans. (2/17/1987), 1095.

149 Narrative by its arrangement of events satisfies the need for order, the most important of which is causation. As Abbott (2021) argues, as much as causation stories (i.e., murder results in the ability to sleep in the victim's blood) are gratifying, they are also treacherous, since they implicitly draw on the fallacy that "things that follow other things are caused by those things" (49).

150 State of Texas v. Michael Morton, Trans. (2/9/1987), 50.

151 State of Texas v. Michael Morton, Trans. (2/17/1987), 1159.

152 State of Texas v. Michael Morton, Trans. (2/17/1987), 1158.

153 Colloff 2012.

154 Colloff 2012.

155 Colloff 2012.

156 Colloff 2012, State of Texas v. Michael Morton, Trans. (2/16/1987), 1027, 1034.

157 Abbott 2021, 196.

158 See Abbott 2021, 196.

159 State of Texas v. Michael Morton, Trans. (2/17/1987), 1127.

160 See Dershowitz 1996a.

161 State of Texas v. Michael Morton, Trans. (2/17/1987), 1129.

162 Hall 2008, 88.

163 Hall 2008, 88.

164 Presser and Sandberg 2015.

165 State of Texas v. Michael Morton, Trans. (2/17/1987), 1092.

166 Herrera v. Collins, 506 U.S. 390, 416 (1993).

167 Brooks 2006, 21.

168 Jackson v. Virginia, 443 U.S. 307 (1974).

169 Morton v. State, 761 S.W.2d 876, 880 (Tex. App. 1988). This is based on *Jackson v. Virginia*, but see also United States v. Dessart, 823 F.3d 395, 403 (7th Cir. 2016) (citation omitted) (quoting United States v. Warren, 593 F.3d 540, 546 (7th Cir. 2010)).

170 Jackson v. Virginia, 443 U.S. 307, 318–319 (1979).

171 See chapters 4 and 5 for a discussion of the German system, which allows for factual appeals and postconviction appeals based on newly discovered evidence.

172 In Cullen v. Pinholster, 563 U.S. 170, 181 (2011) the Court held that appellate review "is limited to the record that was before the state court that adjudicated the claim on the merits."

173 Morton v. State, 761 S.W.2d 876, 880 (Tex. App. 1988), referencing Freeman v. State, 654 S.W.2d 450, 456 (Tex. Cr. App. 1983).

174 Jackson v. Virginia, 443 U.S. 307, 333 (1979).

175 See Strassfeld 1992, 349.

176 Morton v. State, 761 S.W.2d 876, 877 (Tex. App. 1988).

177 Morton v. State, 761 S.W.2d 876, 878 (Tex. App. 1988).

178 Morton v. State, 761 S.W.2d 876, 879 (Tex. App. 1988).

179 Morton v. State, 761 S.W.2d 876, 879 (Tex. App. 1988).

180 See Strassfeld 1992, 345.

181 Brooks 2003.

182 Strassfeld 1992, 350.

183 Morton v. State, 761 S.W.2d 876, 879 (Tex. App. 1988).

184 Morton v. State, 761 S.W.2d 876, 879 (Tex. App. 1988).

185 Epps 2018, 2152.

186 Morton v. State, 761 S.W.2d 876, 880 (Tex. App. 1988).

187 Morton v. State, 761 S.W.2d 876, 881 (Tex. App. 1988).

188 Morton v. State, 761 S.W.2d 876, 881 (Tex. App. 1988).

189 Dramatic here means having a certain relevance for the narrative. As Dershowitz (1996a), points out, life is not a Chekhovian narrative, and life events do not imitate art. They are often "irrelevant to what comes next; events can be out of sequence, random, purely accidental, without purpose" (100).

190 Morton v. State, 761 S.W.2d 876, 881 (Tex. App. 1988).

191 State of Texas v. Michael Morton, Trans. (2/10/1987), 226.

192 Colloff 2012.

193 See Ahmed 2004, 118.

194 Lempert 1991, 560. That mold differs from juror to juror depending on culture, education, social status, and the like. Lempert 1991, 571.

195 This is an example of "life" imitating "art" in which a masterplot, like violent reaction to sexual rejection as motive, organizes the narrative with the purpose of represent actual events. See Bruner 1991, 21.

196 Brooks 2006, 2.

197 Herrera v. Collins, 506 U.S. 390, 415 (1993): "Recent authority confirms that over the past century clemency has been exercised frequently in capital cases in which demonstrations of 'actual innocence' have been made."

198 Rossmo and Pollock 2019, 806.

199 State of Texas v. Michael Morton, Trans. (2/17/1987), 1151–52.

200 Abbott (2021) calls these "reflexive narratives," in which "one side or the other will look back from time to time to relate their own or their opposition's actions to gain a rhetorical advantage" (189).

201 "That is as good as a confession when you tie it into that picture of the body." State of Texas v. Michael Morton, Trans. (2/17/1987), 1151.

202 Norris (2017, 67) speaks of the early 1990s as the "DNA-exoneration era," arguing that the "importance of DNA to the innocence movement cannot be overstated" (70). In *Actual Innocence*, Dwyer, Neufeld, and Scheck (2001) discuss the invention of PCR analysis and that no one could have imagined that it "would travel through the history of the American judicial system" (52).

203 The concept of evidence is relative in nature. Evidence can be anything presented in support of a proposition. Whether or not a thing is evidence depends on the legal facts the investigator needs to establish for a narrative. As Ginzburg (1979) points out, "a detective . . . establishes the author of a 'crime' . . . on the basis of clues that are not perceptible to most people" (276). They are perceptible to the detective (in Ginzburg's example it is Sherlock Holmes). Without a preconceived, rudimentary narrative, there cannot be evidence. A footprint *is* not evidence per se; it becomes evidence through narrativization.

204 For a discussion of the tension between factual accuracy, legal truth, and the "story model," see Griffin (2012), who argues that the adversarial trial is hybrid in that it includes "subjective and objective approaches to the interpretation of facts" (285).

205 Findley (2011b, 1182) mentions the case of Kirk Bloodsworth, who was the first person sentenced to death and later exonerated by DNA evidence. Nine years after the exoneration, the chief prosecutor said she was "not sure" of the innocence and that that police still believe Bloodsworth committed the crime. Prosecutors, as Findley puts it, are often protective of their convictions, which shows how little scientific thinking is intrinsic to the legal discourse (1183). If new evidence could show that a defendant is innocent, why do prosecutors consent to DNA testing only half the time and have the Innocence Project fight their requests for DNA testing in court? See Neufeld 2001, 640. At the same time, the scientific discourse itself is not free of narratives. Probably one of the most notorious statements in the history of science is the one made in 1616 by a team of consultants for the Inquisition in Rome, which declared the heliocentric system of Nicolaus Copernicus to be "foolish and absurd in philosophy" and "formally heretical."

206 That term has become a trope for this constellation. Godsey 2017, 14.

207 Griffin 2012, 302.

208 Bruner 1990, 44.

209 Heller 2006, 252.

210 Heller 2006, 252.

211 When pretrial DNA testing is done in sexual assault cases, the primary suspect, when identified by other traditional sorts of evidence, was innocent in more than 25% of the cases. Findley 2011b, 1171.

212 Snyder et al. 2007, 6.

213 State of Texas v. Michael Morton, Trans. (2/10/1987), 227.

214 The prosecutor continues in a similar way: "And it's important that you listen to every piece of evidence and think of every piece of evidence as a whole. And based upon that evidence, all the facts and circumstances, . . . we are going to convince you beyond any reasonable doubt that the Defendant did exactly did what we said he did, and that he beat his wife to death." State of Texas v. Michael Morton, Trans. (2/10/1987), 223.

215 State of Texas v. Michael Morton, Trans. (2/17/1987), 1147.

216 State of Texas v. Michael Morton, Trans. (2/17/1987), 1130–31.

217 State of Texas v. Michael Morton, Trans. (2/17/1987), 1162.

218 Camus 1989, 96.

219 Camus 1989, 96.

220 Old Chief v. United States, 519 U.S. 172, 189 (1997).

221 Old Chief v. United States, 519 U.S. 172, 187.

222 Old Chief v. United States, 519 U.S. 172, 187.

223 Griffin 2016, 169.

224 Old Chief v. United States, 519 U.S. 172, 187–88.

225 Old Chief v. United States, 519 U.S. 172, 190. "The fact of the qualifying conviction is alone what matters under the statute." In her dissent, Justice O'Connor argues that "a person is not simply convicted of 'a crime' or 'a felony.' Rather, he is found guilty of a specified offense." Therefore, jurors would have a right to learn about the circumstances of the prior conviction.

226 Lempert 2001, 407–08.

227 Lempert 2001. 407.

228 See Feigenson 2010, 63.

229 Lempert 2001, 408.

230 Lempert 2001, 408.

231 Lempert 2001, 409.

232 Lempert 2001, 408.

233 Lempert 2001, 411.

234 See Pizzi 1999, 16.

235 Rule 403 states that a "court may exclude relevant evidence if its probative value is substantially outweighed by a danger of one or more of the following: unfair prejudice, confusing the issues, misleading the jury, undue delay, wasting time, or needlessly presenting cumulative evidence."

236 Lempert 2001, 410.

237 Doran, Jackson, and Seigel 1995, 22; see also Damaška 1973, 581–82 (observing that the primary goal of the adversarial system is to resolve disputes between parties, whereas the inquisitorial system's central goal is to seek truth); Freedman 1998, 57: "[A]n adversary system resolves disputes by presenting conflicting views of fact and law to an impartial and relatively passive arbiter, who decides which side wins what."

238 Doran, Jackson, and Seigel 1995, 14.

239 Goodpaster (1987, 125) describes this view as concordant with the "fair decision theory."

240 Arnella 1983, 206; see also Frankel 1975, 1037: "Employed by interested parties, the process often achieves truth only as a convenience, a byproduct, or an accidental approximation." Weinreb (1999, 61) notes that the same attributes that make the adversarial system great—for example the single-minded, zealous representation of each party—also hamper the pursuit of truth because of tactics or "tricks of persuasion" used by advocates to achieve favorable results for those whom they represent.

241 Frase 2000, 809.

242 Trüg and Kerner 2007, 197.

243 Häberle 1995, 23.

244 Trüg and Kerner 2007, 197. This description is imprecise in that it does not differentiate between truth as the ultimate goal of an inquiry and the process that is used to achieve it. However, the statement holds true for what at the end of a trial and the criminal process in general is an acceptable truth.

245 Goodpaster 1987, 152.

246 Bennett and Feldman 1984, 4.

247 Burns 1999, 164, "[A]t trial, there is not one narrative, there are two that become rival suitors for the jury's imagination." He continues by arguing a "deep in personal history" of the "two-story" scheme as a reflection of "ordinary moral experience, in which we often construct competing narratives." Sherrod (2019) states that "a jury trial is . . . a contest of stories." Heffer 2005, 66: "[H]istory reveals that criminal trials have always consisted in three distinct, though interrelated, elements: an adversarial contest, ritual procedures, and a means of adjudication of guilt and punishment." Ralph 2018, 587: "The contest of narrative is a fundamental part of the way law operates."

248 Johnston and Lufrano 2002, 148: "[T]ruth is best served by placing the responsibility on the parties themselves to formulate their case and destroy the case of their adversary."

249 The contest metaphor is probably rooted in the idea of adversarialism itself. See Freedman (1998), who concludes that "there is good reason to believe that the adversary system is superior in determining truth when facts are in dispute between contesting parties" (90).

250 When Richard Danziger said that he was falsely incriminated by Chris Ochoa's (false) confession and testimony, the prosecutor immediately introduced the conspiracy narrative: "And the cops have joined in? . . . And all these people that said they didn't tell you about the caliber of the weapon—" (State of Texas v. Richard Danziger, Trans. (10/21/1990), 1248). In the next sentence, the prosecutor accused Danziger of making false statements to the jury about how hard Danziger had been working. So within the minute or less in which this exchange (that went on in a similar way) occurred, the jury sees Danziger's defense (being framed)

and Danziger's character being put into doubt. That functions so well because jurors do not see or learn much about the pretrial stage, specifically how the state prepares its case and how evidence is constructed. On this point, see K. McKillop and Vidmar (2015, 978).

251 Habermas 1990.

252 Goodpaster 1987, 122; see also Frankel 1975, 1036: "[W]e know that others searching after facts—in history, geography, medicine, whatever—do not emulate our adversary system." Even today in the age of science and technology, the faith in adversarial truth-finding remains deeply rooted so much as to it being compared to "the Church's canonization of Saints." Johnston and Lufrano 2002, 147. Freedman 1998, 80, dismisses the analogy to nonlitigation settings of truth-finding more rhetorically than substantively, arguing that a court is not a laboratory and that "in the case of the research scientist, truth is ultimately knowable in an absolute sense—either a cure works or it doesn't. In most litigation, however, we can rarely be certain that a verdict is synonymous with 'truth.'" The main flaw of this argument is that truth is always an approximation in any science and discourse. The potential of falsification is always present, it even drives science. Finality and the concept or legal certainty drive law.

253 Goodpaster 1987, 122 n.10.

254 Goodpaster 1987, 124.

4. STORYTELLING IN AN INQUISITORIAL SYSTEM

1 See BVerfG [Federal Constitutional Court] Mar. 19, 2013, 2 BvR 2628/10 para. 160.

2 Bock et al. 2013, 328.

3 See Frase and Weigend 1995, 342; the role of defense attorneys varies across Europe. In Germany, they are more involved than in France, for instance. This is why some call Germany's system "neo-inquisitorial." Frase and Weigend 1995, 318. Roach (2010, 388) generalizes and equates "inquisitorial" with "Continental."

4 Consider, for instance, that German prosecutors address their charges to the court. That court first decides whether sufficient evidence exists for a trial; if so, it would be the same court that then presides over the case. This raises many narrative questions that are unique for the German criminal justice system. At the same time, German scholars must be careful in assessing the American system without consideration of its context. Blufarb (2018, 354), for instance, qualifies the cross-examination of witnesses in the United States as "vehement rhetoric," which in its dramatic form is used to attack the credibility of witnesses. This is an oversimplification.

5 See Olson 2018, 23. Blufarb (2018) asks whether the narratological approach is transferrable to Germany, but this question seems to misunderstand that all systems narrate in their specific ways and that there are multiple narratologies.

6 Machura and Robson 2001, 123.

7 Machura and Robson 2001, 117.

8 Von Arnold 2008, 48.

9 Von Arnold 2008, 43.

10 Olson 2010, 353.

11 Blufarb 2018, 515.

12 See Blufarb (2018, 517), who suggests a concept of narrativity (Narrativität)— probably meaning "narrative"—specific to the German legal context. That definition does not differ much from classical approaches and is not specifically German at all.

13 See, e.g., Bruner 2002, 37.

14 Olson 2010, 339; also Olson 2018, 26.

15 For a disclaimer, see Zalman and Grunewald (2015–2016, 193).

16 Reichel 2013, 80. That is a contrast to German civil procedure, which resembles adversarial structures. Litigants must present facts and evidence (so-called Beibringungsgrundsatz) to the court, which is under no obligation to investigate the true facts and must decide based on the submitted evidence. Zippelius 2008, 127. Blufarb (2018, 519) argues without offering much support that the procedural layout has little influence on narrative processes.

17 See Olson 2018, 27.

18 Grimm 2019, 26: "Dasz recht und poesie miteinander aus einem bette aufgestanden waren, hält nicht schwer zu glauben."

19 Renner 2010, 174.

20 Renner 2010, 174.

21 For instance, Grimm claims that judges and poets do not have almost the same name by chance, namely Schöffen ("lay judges") and Schöpfer "creator(s)" respectively. These terms not only sound similar in German; they also share a common function that refers to "creation," in the sense of re-creating those songs and laws as they are stored in the archive of the people's "soul." See Renner 2010, 175.

22 Grimm 2019, 64.

23 For example, to resolve a border dispute between two municipalities, "it was agreed to take a crab and let it run over the disputed field. Its tracks were followed and traced with stones. Because it ran so strangely in a crisscross, there is a strange border with many corners to this day." Grimm 2019, 85.

24 Blufarb 2018, 28.

25 Von Arnold 2008, 43.

26 Olson 2018, 28.

27 Merryman and Pérez-Perdomo 2007, 81.

28 Gräfin von Schlieffen 2009, XVI. Law is taught at "rechtswissenschaftliche Fakultäten," (departments of juridical science).

29 Von Arnold 2008, 43.

30 Olson 2010, 352.

31 Merryman and Pérez-Perdomo 2007, 23.

32 Certain exceptions exist so that laws are applied uniformly. Decisions from the Federal Constitutional Court are binding on all courts. Also, if a higher regional court (Oberlandesgericht) intends to deviate from a decision from another higher

regional court or federal court, the issue in question must be presented to the federal court (121 II GVG).

33 Zippelius 2008, 16.

34 According to Zippelius (2008), "it goes without saying that the principle of equal treatment is the heart and soul of legal hermeneutics; at the very least it is an incredibly important form in which a problem of justice is made accessible in hermeneutics" (100).

35 Zippelius 2008, 91.

36 Merryman and Pérez-Perdomo 2007, 62; see also Zippelius 2008, 3.

37 Olson 2010, 352.

38 Kelsen 1941. 44.

39 Kelsen 1941, 49.

40 Kelsen 1941, 47.

41 Adomeit 2003, 165.

42 Von Arnold 2008, 43.

43 Certainty of law and what it means are objectives in all legal systems, "but in the civil law tradition [this] has come to be a kind of supreme value, an unquestioned dogma, a fundamental goal." Therefore, the "process of interpretation and application of the law should be as automatic as possible, again in the interest of certainty. In this sense, the emphasis on certainty is an expression of a desire to make the law judge-proof." Merryman and Pérez-Perdomo 2007, 48.

44 Naucke 1991, 15–16.

45 See Wetlaufer 1990, 1558.

46 Naucke 1991, 59.

47 This goes back to Aristotle's distinction in Rhetoric Book III, Part 13: "You cannot either state your case and omit to prove it, or prove it without having first stated it; since any proof must be a proof of something, and the only use of a preliminary statement is the proof that follows it." The Internet Classics Archive 2009.

48 Naucke 1991, 59. Bruner 1986, 11: "[A]rguments convince one of their truth, stories of their lifelikeness. The one verifies by eventual appeal to procedures for establishing formal and empirical proof. The other establishes not truth but verisimilitude."

49 Naucke 1991, 61.

50 Zippelius 2008, 130. "[A] fact of behavior in its specific form and the question of its subsumption-ability gives the impetus to weigh and to make precise the range of meaning of the norm—with regard to the submitted facts of behavior. 'Substantiating' the norm takes place with reference to the extant reality of life in a 'back and forth wandering glance' between the norm and those facts of behavior relevant to the norm." Zippelius 2008, 132.

51 Mosbacher 2015, 85.

52 Hoffmann 1991, 88 (translation by the author); Mosbacher (2015, 85) says that the personal conviction of facts required by law is a "highly personal actualization (*Leistung*)," which has a different structure than the process of subsuming these facts under the law.

53 Naucke 1991, 60 (translation by the author). In comparison to the complexity of even a very simple crime, the legally reduced version that is necessary to fulfill the requirements of the law is a "leathery assumption." By separating motives and dispositions from technical intent, a legal narrative deteriorates to "the case." Naucke 1991, 64.

54 Naucke 1991, 60.

55 Von Arnauld 2017, 325.

56 Bruner 2002, 39.

57 Naucke 1991, 60.

58 Naucke 1991, 59.

59 See Wetlaufer 1990, 1559.

60 Hannken-Illjes 2006, 216.

61 See Hoffmann 1991, 88.

62 Grasnick 2010, 206.

63 Hannken-Illjes 2006, 216 ff.

64 Sec. 6 (2) 1 Pflichtversicherungsgesetz (Mandatory-Insurance Law).

65 Hannken-Illjes 2006, 217.

66 Hannken-Illjes 2006, 221.

67 See von Arnold 2008, 31. Hruschka's (1965, 11–12) point, which likely refers to judicial decision-making, is applicable to other stages of narrativization. He argues that, before any kind of legal assessment can happen, the "facts" are the result of a complex process of thought. Only what in the opinion of the judge or the narrator has any relation to the essence of the event and what is subject to a legal judgment is included in the factual presentation of the case. Through that presentation a "certain order" is achieved: recognition, selection and interpretation of the facts are the products of fact-finding, which results in a finished statement of facts.

68 "The legal case is the ontic correlate of the facts; it is what is described in the description, what is intended in the imagination, it is what is extracted from the life narrative into the statement of facts." Hruschka 1965, 12.

69 Von Arnauld 2017, 21.

70 Schönert 2015, 2.

71 Schönert (2015, 2) uses the term "Erzählspiel" (narrative play), which in combination with "regulated" reminds us of the term "regulated storytelling contest."

72 Schönert 2015, 3.

73 Luhmann 1993, 347.

74 Luhmann 1993, 348.

75 Luhmann 1993, 347.

76 Hruschka 1965, 5.

77 Hruschka (1965, 15) describes "meta-juridical" as the prelegal possibility of a certain way of thinking.

78 Hruschka 1965, 11.

79 Hruschka 1965, 32.

80 "Lebensverhalt" as a term is not common in the German language. Hruschka probably uses it to show a difference to Lebenssachverhalt, a term that has legal connotations.

81 Zippelius 2008 121.

82 Hruschka 1965, 12. Quite in contrast, Zippelius (2008, 122) posits that these "possible premises of the judicial decision then increasingly narrow themselves. Upon reflection within included norms some will then be recognized as 'not relevant here.'" What is striking (and typical for German legal thinking) is the agentless construction of these statements, for "premises . . . narrow themselves" and "norms . . . will then be recognized as not relevant." Processes of interpretation, application of law, and judgment are not without an agent. Facts do not tell themselves; they are told.

83 Hruschka 1965, 32.

84 Hruschka 1965, 38.

85 Hruschka 1965, 20.

86 Hruschka 1965, 22.

87 Hruschka 1965, 29.

88 Hruschka 1965, 23.

89 Hruschka 1965, 61.

90 What is happening in its immediacy is not the object of the specific legal assessment but rather an image that is preformed by consciousness based on perceptions categorically arranged and interpreted. Hruschka 1965, 11–12.

91 Trüg and Kerner 2007, 193.

92 Trüg and Kerner 2007, 194; see also Grunewald 2014.

93 Most inquisitorially oriented systems include adversarial elements, just as adversarial systems have inquisitorial elements. But there are noticeable differences. See Stamp (1998, 19), who points out that it is characteristic of the German criminal process that the agencies (police, prosecutors, judges, etc.) "instruct themselves," meaning that that they autonomously and independently look for a comprehensive picture of the facts.

94 Merryman and Pérez-Perdomo 2007.

95 See Brants 2012, 1069.

96 See Merryman and Pérez-Perdomo 2007, 127.

97 See Amboss 2008, 590, and Damaška 2012, 919.

98 Reichel 2013, 130. Although torture has been condemned as a way of obtaining a confession in all civilized countries, many scholars consider the suspect a central figure for finding facts in the inquisitorial system. See, e.g., Mack 1996, 70–71. That is a misconception.

99 Reichel (2013, 129), among others, claims that a defendant is expected but not required to cooperate with an investigation. Apart from questions about their identity, defendants are under no obligation to cooperate. When they do, there is less at stake for them, since, for instance, they cannot commit perjury and are considered a subject (as opposed to an object) of all proceedings.

100 Weinreb 1999, 63.

101 Findley 2011a, 913. German prosecutors, in fact, have the duty to "ascertain not only incriminating but also exonerating circumstances." Sec. 160 (2) StPO (Strafprozessordnung, Code of Criminal Procedure). In France, the examining magistrate (*juge d'instruction*) has to carry out "any investigative step he deems useful for the discovery of the truth." Code de Procédure Pénale, Article 81 (Fr.).

102 Vogler (2008a, 179) explains that the French system is a mixed system and lacks crucial procedural safeguards (like the exclusionary rule) that the German system offers.

103 Vogler 2008a, 202.

104 Vogler 2008a, 205.

105 Vogler 2008a, 205.

106 Frase and Weigend 1995, 322.

107 Findley 2011a, 931.

108 Groenhuijsen and Simmelink 2008, 385.

109 Groenhuijsen and Simmelink 2008, 386.

110 The scope of theoretical and practical prosecutorial discretion deserves its own discussion but is not relevant for the analysis here.

111 Vogler 2008b, 25.

112 Groenhuijsen and Simmelink 2008, 392.

113 Germany, Spain, and Italy trust the principle of legality, whereas England, Belgium, the Netherlands, and France operate systems of prosecutorial discretion. See Vogler 2008b, 24–25.

114 See Vogler 2008a, 229.

115 Whitman (2003) describes a strong state as one that is relatively *powerful* in its ability to "intervene in civil society without losing political legitimacy" and autonomous in that its bureaucracies "are relatively immune to the vagaries of public opinion" (13–14). In these respects, France and Germany are strong states; in contrast, governments in the United States are weak.

116 Frase and Weigend 1995, 323.

117 Frase and Weigend 1995, 323. The great majority of police officers are called "auxiliary officers" of the prosecutor and can be dispatched to conduct further investigations without direct oversight from the prosecutor.

118 Leigh and Zedner 1992, 26.

119 Leigh and Zedner 1992, 71.

120 Sec. 147 (2) StPO.

121 H. V. White 1980, 9.

122 Sec. 169a StPO.

123 Sec. 147 (1) StPO. In general, most documents included in the dossier are sent to the attorney's place of practice, where they are free to make copies/scans. Sec. 147 (2) StPO gives prosecutors the discretion to let the defense review the files even before that point in the process if such a review does not interfere with the investigation.

124 Frase and Weigend 1995, 352.

125 Berger v. United States, 295 U.S. 78, 88 (1935).

126 Vismann 2000, 89.

127 According to the law, the facts recorded in the record form the basis of the procedure; regardless of what actually occurred in the trial. See BGHSt 2, 125, 126.

128 BGHSt 2, 125, 126.

129 Vismann 2000, 28.

130 Frase and Weigend 1995, 344.

131 Mosbacher 2015, 85.

132 Merryman and Pérez-Perdomo 2007, 37.

133 Olson 2010, 352.

134 "The presiding judge presides over the trial, interrogates the defendant and takes the evidence." Sec. 238(1) StPO.

135 In the United States, there is only little criticism of the jury as a fact finder and contributor to wrongful convictions. Kent Roach (2010), for instance, acknowledges that bench trials in the United States reflect values of reasoned decision-making that are found in judge-dominated inquisitorial systems. "Decreased use of juries might increase the ability of the justice system to reach accurate results, especially in cases involving complex scientific evidence" (418).

136 This is accomplished by requesting the police or prosecutor to collect more evidence. See Huber 2008, 332.

137 Frase and Weigend 1995, 342.

138 Frase and Weigend 1995, 342.

139 Weigend 2003, 162.

140 "Continental fact finders are continuously awash in hearsay." Damaška 1997, 49. The American exclusion of hearsay at trial has more to do with the bifurcated nature of American trial courts than with the usual story that hearsay will be given undue credence by amateur jurors. Damaška 1997, 48–52.

141 See Frase and Weigend 1995, 342–43. The principle of immediacy regulates the preference of oral over written proof if the "original" evidence was oral. Frase and Weigend 1995, 343. A witness's statement cannot be introduced by reading a transcript.

142 Finding the truth is mandated by the German Constitution through the Schuldprinzip ("guilt principle," the standard that individual guilt/blameworthiness is the basis for and limit of any sentence or intervention). See BVerfG [Federal Constitutional Court], Mar. 19, 2013, 2 BVR 2628/10.

143 See BVerfG [Federal Constitutional Court], Mar. 19, 2013, 2 BVR 2628/10. An equivalent to "plea bargaining" exists in Germany, but it is regulated and requires judicial oversight (Sec. 257b StPO). As Slobogin (2015, 21) argues, that results in well-honed punishments because the judges equalize the existing power differential.

144 See Sec. 261 StPO, which states that "[t]he court shall decide on the result of the evidence taken according to its free conviction gained from the hearing as a whole." See also Weigend and Iontcheva Turner 2014, 81.

145 See generally Weigend 2003, 162. Wells (1994, 100) observes that French law is not as formal as its courts' opinions might otherwise suggest.

146 Dressler and Michaels 2013, 29–30. Also Pizzi 1999, 65: Inquisitorial systems "permit considerable pressure to be put on suspects to cooperate with legitimate police inquiries." But see Damaška (1973, 506), who critically comments on Justice Douglas's claim in his dissent in Johnson v. Louisiana, 406 U.S. 356 (1972), that higher evidentiary barricades to conviction emanate from the very nature of adversary proceedings and that their lowering smacks of the inquisitorial Continental procedure.

147 See Roach 2010, 435.

148 Findley 2011a, 917. Similar Bakken (2008), who describes the inquisitorial process as comparatively less protective because it has defendants relinquish rights that are usually afforded in American criminal litigation (567–68).

149 Cho 2001, 18 (quoting the German Federal Court of Justice for Criminal matters).

150 The French system allows defendants to intervene actively in their own defense. That includes the right to know the details of the accusation, the right to silence, and the right to counsel. These rights are strongest in the *instruction* period. but not that well protected in the earlier stages in the proceedings. Vogler 2008a, 192. For a detailed description of a French murder trial, see B. McKillop (1997, 527).

151 See Huber 2008 for an overview of German criminal procedure.

152 German criminal procedure is not bifurcated into a guilt and a sentencing stage. For example, if, in light of the incriminating evidence, the defense wants to introduce mitigating aspects relevant for the sentence, that has to happen during the trial.

153 Leigh and Zedner 1992, 35.

154 Huber 2008, 301–02. United States constitutional law is to the contrary: Stansbury v. California, 511 U.S. 318 (1994), holds that officer's subjective and undisclosed view concerning whether an interrogee is a suspect is irrelevant to the assessment of whether that person is in custody.

155 Sec. 136a (2) StPO.

156 United States constitutional law is to the contrary: Frazier v. Cupp, 394 U.S. 731 (1969).

157 Frase and Weigend 1995, 343.

158 See Heyl 2014, 931.

159 Sec. 52, 53 StPO. See also Frase and Weigend 1995, 343.

160 See Frase and Weigend 1995, 335.

161 See Cho 2001, 26.

162 See BVerfGE 80, 367, 374.

163 BVerfGE 80, 367, 374–75: "Privacy rights protected by the Fourth Amendment, for example, can lead to the exclusion of undeniably relevant and reliable evidence."

164 Whitman 2003, 194; Haney 2006.

165 Pizzi 1999, 181.

166 Weigend 2003, 167.

167 Lepore 2015, 1145.

168 The reason for a limited review is the (higher) number of judges that conduct the trial; see Huber 2008, 320.

169 Frase and Weigend 1995, 349.

170 See Huber 2008, 322.

171 Sec. 359 [Reopening for the Convicted Person's Benefit]: "Reopening of the proceedings concluded by a final judgment shall be admissible for the convicted person's benefit: . . . 5. if new facts or evidence were produced, which, independently or in connection with the evidence previously taken, tend to support the defendant's acquittal, or, upon application of a less severe penal norm, a lower penalty or an essentially different decision on a measure of reform and prevention."

172 That view is common; see Smidt in Pfeiffer 2003, Vorbemerkungen Sec. 359 Rn. 1.

173 Smidt in Pfeiffer 2003, Vorbemerkungen Sec. 359 Rn. 4.

174 Dunkel and Kemme 2016, 141. Within narrow circumstances, a case can be reopened to the disadvantage of a defendant. Sec. 362 StPO mentions forged documents, perjured testimony, and other items.

175 Smidt in Pfeiffer 2003, Sec. 359 Rn. 24.

176 Pizzi 1999, 181.

177 See Grasnick 2010, 201.

178 Another aspect that explains a different approach to narrative is the role of cases as law. In a civil law system, decisions are generally not a source of law (only statutory law is) and therefore not binding on other courts. Merryman and Pérez-Perdomo 2007, 46–47. Practically, a lower court would abide by a ruling from a higher court, so its decision is not reversed; however, there is no law that forces the hands of a lower court judge. This suggests that narratives cannot that easily make it into law; in other words, they have little relevance for it. An exemplary narrative, as Gordon (2013, 361) argues, "functions both as and of law," but only in a system that allows for precedent as being a binding type of law.

179 Naucke 1991, 60.

180 Von Arnold 2008, 39.

181 Von Arnold 2008, 37.

182 Machura and Robson 2001.

183 Grasnick 2010, 201.

184 Grasnick 2010, 205.

185 See Olson 2018, 35.

186 Von Arnold 2008, 40.

5. ANATOMY OF A GERMAN WRONGFUL CONVICTION

1 Baker Trans., 34. Transcripts are not public record in Germany. The author was given access to them with the permission of the district attorneys' offices.

2 This is a well-known case, but in compliance with the terms of the offices that granted access to the case files, all names have been changed to protect the privacy of those involved.

3 Kotsoglou 2017; Kotsoglou 2017, 123, explicitly referring to Judge Learned Hand's claim (129).

4 Kotsoglou 2017, 124, referring to Nesson (1985), who argues that the public can accept a verdict as exemplifying a legal rule when it projects as a "statement about what happened" (1358). If such a belief does not exist, "then we cannot feel secure about the imposition of punishment" (1367).

5 Fischer 2015.

6 Kotsoglou 2017, 131.

7 Kotsoglou 2017, 132.

8 Barton 2019, 20.

9 Böhme 2016, 49.

10 See Barton 2019, 19; Velten 2015 394.

11 Mosbacher 2015, 87 (also 11–12); see also Dunkel and Kemme 2016, 17, following Peters; Schwenn 2013 (the alleged perpetrator did not commit the crime); and Jehle 2013, who distinguishes "false" (including procedural errors) and "wrongful convictions."

12 Leuschner, Rettenberger, and Dessecker 2019, 9.

13 The study conducted by the Center for Criminology analyzed 29 cases; see Leuschner et al. 2019, 9.

14 Findley (2011b, 1162) brings up the point that factual innocence is, in the end, a question of a legal standard, which blurs the line between legal and factual innocence.

15 Dunkel and Kemme 2016, 140, follow the same definition of "wrongful conviction." In their study, Leuschner, Rettenberger, and Dessecker (2019, 9) also limit the scope of their analysis to these cases.

16 See, e.g., Darnstädt 2013 and Rückert 2007.

17 Two federal judges guessed with little statistical support that the wrongful conviction rate is "in the lower single digit percentage range" (Mosbacher 2015, 86) or around 10% according to Eschelbach 2017.

18 The easiest way to assess the number of wrongful convictions would be to count how many cases were successfully reopened according to Sec. 359 Nr. 5 StPO and then count how many of these led to an acquittal. But German statistics record only the total number of initiated reopening proceedings (not just new-evidence cases), including proceedings for and against the defendant. A small-scale quantitative study (Dunkel 2018) faced similar issues and could not reveal how many of the reopened cases were successful, if any at all.

19 Leuschner, Rettenberger, and Dessecker 2019, 9.

20 Leuschner, Rettenberger, and Dessecker 2019, 7.

21 Leuschner, Rettenberger, and Dessecker 2019, 12. Robert Stellwag spent eight years in prison for a bank robbery he did not commit. Despite eight witnesses testifying that he was 350 kilometers away from the crime, an expert conducted an anthropological analysis of camera footage from the bank and then testified that based on the shape of Stellwag's ears he is the person in the photo. It would

be difficult given the degree of scrutiny to argue that this shows a fundamental issue with witness identifications. If anything, it is proof of the distinct trust that German judges put in experts and the reliability of their methods.

22 See, e.g., Kröber 2013, 2013; Mosbacher, 2015; Schwenn 2013.

23 Leuschner, Rettenberger, and Dessecker 2019, 13.

24 Schwenn 2013.

25 In the notorious "Wormser Prozesse" (Worms Trials) between 1994 and 1997, 25 innocent people were accused of having sexually assaulted multiple children. Suspicion arose when children made remarks to daycare staff that were misinterpreted, triggering an investigation. All 25 suspects were later acquitted. Schwenn (2010, 708) points out the reality-defining force of such framing narratives and how the system is all too ready to aid in "contouring" a victim's story and "inventing signs of abuse."

26 Leuschner, Rettenberger, and Dessecker 2019, 13. False confessions play a role in 12% of wrongful convictions in the United States.

27 Leuschner, Rettenberger, and Dessecker 2019, 14.

28 There has been an increasing debate in German scholarship about the problem of cognitive biases that judges develop by being too close to the experts they pick. It has long been argued that judges, especially in cases of false accusations of sexual assaults, tend to trust experts to a high degree and are rarely able to consider "dissonant" aspects. Grunewald 2014, 1191.

29 Bundesgerichtshof, Beschluss vom 24.06.1982–4 StR 183/82. NStZ:478.

30 Bundesgerichtshof, Beschluss vom 24.06.1982–4 StR 183/82. NStZ:478. See also Mosbacher 2015, 84.

31 In de Montgazon's case, the trial court supported the guilty verdict by relying on two out of six contradictory scientific reports. The Federal Court of Justice openly criticized the one-dimensional analysis and lack of methodological awareness of the trial judges. BGH 5 StR 372/05 (January 11, 2005) 5.

32 Findley and Scott 2006, 292.

33 See Dunkel 2018, 90.

34 In his study, Schünemann (2000, 161) showed that judges are significantly more likely to convict if they have seen the dossier before they conducted the trial and less likely if they have to base their verdict on the trial itself.

35 See Dunkel 2018, 63.

36 Dunkel 2018, 71.

37 In an experimental study, Schünemann (2000, 162) showed that judges are more likely to proceed to a trial of a case with ambivalent evidence if the prosecutor filed an indictment. The same dossier without an indictment led to a significantly lower number of decisions to move to the trial stage.

38 Heller 2006, 294.

39 Perseverance is the tendency to retain existing beliefs even after the original evidence that fostered those beliefs has been shown to be invalid. See Lord, Preson, and Lepper 1984, 1239–40.

40 Lord, Preson, and Lepper 1984, 1240.

41 See Heller 2006, 294.

42 Bruner 1986, 12.

43 Caracciolo 2013, 22.

44 Caracciolo 2013, 22.

45 Baker, Trans., 20.

46 Baker, Trans., 34.

47 Baker, Trans., 36.

48 Genette 1982, 136.

49 Hart, the scrap-metal dealer, knew the Bakers and Michael Smith. When being interviewed, he was asked about his German Shepheard and "what do you feed your dog?" (Baker, Trans., 937). This question can be considered relevant only in light of the underlying suspicion of how the suspects disposed of Hans's body.

50 Baker, Trans., 47.

51 Baker, Trans., 47.

52 Baker, Trans., 70.

53 Baker, Trans., 74.

54 In a variation of Carlo Ginzburg's point on the Morellian method, it can be argued that the detective as a reader of a case should not look at the most striking features of a potential narrative but scrutinize the more subtle, negligible details— those that do not so easily fit in. See Ginzburg 1979, 274.

55 Baker, Trans., 138.

56 Baker, Trans., 136.

57 Baker, Trans., 35.

58 Brooks 2006, 9.

59 The point that Brooks (2006, 9) makes about the lack of "recognition in Court opinions that there may be a general problem of narrative" applies here as well. The problem is that, in an inquisitorial system, rhetorical issues are even less scrutinized because of the idea that the objective fact finder will reconstruct the whole case.

60 Baker, Trans., 188 [author translation].

61 Baker, Trans., 191.

62 Baker, Trans., 235.

63 Baker, Trans., 259.

64 Baker, Trans., 262.

65 Baker, Trans., 267.

66 Spiegel, September 11, 2012.

67 See Von Arnold 2008, 34.

68 Arntzen 2011, 15–16. Title is my translation, as this work has not appeared in English. Von Arnauld and Martini (2015) also stress the relevance of details for a reliable narrative, arguing that it should match the "normality range of testimonial reliability" (358). Whatever that is.

69 Baker, Trans., 1230.

70 Baker, Trans., 1237.

71 In a radio interview, the forensic psychologist Renate Volbert confirmed that such detailed confessions appear authentic but speculates that "[i]f these are not verbatim records, however, the interrogation protocol may reflect information that does not stem from the accused but has been communicated in the course of the interrogations and then repeated by the accused." Schmidt-Langels and Langels 2011.

72 Baker, Trans., 1654.

73 Baker, Trans., 1654.

74 The criminal act must be described as a historical event, including time and place. BGHSt 5. 227; 16, 47, 48; 29, 124, 126.

75 See Baker, Trans., 1751.

76 Baker, Trans., 1752.

77 For instance, Baker, Trans., 1745: "The head of the murdered Hans Baker was boiled in a washing boiler and then crushed."

78 Baker, Trans., 1754.

79 Baker, Trans., 1754.

80 Baker, Trans., 1756.

81 Baker, Trans., 34.

82 Baker, Trans., 1772.

83 Baker, Trans., 1773.

84 Baker, Trans., 1775.

85 Sec. 261 StPO stipulates that the fact finder "shall decide on the result of the evidence taken according to its free conviction gained from the hearing as a whole."

86 Baker, Trans., 2640.

87 Baker, Trans., 2499.

88 Baker, Trans., 2503.

89 Baker, Trans., 2505.

90 Baker, Trans., 2511.

91 Baker, Trans., 2542.

92 Baker, Trans., 2540.

93 Baker, Trans., 2539.

94 Baker, Trans., 2539.

95 Baker, Trans., 2524.

96 Baker, Trans., 2543.

97 Baker, Trans., 2546. Another detail the court stresses is the dialect word Michael Smith used for the process of getting the hammer out of Hans Baker's skull when it stuck. The word he uses is "naggeln," which can refer to shaking, rattling, rocking, or wobbling. The expert confirms that such a complication can occur, and the court again "adopts" that view (2584).

98 Baker, Trans., 2547.

99 Baker, Trans., 2548.

100 Baker, Trans., 2549.

101 Baker, Trans., 2620.

102 The court argued that "[i]n particular, the narrative contains several details which speak for an actual experience. On the one hand, the margarine cup . . . , which the defendant brings up constantly and with which he has scooped the blood from the abdominal cavity, must be mentioned here" (Baker, Trans., 2620).

103 Baker, Trans., 2635.

104 Baker, Trans., 2628.

105 Baker, Trans., 2630.

106 Baker, Trans., 2632.

107 Baker, Trans., 2633.

108 Baker, Reopening Trans., 307.

109 Baker, Reopening Trans., 312.

110 Baker, Reopening Trans., 483.

111 Baker, Reopening Trans., 483.

112 Baker, Reopening Trans., 483.

113 Baker, Reopening Trans., 495–496.

114 Baker, Reopening Trans., 581.

115 Baker, Acquittal Trans., 1706.

116 Baker, Acquittal Trans., 1709.

117 Trüg and Kerner 2007, 202.

118 Trüg and Kerner 2007, 203.

119 Larson 2000.

6. CONCLUSION

1 Borchard 1932, preface, quoting a district attorney in Worcester County, Massachusetts.

2 The model of having a nonprofit innocence project has been described as a success-model worth exporting. See Gerrett 2017, 54.

3 Medwed 2017, 8.

4 Gerrett 2017, 53.

5 In Italy, as Lupária and Greco (2020, 107) note, there were 153 cases of wrongful convictions in the last thirty years and almost 28,000 cases of wrongful preliminary detention. In their discussion of these cases, it becomes evident that what led to these numbers is intrinsically tied to underlying procedural structures. This is why it is problematic to project the catalog of factors—a catalog developed in different system—to the mixed adversarial and inquisitorial Italian criminal justice system.

6 Gerrett 2017, 54.

7 See, e.g., Roper v. Simmons, 543 U.S. 551 (2005): "In sum, it is fair to say that the United States now stands alone in a world that has turned its face against the juvenile death penalty."

8 Nolan 2011, 161.

9 Whitman 2003, 76.

10 See Hoffman 2014, 278.

11 Hoffman (2014, 278) notes that jurors often do not recall evidence that stood in conflict with their verdict.

12 Von Arnauld 2017, 325.

13 Bruner Making Stories 39.

14 See Becker 1963, 1ff, 9.

15 Presser 2009, 178.

16 Presser 2009, 179.

17 Fleetwood et al. 2019, 2.

18 See Presser 2009, 178. Much scholarship (including aspects of criminalization) has developed since Presser's inaugural conceptualization of narrative criminology.

19 Fleetwood et al. 2019, 13.

20 Doležel 1998, 792.

21 Abbott (2021, 155) mentions elements like rich internal accounts of events expressed through indirect thought, interior monologue, free indirect thought, and the like that won't be found in histories or biographies. But false confessions, for instance, are full of them, and such made-up details are used to underline the veracity of such statements.

22 Abbott 2021, 153.

23 Abbott 2021, 155.

24 Abbott 2021, 154.

25 Abbott 2021, 161 (referring to Barthes, who coined that term).

26 Doležel (1998) makes the point that gaps in fiction are ontological—they are "irrecoverable lacunae which cannot be filled by legitimate interference" (795). Gaps in history are epistemological—they are due to "the limitations of human cognition" because of either the historian's selectivity or the lack of evidence. In law, such a distinction is difficult to uphold because legal narratives have fictional and factual elements, and both correspond to each other.

27 For the historical context, see Doležel 1998, 791.

BIBLIOGRAPHY

Abbott, H. Porter. 2010. "Narrating Conversion in an Age of Darwinian Gradualism." *Storyworlds: A Journal of Narrative Studies* 2(1): 1–18. www.jstor.org/stable/10.5250/storyworlds.2.1.1.

———. 2021. *The Cambridge Introduction to Narrative.* 3rd ed. Cambridge Introductions to Literature. Cambridge, UK, and New York: Cambridge University Press.

Abelson, Robert P. 1981. "Psychological Status of the Script Concept." *American Psychologist* 36(7): 715–29. doi:10.1037/0003-066X.36.7.715.

Acker, James R., Allison D. Redlich, Robert J. Norris, and Catherine L. Bonventre. 2014. "Stepping Back—Moving Beyond Immediate Causes: Criminal Justice and Wrongful Convictions on Social Context." In *Examining Wrongful Convictions: Stepping Back, Moving Forward,* 3–15. Durham: Carolina Academic Press.

Adomeit, Klaus. 2003. "Der Rechtspositivismus im Denken von Hans Kelsen und Gustav Radbruch." *JuristenZeitung,* 161–216.

Ahmed, Sara. 2004. "Affective Economies." *Social Text* 79: 117–39.

Amboss, Kai. 2008. "Zum heutigen Verständnis von Akkusationsprinzip und –verfahren aus historischer Sicht." *JURA: Juristische Ausbildung* 8: 586–94.

American Bar Association. 2017. "Criminal Justice Standards for the Prosecution Function." www.americanbar.org.

Amsterdam, Anthony G., and Jerome S. Bruner. 2000. *Minding the Law.* Cambridge, MA: Harvard University Press.

Appleby, Sara C., and Saul M. Kassin. 2016. "When Self-Report Trumps Science: Effects of Confessions, DNA, and Prosecutorial Theories on Perceptions of Guilt." *Psychology, Public Policy, and Law* 22(2): 127–40. doi:10.1037/law0000080.

Arnella, Peter. 1983. "Rethinking the Functions of Criminal Procedure: The Warren and Burger Courts' Competing Ideologies." *Georgetown Law Journal* 72: 185–249.

Arntzen, Friedrich. 2011. *Psychologie der Zeugenaussage: System der Glaubhaftigkeitsmerkmale.* 5. Aufl. München: Beck.

Ashworth, Andrew, and Jeremy Horder. 2013. *Principles of Criminal Law.* 7th ed. Oxford, UK: Oxford University Press.

The Associated Press. 2001. "O'Connor Questions Death Penalty." *New York Times,* July 4. www.nytimes.com.

Bakken, Tim. 2008. "Truth and Innocence Procedures to Free Innocent Persons: Beyond the Adversarial System." *University of Michigan Journal of Law Reform* 41(3): 547–83.

Bandes, Susan. 1996. "Empathy, Narrative, and Victim Impact Statements." *University of Chicago Law Review* 63(2): 361–412.

———. 2008. "Framing Wrongful Convictions." *Utah Law Review* 1: 5–24.

Banks-Anderson, Liz. 2016. "The 'Making a Murderer' Effect." *Pursuit* (University of Melbourne website for research and commentary), March 15. https://pursuit.unimelb.edu.au.

Barthes, Roland. 1977a. "Introduction to the Structural Analysis of Narratives." In *Image, Music, Text*, edited by Stephen Heath, 79–124. London: Fontana.

———. 1977b. "The Death of the Author." In *Image, Music, Text*, edited by Stephen Heath, 142–48. London: Fontana.

Barton, Stephan. 2016. "Absorption von Ungewissheit." In *Verdacht*, edited by Thomas Fischer and Elisa Hoven, 19–28. Baden-Badener Strafrechtsgespräche Band 2. Baden-Baden: Nomos.

———. 2019. "„Das Fehlurteil gibt es nicht"—Gibt es doch!" In *Für die Sache—Kriminalwissenschaften aus unabhängiger Perspektive: Festschrift für Ulrich Eisenberg zum 80. Geburtstag*, edited by Ingke Goeckenjan, Jens Puschke, and Tobias Singelnstein, 15–29. Schriften zum Strafrecht Band 335. Berlin: Duncker & Humblot.

Bazelon, Emily. 2021. "I Write About the Law. But Could I Really Help Free a Prisoner?" *New York Times Magazine*, July 4. www.nytimes.com.

Becker, Howard Saul. 1963. *Outsiders: Studies in the Sociology of Deviance*. London: Free Press of Glencoe.

Bennett, W. Lance, and Martha S. Feldman. 1984. *Reconstructing Reality in the Courtroom: Justice and Judgment in American Culture*. Crime, Law, and Deviance series. New Brunswick, NJ: Rutgers University Press.

Bennett, W. Lance. 1997. "Storytelling in Criminal Trials." In *Memory, Identity, Community: The Idea of Narrative in the Human Sciences*, edited by Lewis P. Hinchman and Sandra Hinchman, 72–103. SUNY series in the Philosophy of the Social Sciences. Albany: State University of New York Press.

Berlow, Alan. 2000. "Texas Justice: What Made Timid Honors Student Christopher Ochoa Confess to a Rape and Murder That He Almost Certainly Did Not Commit?" www.salon.com.

Blufarb, Ruth. 2018. *Geschichten im Recht: Übertragbarkeit von „Law as Narrative" auf die deutsche Rechtsordnung*. Recht und Literatur v. 3. Baden-Baden: Nomos Verlagsgesellschaft.

Blume, John H., Shari L. Johnson, and Emily C. Paavola. 2007. "Every Juror Wants a Story: Narrative Relevance, Third Party Guilt and the Right to Present a Defense." *American Criminal Law Review* 44: 1069–1113.

Bock, Michael, Ralf Eschelbach, Andreas Geipel, Michael Hettinger, Joachim Röschke, and Florian Wille. 2013. "Die erneute Wiederaufnahme des Strafverfahrens." *Goltdammer's Archiv für Strafrecht* (6): 328–45.

Böhme, Toni. 2016. "Das Fehlurteil im Strafprozess—Zum Begriff und zur Häufigkeit." In *Einheit der Prozessrechtswissenschaft? Tagung junger Prozessrechtswissenschaftler am 18./19. September 2015 in Köln*, edited by Daniel O. Effer-Uhe, 39–54. Stuttgart: Boorberg.

Borchard, Edwin M. 1913. "European Systems of State Indemnity for Errors of Criminal Justice." *Journal of Criminal Law & Criminology* 3: 684–718.

———. 1932. *Convicting the Innocent: Sixty-Five Actual Errors of Criminal Justice.* Garden City, NY: Garden City Pub. Co.

Bornstein, Brian H., and Edie Greene. 2011. "Jury Decision Making: Implications for and from Psychology." *Current Directions in Psychological Science* 20(1): 63–67. doi:10.1177/0963721410397282.

Brandt, Christina. 2017. "Wissenschaft." In *Erzählen*, edited by Matías Martínez, 210–18. Stuttgart: J. B. Metzler.

Brants, Chrisje. 2012. "Wrongful Convictions and Inquisitorial Process: The Case of the Netherlands." *University of Cincinnati Law Review* 80: 1069–1114.

Brooks, Peter. 1984. "Narrative Desire." *Style* 18(3): 312–27.

———. 1996. "The Law as Narrative and Rhetoric." In *Law's Stories: Narrative and Rhetoric in the Law*, edited by Peter Brooks and Paul D. Gewirtz, 14–22. New Haven: Yale University Press.

———. 2003. "'Inevitable Discovery': Law, Narrative, Retrospectivity." *Yale Journal of Law & the Humanities.* 15: 71–101.

———. 2006. "Narrative Transactions: Does the Law Need a Narratology?" *Yale Journal of Law & the Humanities* 18(1): 1–28.

———. 2017. "Clues, Evidence, Detection: Law Stories." *Narrative* 25(1): 1–27.

Brooks, Peter, and Paul D. Gewirtz, eds. 1996. *Law's Stories: Narrative and Rhetoric in the Law*. New Haven: Yale University Press.

Bruner, Jerome S. 1986. *Actual Minds, Possible Worlds*. Cambridge, MA: Harvard University Press.

———. 1990. *Acts of Meaning: Four Lectures on Mind and Culture*. The Jerusalem-Harvard Lectures. Cambridge, MA: Harvard University Press.

———. 1991. "The Narrative Construction of Reality." *Critical Inquiry* 18(1): 1–21.

———. 2002. *Making Stories: Law, Literature, Life*. New York: Farrar, Straus, and Giroux.

Burnett, D. Graham. 2001. *A Trial by Jury*. New York: A.A. Knopf.

Burns, Robert P. 1999. *A Theory of the Trial*. Princeton, NJ: Princeton University Press.

Camus, Albert. 1989. *The Stranger*. First Vintage International ed. New York: Vintage International.

Caracciolo, Marco. 2013. "Patterns of Cognitive Dissonance in Readers' Engagement with Characters." *Enthymema* 8: 22–37. doi: 10.13130/2037-2426/2903.

Champagne, Farrah. 2015. "5 Tips for Engaging Opening Statements." www.americanbar.org.

Cho, Kuk. 2001. "'Procedural Weakness' of German Criminal Justice and Its Unique Exclusionary Rules Based on the Right of Personality." *Temple International & Comparative Law Journal* 15: 1–30.

Cohn, Dorrit. 1999. *The Distinction of Fiction*. Baltimore and London: Johns Hopkins University Press.

Colloff, Pamela. 2012. "The Innocent Man." *Texas Monthly*. www.texasmonthly.com.

Cooper, Sarah Lucy. 2016. *Controversies in Innocence Cases in America*. Controversies in American Constitutional Law. London and New York: Routledge.

Cover, Robert M. 1983. "Nomos and Narrative." *Harvard Law Review* 97(4): 4–68.

Cruz, Lenika. 2015. "The New True Crime." *The Atlantic*, June 11. www.theatlantic.com.

Culler, Jonathan. 2002. *The Pursuit of Signs: Semiotics, Literature, Deconstruction*. An augmented ed. Ithaca: Cornell University Press.

Currie, Gregory. 2006. "Narrative Representation of Causes." *Journal of Aesthetics and Art Criticism* 64(3): 309–16.

Damaška, Mirjan. 1973. "Evidentiary Barriers to Conviction and Two Models of Criminal Procedure: A Comparative Study." *University of Pennsylvania Law Review* 121: 506–89.

———. 1997. *Evidence Law Adrift*. New Haven: Yale University Press.

———. 1998. "Truth in Adjudication." *Hastings Law Journal* 49: 289–308.

———. 2012. "The Quest for Due Process in the Age of Inquisition." *American Journal of Comparative Law* 60: 919–54.

Danto, Arthur Coleman. 2007. *Narration and Knowledge*. Columbia Classics in Philosophy. New York: Columbia University Press.

Darnstädt, Thomas. 2013. *Der Richter und sein Opfer: Wenn die Justiz sich irrt*. München [u.a.]: Piper.

Del Mar, Maksymilian, and Randy Gordon. 2013. "Preface." *Law & Literature* 25(3): 331–36.

Dershowitz, Alan M. 1996a. "Life Is Not a Dramatic Narrative." In *Law's Stories: Narrative and Rhetoric in the Law*, edited by Peter Brooks and Paul D. Gewirtz, 99–105. New Haven: Yale University Press.

———. 1996b. *Reasonable Doubts: The O.J. Simpson Case and the Criminal Justice System*. New York: Simon & Schuster.

Doctorow, E. L. 1983. "False Documents." In *E. L. Doctorow: Essays and Conversations*, edited by Richard Trenner, 16–26. Ontario Review Press critical series. Princeton and New York: Ontario Review Press.

Doležel, Lubomír. 1998. "Possible Worlds of Fiction and History." *New Literary History* 29(4): 785–809. www.jstor.org/stable/20057512.

Doran, Sean, John D. Jackson, and Michael L. Seigel. 1995. "Rethinking Adversariness in Nonjury Criminal Trials." *American Journal of Criminal Law* 23(1): 1–59.

Dressler, Joshua, and Alan C. Michaels. 2013. *Understanding Criminal Procedure*. 6th ed. The Understanding series. Durham: Carolina Academic Press.

Drizin, Steven A. 2014. "Knox and Sollecito: Victims of a Prosecutor's 'Conspiracy Theories' to Explain Away DNA." www.huffpost.com.

Dunkel, Barbara. 2018. *Fehlentscheidungen in der Justiz: Systematische Analyse von Wiederaufnahmeverfahren in Strafverfahren im Hinblick auf Häufigkeit und Risikofaktoren*. Deutsches und Europäisches Strafprozessrecht und Polizeirecht Band 8. Baden-Baden: Nomos.

Dunkel, Barbara, and Stefanie Kemme. 2016. "Fehlurteile in Deutschland: Eine Bilanz der empirischen Forschung seit fünf Jahrzehnten." *Neue Kriminalpolitik* 28(2): 138–54. doi:10.5771/0934-9200-2016-2-138.

Dworkin, Ronald. 1986. *Law's Empire*. Cambridge MA: Belknap Press.

Dwyer, Jim, Peter Neufeld, and Barry Scheck. 2001. *Actual Innocence: When Justice Goes Wrong and How to Make It Right*. New York: New American Library.

Edwards, Linda L., and J. Stanley Edwards. 2002. *Introduction to Paralegal Studies and the Law: A Practical Approach*. West Legal Studies series. Albany, NY: West/Thomson Learning.

Eligon, John. 2011. "If Truth Is Elusive, Rape Trial May Turn on Prosecutor's Tug of War with Officer." *New York Times*, May 15. www.nytimes.com.

Epps, Daniel. 2018. "Harmless Errors and Substantial Rights." *Harvard Law Review* 131(8): 2117–86.

Esser, Josef. 1972. *Vorständnis und Methodenwahl in der Rechtsfindung: Rationalitätsgrundlagen richterlicher Entscheidungspraxis*. Durchgesehene und erg. Ausg. Fischer Athenäum Taschenbücher 6001. Frankfurt am Main: Athenäum.

Fagan, Jeffrey, and Amanda Geller. 2015. "Following the Script: Narratives of Suspicion in Terry Stops in Street Policing." *University of Chicago Law Review* 82: 51–88.

Feigenson, Neil. 2010. "Emotional Influences on Judgments of Legal Blame: How They Happen, Whether They Should, and What to Do About It." In *Emotion and the Law: Psychological Perspectives*, edited by Brian H. Bornstein and Richard L. Wiener, 45–96. Nebraska Symposium on Motivation, vol. 56. New York: Springer.

Feldman Barrett, Lisa. 2017. "The Law's Emotion Problem." *New York Times*, March 12. www.nytimes.com.

Ferguson, Robert A. 1996. "Untold Stories in the Law." In *Law's Stories: Narrative and Rhetoric in the Law*, edited by Peter Brooks and Paul D. Gewirtz, 84–98 New Haven: Yale University Press.

Ferguson-Gilbert, Catherine. 2011. "It Is Not Whether You Win or Lose, It Is How You Play the Game: Is the Win-Loss Scorekeeping Mentality Doing Justice for Prosecutors?" *California Western Law Review* 38: 283–309.

Findley, Keith. 2008. "Toward a New Paradigm of Criminal Justice: How the Innocence Movement Merges Crime Control and Due Process." *Texas Tech Law Review* 41: 133–73.

———. 2011a. "Adversarial Inquisitions: Rethinking the Search for the Truth." *New York Law School Law Review* 56: 911–41.

———. 2011b. "Defining Innocence." *Albany Law Review* 74: 1157–1208.

Findley, Keith, and Michael Scott. 2006. "The Multiple Dimensions of Tunnel Vision in Criminal Cases." *Wisconsin Law Review* 2: 291–397.

Fischer, Thomas. 2015. "Beweis und Überzeugung." www.zeit.de.

Fish, Stanley Eugene. 1994. *There's No Such Thing as Free Speech, and It's a Good Thing Too*. New York: Oxford University Press.

Fleetwood, Jennifer, Lois Presser, Sveinung Sandberg, and Thomas Ugelvik, eds. 2019. *The Emerald Handbook of Narrative Criminology*. Bingley, UK: Emerald Publishing.

Fleischhut, Nadine, Björn Meder, and Gerd Gigerenzer. 2017. "Moral Hindsight." *Experimental Psychology* 64(2): 110–23. doi:10.1027/1618-3169/a000353.

Fludernik, Monika. 2010. "Erzählung aus narratologischer Sicht." In *Erzählen in den Wissenschaften: Positionen, Probleme, Perspektiven: 26. Kolloquium (2009) Der schweizerischen Akademie der Geistes- und Sozialwissenschaften*, edited by Balz Engler, 5–22. Kolloquium der Schweizerischen Akademie der Geistes- und Sozialwissenschaften 26. Fribourg: Academic Press.

Foster, Raymond E. 2010. "Crime Scene Investigation." *GovTech*, July 27. www.govtech.com.

Frankel, Marvin E. 1975. "The Search for Truth: An Umpireal View." 123(5): 1031–59.

Frase, Richard S. 2000. "The Search for the Whole Truth: About American and European Criminal Justice." *Buffalo Criminal Law Review* 3: 785–849.

Frase, Richard S., and Thomas Weigend. 1995. "German Criminal Justice as a Guide to American Law Reform: Similar Problems, Better Solutions?" *Boston College International and Comparative Law Review* 18: 317–360.

Freedman, Monroe H. 1998. "Our Constitutionalized Adversary System." *Chapman Law Review* 57(1): 57–90.

Fuller, Lon L. 1967. *Legal Fictions*. Stanford: Stanford University Press.

Gadamer, Hans-Georg. 2004. *Truth and Method*. 2nd rev. ed. New York: Continuum.

———. 2016. "Language and Understanding." *Theory, Culture & Society* 23(1): 13–27. doi:10.1177/0263276406063226.

Gallup, Inc. 2021. "Confidence in Institutions." https://news.gallup.com.

Garrett, Brandon. 2010. "The Substance of False Confessions." *Stanford Law Review* 62: 1051–1119.

———. 2011. *Convicting the Innocent: Where Criminal Prosecutions Go Wrong*. Cambridge, MA: Harvard University Press.

Genette, Gérard. 1982. *Figures of Literary Discourse*. European Perspectives. New York: Columbia University Press.

Garrett, Brandon L. 2017. "Convicting the Innocent Redux." In *Wrongful Convictions and the DNA Revolution: Twenty-Five Years of Freeing the Innocent*, edited by Daniel S. Medwed, 40–56. Cambridge, UK: Cambridge University Press.

Gerrig, Richard J., and Giovanna Egidi. 2003. "Cognitive Psychological Foundations of Narrative Experiences." In *Narrative Theory and the Cognitive Sciences*, edited by David Herman, 33–55. CSLI Lecture Notes no. 158. Stanford: CSLI Publications.

Gilbert, David I., Michael E. Gilfarb, and Stephen K. Talpins, eds. 2005. "Basic Trial Techniques for Prosecutors." Special issue for the Special Topics Series of the American Prosecutors Research Institute, a nonprofit affiliate of the National District Attorneys Association. PDF available at https://ndaa.org/wp-content/uploads/basic_trial_techniques_05.pdf.

Ginzburg, Carlo. 1979. "Clues: Roots of a Scientific Paradigm." *Theory and Society* 7(3): 273–88. doi:10.1007/BF00207323.

———. 1991. "Checking the Evidence: The Judge and the Historian." *Critical Inquiry* 18(1): 79–92.

Godsey, Mark. 2017. *Blind Injustice: A Former Prosecutor Exposes the Psychology and Politics of Wrongful Convictions*. Oakland: University of California Press.

Golob, Brandon. 2018. "Un-Making a Murderer: New Media's Impact on (Potential) Wrongful Conviction Cases." *California Western Law Review* 54(1): 137–50.

Goode, Erica. 2011. "DNA Evidence of Innocence Rejected by Some Prosecutors." *New York Times*, November 15. www.nytimes.com.

Goodpaster, Gary. 1987. "Criminal Law: On the Theory of American Adversary Criminal Trial." *Journal of Criminal Law & Criminology* 78: 118–154.

Gordon, Randy. 2013. "Institutionalizing Exemplary Narratives: Stories as Models for and Movers of Law." *Law & Literature* 25: 337–65. http://dx.doi.org.

Gould, Jon B., Julia Carrano, Richard Leo, and Joseph Young. 2013. "Predicting Erroneous Convictions: A Social Science Approach to Miscarriages of Justice." Final report to the National Institute of Justice, grant number 2009-IJ-CX-4110. www.ncjrs.gov.

Goyal, Rishi. 2014. "Narration in Medicine." In Hühn 2014.

Gräfin von Schlieffen, Katharina. 2009. "Zur analytischen Rhetorik von Ottmar Ballweg." In *Analytische Rhetorik: Rhetorik, Recht und Philosophie*, edited by Katharina von Schlieffen, XIII–XXXVII. Recht und Rhetorik Band 1. Frankfurt am Main, Berlin, Bern, Bruxelles, New York, Oxford, Wien: Peter Lang Internationaler Verlag der Wissenschaften.

Grasnick, Walter. 2010. "Die Erzählbarkeit des Rechts." In *Festschrift für Jan Schapp zum siebzigsten Geburtstag*, edited by Patrick Gödicke, Horst Hammen, Wolfgang Schur, and Wolf-Dietrich Walker, 195–212. Tübingen: Mohr Siebeck.

Greenbaum, Rosa. 2019. "Investigating Innocence: Comprehensive Pre-Trial Defense Investigation to Prevent Wrongful Convictions." Master of Arts in Social Ecology, University of California Irvine. https://escholarship.org.

Grice, H. P. 1989. *Studies in the Way of Words*. Cambridge, MA: Harvard University Press.

Griffin, Lisa Kern. 2012. "Narrative, Truth & Trial." *Georgetown Law Journal* 101: 281–335.

———. 2016. "Criminal Adjudication, Error Correction, and Hindsight Blind Spots." *Washington and Lee Law Review* 73: 165–215.

Grimm, Jacob. 2019. *Von der Poesie im Recht*. Nachdruck der Ausgabe von 1882. Norderstedt: Hansebooks GmbH.

Groenhuijsen, Marc, and Joep Simmelink. 2008. "Criminal Procedure in the Netherlands." In *Criminal Procedure in Europe*, edited by Richard Vogler and Barbara Huber, 373–481. Schriftenreihe des Max-Planck-Instituts für ausländisches und internationales Strafrecht. Reihe S: Strafrechtliche Forschungsberichte 112. Berlin, Freiburg i. Br. Duncker & Humblot; Max-Planck-Institut.

Gross, Samuel R. 2008. "Convicting the Innocent." *Annual Review of Law and Social Science* 4: 173–92. doi:10.1146/annurev.lawsocsci.4.110707.172300.

Gross, Samuel R., and Kaitlin Jackson. 2015. "Snitch Watch." www.law.umich.edu.

Gross, Samuel R., Kristen Jacoby, Daniel J. Matheson, and Nicholas Montgomery. 2005. "Exonerations in the United States 1989 Through 2003." *Journal of Criminal Law & Criminology* 95(2): 523–60.

Grunewald, Ralph. 2014. "Comparing Injustices: Truth, Justice, and the System." *Albany Law Review* 77(3): 1139–1200.

———. 2021. "Forces Beyond Linear Reasoning: The Evidentiary Power of Narrative in Wrongful Conviction Cases." In *Narratives in the Criminal Process*, edited by Frode H. Pedersen, Espen Ingebrigtsen, and Werner Gephart, 189–218. Schriftenreihe des Käte-Hamburger-Kollegs "Recht als Kultur" 26. Frankfurt am Main: Vittorio Klostermann GmbH.

Gudjonsson, Gisli H. 2003. *The Psychology of Interrogations and Confessions: A Handbook*. Chichester, West Sussex, England, Hoboken, NJ: Wiley.

Häberle, Peter. 1995. *Wahrheitsprobleme im Verfassungsstaat*. Baden-Baden: Nomos.

Habermas, Jürgen. 1990. *Moral Consciousness and Communicative Action*. Studies in contemporary German social thought. Cambridge, MA: MIT Press.

Hall, Jerome. 2010. *General Principles of Criminal Law*. 2nd ed. Clark, NJ: Lawbook Exchange.

Hamilton, Ross. 2007. *Accident: A Philosophical and Literary History*. Chicago: University of Chicago Press. www.loc.gov.

Hand, David. 2015. *The Improbability Principle: Why Coincidences, Miracles and Rare Events Happen All the Time*. London, London: Corgi Books.

Haney, Craig. 2006. *Reforming Punishment: Psychological Limits to the Pains of Imprisonment*. Washington, DC: American Psychological Association.

Hanne, Michael, and Robert Weisberg. 2018a. "Editors' Introduction." In *Narrative and Metaphor in the Law*, edited by Michael Hanne and Robert Weisberg, 15–18. Cambridge, UK: Cambridge University Press.

———. 2018b. "Introduction." In *Narrative and Metaphor in the Law*, edited by Michael Hanne and Robert Weisberg, 1–12. Cambridge, UK: Cambridge University Press.

———, eds. 2018. *Narrative and Metaphor in the Law*. Cambridge, UK: Cambridge University Press.

Hannken-Illjes, Kati. 2006. "Mit Geschichten argumentieren: Argumentation und Narration im Strafverfahren." *Zeitschrift für Rechtssoziologie* 27: 211–23.

Hans, Valerie P. 2007. "Deliberation and Dissent: 12 Angry Men Versus the Empirical Reality of Juries." *Chicago-Kent Law Review* 82: 579–89.

Harmon-Jones, Eddie, ed. 2019. *Cognitive Dissonance: Reexamining a Pivotal Theory in Psychology*. 2nd ed. Washington, DC: American Psychological Association.

Heath, Stephen, ed. 1977. *Image, Music, Text*. London: Fontana.

Heffer, Chris. 2005. "The Trial as Complex Genre." In *The Language of Jury Trial*, edited by Chris Heffer, 65–91. London: Palgrave Macmillan UK.

Heller, Kevin Jon. 2006. "The Cognitive Psychology of Circumstantial Evidence." *Michigan Law Review* 105: 241–305.

Henry, Jessica. 2016. "Wrongly Convicted: Arson or Accident?" www.huffingtonpost.com.

Heyl, Dorothy. 2014. "The Limits of Deception: An End to the Use of Lies and Trickery in Custodial Interrogations to Elicit the 'Truth'?" *Albany Law Review* 77: 931–53.

Hoffman, Morris B. 2014. *The Punisher's Brain: The Evolution of Judge and Jury*. Cambridge Studies in Economics, Choice, and Society. Cambridge, UK: Cambridge University Press.

Hoffmann, Ludger. 1991. "Vom Ereignis zum Fall: Sprachliche Muster zur Darstellung und Überprüfung von Sachverhalten vor Gericht." In *Erzählte Kriminalität: Zur Typologie und Funktion von narrativen Darstellungen in Strafrechtspflege, Publizistik und Literatur zwischen 1770 und 1920: Vorträge zu einem interdisziplinären Kolloquium, Hamburg, 10.–12. April 1985*, edited by Jörg Schönert, Konstantin Imm, and Joachim Linde, 87–113. Studien und Texte zur Sozialgeschichte der Literatur Bd. 27. Tübingen: Niemeyer.

Holbrook, James. 2015. "How and Why We Tell Stories in the Law." *Legal Studies Forum* 39(1): 45–48.

Horowitz, Evan. 2011. "Narrative Accidents and Literary Miracles." *Philosophy and Literature* 35(1): 65–78. doi:10.1353/phl.2011.0005.

Hruschka, Joachim. 1965. *Die Konstitution des Rechtsfalles: Studien zum Verhältnis von Tatsachenfeststellung und Rechtsanwendung*. Schriften zur Rechtstheorie. Berlin: Duncker & Humblot.

Huber, Barbara. 2008. "Criminal Procedure in Germany." In *Criminal Procedure in Europe*, edited by Richard Vogler and Barbara Huber, 269–371. Schriftenreihe des Max-Planck-Instituts für ausländisches und internationales Strafrecht. Reihe S, Strafrechtliche Forschungsberichte 112. Berlin, Freiburg i. Br. Duncker & Humblot; Max-Planck-Institut.

Hühn, Peter. 1987. "The Detective as Reader: Narrativity and Reading Concepts in Detective Fiction." *MFS Modern Fiction Studies* 33(3): 451–66. doi:10.1353/mfs.0.1310.

———, ed. 2014. *Handbook of Narratology*. 2nd ed., fully revised and expanded. De Gruyter reference. Berlin: De Gruyter.

Innocence Project. 2018. "Michael Morton." https://innocenceproject.org.

———. 2019. "Richard Danziger Celebrates 17 Years of Freedom." https://innocenceproject.org.

The Internet Classics Archive. 2009. "Rhetoric by Aristotle." http://classics.mit.edu.

Jackson, Bernard S. 1988. *Law, Fact, and Narrative Coherence*. Legal Semiotics Monographs 1. Roby, Merseyside, UK: Deborah Charles Publications.

Jackson, J. D. 1990. "Law, Fact and Narrative Coherence: A Deep Look at Court Adjudication." *International Journal for the Semiotics of Law* 3(1): 81–95. doi:10.1007/BF01130271.

Jehle, Jörg-Martin. 2013. "Was und wie häufig sind Fehlurteile?" *Forensische Psychiatrie, Psychologie, Kriminologie* 7(4): 220–29. doi:10.1007/s11757-013-0237-0.

Johnston, Robert G., and Sara Lufrano. 2002. "The Adversary System as a Means of Seeking Truth and Justice." *John Marshall Law Review* 35: 147–61.

Jolly, Roslyn. 1993. "The Unreliable Reader: The Problem of Circumstantial Evidence in Nineteenth-Century Narrative." *Australian Journal of Law and Society* 9: 81–88.

Kaiser, Jeanne, and Scott Brown. 2015. "When the Story is Too Good to be True: A Lawyer's Role in Resisting the Lure of Narrative." *Western New England Law Review* 37: 233–63.

Kalven, Harry, Jr., and Hans Zeisel. 1966. *The American Jury*. Boston: Little, Brown and Company.

Kelsen, Hans. 1941. "The Pure Theory of Law and Analytical Jurisprudence." *Harvard Law Review* 55: 44–70.

Klein, Christian, and Matías Martínez, eds. 2008. *Wirklichkeitserzählungen: Formen und Funktionen nicht-literarischen Erzählens*. Stuttgart: J. B. Metzler.

Knauer, Nancy J. 2010. "Legal Fictions and Juristic Truth." *St. Thomas Law Review* 23: 70–120.

Kotsoglou, Kyriakos N. 2017. "Das Fehlurteil gibt es nicht. Zur Aufgabe des Tatrichters." *JuristenZeitung* 72(3): 123–31. doi:10.1628/002268816X14730875882914.

Kröber, Hans-Ludwig. 2013. "Die schrittweise interaktive Entstehung einer Fehlbeschuldigung sexuellen Missbrauchs." *Forensische Psychiatrie, Psychologie, Kriminologie* 7(4): 240–49. doi:10.1007/s11757-013-0240-5.

Landsman, Stephan. 1983. "A Brief Survey of the Development of the Adversary System." *Ohio State Law Journal* 44: 713–39.

Langbein, John H. 1977. *Comparative Criminal Procedure: Germany*. American casebook series. St. Paul: West Publishing Co.

Laporte, Gerald. 2018. "Wrongful Convictions and DNA Exonerations: Understanding the Role of Forensic Science." *National Institute of Justice Journal* (279): 1–15.

Laudan, Larry. 2006. *Truth, Error, and Criminal Law: An Essay in Legal Epistemology*. Cambridge studies in philosophy and law. Cambridge, UK: Cambridge University Press. https://doi.org/10.1017/CBO9780511617515.

Leigh, Leonard Herschel, and Lucia Zedner. 1992. *A Report on the Administration of Criminal Justice in the Pre-trial Phase in France and Germany*. Vol. 1. Royal Commission on Criminal Justice. London: HM Stationery Office.

Lemert, Edwin McCarthy. 1967. *Human Deviance, Social Problems, and Social Control*. Prentice-Hall Sociology series. Englewood Cliffs NJ: Prentice-Hall.

Lempert, Richard. 1991. "Telling Tales in Court: Trial Procedure and the Story Model." *Cardozo Law Review* 13: 559–74.

———. 2001. "Narrative Relevance, Imagined Juries, and a Supreme Court Inspired Agenda for Jury Research." *Revue Internationale de Droit Pénal* 72(1): 405–13. doi:10.3917/ridp.721.0405.

Leo, Richard A. 2009. "False Confessions: Causes, Consequences, and Implications." *Journal of the American Academy of Psychiatry and the Law Online* 37(3): 332–34.

Leo, Richard A., and Steven A. Drizin. 2010. "The Three Errors: Pathways to False Confession and Wrongful Conviction." In *Police Interrogations and False Confessions: Current Research, Practice, and Policy Recommendations*, edited by G. D. Lassiter and Christian A. Meissner, 9–30. Decade of Behavior. Washington, DC: American Psychological Association.

Lepore, Jill. 2015. "On Evidence: Proving Frye as a Matter of Law, Science, and History." *Yale Law Journal* 124: 1092–1158.

Leuschner, Fredericke, Martin Rettenberger, and Axel Dessecker. 2019. "Imprisoned but Innocent: Wrongful Convictions and Imprisonments in Germany, 1990–2016." *Crime & Delinquency* 76:1–25. doi:10.1177/0011128719833355.

Leverick, Fiona, Kathryn Campbell, and Isla Callander. 2017. "Post-Conviction Review: Questions of Innocence, Independence, and Necessity." *Stetson Law Review* 47: 45–84.

Levit, Nancy. 2009. "Legal Storytelling: The Theory and the Practice—Reflective Writing Across the Curriculum." *Journal of the Legal Writing Institute* 15: 259–83.

LinkedIn. 2022. "What Makes a Portrait Narrative?—Narrative Portraiture: Foundations of Portraiture Video Tutorial | LinkedIn Learning, Formerly Lynda.Com." www.linkedin.com.

Lisska, Anthony J. 1996. *Aquinas's Theory of Natural Law: An Analytic Reconstruction.* Oxford, UK: Clarendon Press.

Little, Joseph W. 2007. "Palsgraf Revisited (Again)." *Pierce Law Review* 6(1): 75–110.

Loftus, Elizabeth F. 1979. *Eyewitness Testimony.* Cambridge, MA, and London: Harvard University Press.

Lord, Charles G., Elizabeth Preson, and Mark R. Lepper. 1984. "Considering the Opposite: A Corrective Strategy for Social Judgment." *Journal of Personality and Social Psychology* 47(6): 1231–43.

Luhmann, Niklas. 1983. *Legitimation durch Verfahren.* Frankfurt am Main: Suhrkamp.

———. 1993. *Das Recht der Gesellschaft.* Frankfurt am Main: Suhrkamp.

Lupária, Luca, and Chiara Greco. 2020. "Unveiling Wrongful Convictions Between the U.S. and Italy." *Wrongful Conviction Law Review* 1(1): 101–23. doi:10.29173/wclawr12.

MacFarlane, Bruce A. 2006. "Convicting the Innocent: A Triple Failure of the Justice System." *Manitoba Law Journal* 13(3): 403–84.

Machura, Stefan, and Peter Robson. 2001. "Law and Film." *Journal of Law and Society* 28: 117–32.

Mack, Raneta Lawson. 1996. "It's Broke So Let's Fix It: Using a Quasi-Inquisitorial Approach to Limit the Impact of Bias in the American Criminal Justice System." *Indiana International & Comparative Law Review* 7: 63–94.

Marian, David. 2016. "The Correspondence Theory of Truth." Stanford Encyclopedia of Philosophy. https://plato.stanford.edu.

Maroney, Terry A. 2011. "The Persistent Cultural Script of Judicial Dispassion." *California Law Review* 99: 629–81.

Martelle, Scott. 2010. "Authors & Ideas: Scott Turow Revisits 'Presumed Innocent's' Rusty Sabich." *Los Angeles Times*, May 2. www.latimes.com.

Martinez, Matias, and Michael Scheffel. 2009. *Einführung in die Erzähltheorie.* 8. Aufl. C.-H.-Beck-Studium. München: Beck.

Matthews, Karen. 2021. "Author Alice Sebold Apologizes to Man Cleared in 1981 Rape." https://apnews.com.

McKillop, Bron. 1997. "Anatomy of a French Murder Case." *American Journal of Comparative Law* 45(3): 527. doi:10.2307/840949.

McKillop, Kara, and Neil Vidmar. 2015. "Decision-Making in the Dark: How Pre-Trial Errors Change the Narrative in Criminal Jury Trials." *Chicago-Kent Law Review* 90: 957–80.

Medwed, Daniel S. 2017. "Talking About a Revolution: A Quarter Century of DNA Exonerations." In *Wrongful Convictions and the DNA Revolution: Twenty-Five Years of Freeing the Innocent*, edited by Daniel S. Medwed, 2–13. Cambridge, UK: Cambridge University Press.

———, ed. 2017. *Wrongful Convictions and the DNA Revolution: Twenty-Five Years of Freeing the Innocent*. Cambridge, UK: Cambridge University Press.

Merryman, John, and Rogelio Pérez-Perdomo. 2007. *The Civil Law Tradition: An Introduction to the Legal Systems of Europe and Latin America*. 3rd ed. Palo Alto: Stanford University Press.

Merten, Martina. 2003. "Ärztliche Leichenschau: Qualität mangelhaft." *Deutsches Ärzteblatt* 100(40): 2558.

Miller, J. Hillis. 1995. "Narrative." In *Critical Terms for Literary Study*, edited by Frank Lentricchia and Thomas McLaughlin, 66–79. 2nd ed. Chicago: University of Chicago Press.

Mnookin, Jennifer L., and Nancy West. 2008. *Theaters of Proof: Visual Evidence and the Law in "Call Northside 777."* Aldershot, UK: Ashgate.

Morton, Michael. 2014. *Getting Life: An Innocent Man's 25-Year Journey from Prison to Peace*. New York: Simon & Schuster.

Mosbacher, Andreas. 2015. "Das Ideal richterlicher Wahrheitsfindung und die Betrübnisse des wirklichen Lebens." *Forensische Psychiatrie, Psychologie, Kriminologie* 9(2): 82–91. doi:10.1007/s11757-015-0309-4.

National Registry of Exonerations. "Christopher Ochoa." www.law.umich.edu.

———. "Data Spreadsheet." www.law.umich.edu.

———. "Exonerations by Year: DNA and Non-DNA." www.law.umich.edu.

———. "Homepage." National Research Council. 2009. *Strengthening Forensic Science in the United States: A Path Forward*. Washington, DC National Academies Press.

Naucke, Wolfgang. 1991. "Die Stilisierung von Sachverhaltsschilderungen durch materielles Strafrecht und Strafprozeßrecht." *Erzählte Kriminalität: Zur Typologie und Funktion von narrativen Darstellungen in Strafrechtspflege, Publizistik und Literatur zwischen 1770 und 1920: Vorträge zu einem interdisziplinären Kolloquium, Hamburg, 10.–12. April 1985*, edited by Jörg Schönert, Konstantin Imm, and Joachim Linde, 59–72. Studien und Texte zur Sozialgeschichte der Literatur Bd. 27. Tübingen: Niemeyer.

Nesson, Charles. 1985. "The Evidence or the Event? The Evidence or the Event? On Judicial Proof and the Acceptability of Verdicts." *Harvard Law Review* 98(7): 1357–92.

Neufeld, Peter. 2001. "Legal and Ethical Implications of Post-Conviction DNA Exonerations." *New England Law Review* 35(3): 639–648.

Nolan, James L. 2011. *Legal Accents, Legal Borrowing: The International Problem-Solving Court Movement*. Princeton: Princeton University Press.

Norris, Robert J. 2017. *Exonerated: A History of the Innocence Movement*. New York: New York University Press.

Nunn, Kenneth B. 1995. "The Trial as Text: Allegory, Myth and Symbol in the Adversarial Criminal Process—a Critique of the Role of the Public Defender and a Proposal for Reform." *American Criminal Law Review* 32: 743–822.

Nünning, Ansgar, and Vera Nünning, eds. 2002a. *Neue Ansätze in der Erzähltheorie.* WVT-Handbücher zum literaturwissenschaftlichen Studium Bd. 4. Trier: Wissenschaftlicher Verlag.

———. 2002b. "Von der strukturalistischen Narratologie zur ‚postklassischen' Erzähltheorie: Ein Überblick über neue Ansätze und Entwicklungstendenzen." In *Neue Ansätze in der Erzähltheorie*, edited by Ansgar Nünning and Vera Nünning, 1–33. WVT-Handbücher zum literaturwissenschaftlichen Studium Bd. 4. Trier: Wissenschaftlicher Verlag.

O'Brian, Barbara, and Keith Findley. 2014. "Psychological Perspectives: Cognition and Decision Making." In *Examining Wrongful Convictions: Stepping Back, Moving Forward*, 35–53. Durham: Carolina Academic Press.

O'Hara, Charles E. 1980. *Fundamentals of Criminal Investigation.* 5th ed. Springfield, IL: Charles C Thomas.

Olson, Greta. 2010. "De-Americanizing Law and Literature Narratives: Opening up the Story." *Law & Literature* 22: 338–64. www.jstor.org.

———. 2014. "Narration and Narrative in Legal Discourse." In *Handbook of Narratology.* 2nd ed. (fully revised and expanded). Ed. Peter Hühn. De Gruyter reference. Berlin: De Gruyter.

———. 2018. "On Narrating and Troping the Law: The Conjoined Use of Narrative and Metaphor in Legal Discourse." In *Narrative and Metaphor in the Law*, edited by Michael Hanne and Robert Weisberg, 19–36. Cambridge, UK: Cambridge University Press.

Otterman, Sharon. 2019. "He Left His Twins in a Hot Car and They Died. Accident or Crime?" *New York Times*, August 1. www.nytimes.com.

Packer, Herbert L. 1968. *The Limits of the Criminal Sanction.* Stanford: Stanford University Press.

Pennington, Nancy, and Reid Hastie. 1992. "A Cognitive Theory of Juror Decision Making: The Story Model." *Cardozo Law Review* 13: 519–57.

Pfeiffer, Gerd. 2003. *Karlsruher Kommentar zur Strafprozessordnung und zum Gerichtsverfassungsgesetz.* 5., neu bearbeitete Aufl. München: Beck.

Pizzi, William T. 1999. *Trials Without Truth: Why Our System of Criminal Trials Has Become an Expensive Failure and What We Need to Do to Rebuild It.* New York: New York University Press.

Posner, Richard A. 1997a. "Legal Narratology." *University of Chicago Law Review* 64: 737–47.

———. 1997b. "Narrative and Narratology in Classroom and Courtroom." *Philosophy and Literature*, 292–305.

Presser, Lois. 2009. "The Narratives of Offenders." *Theoretical Criminology* 13(2): 177–200. doi:10.1177/1362480609102878.

Presser, Lois, and Sveinung Sandberg. 2015. *Narrative Criminology: Understanding Stories of Crime.* Alternative Criminology series. New York: New York University Press.

Przybilla, Steve. 2016. "Jeder zweite Mord bleibt unentdeckt." *Stuttgarter Nachrichten*, January 26, 2016.

Punnett, Ian. 2018. *Toward a Theory of True Crime Narratives: A Textual Analysis*. Routledge Focus on Journalism Studies. London: Routledge.

Rabello, Alfredo Mordechai. 1974. "Non Liquet: From Modern Law to Roman Law." *Israel Law Review* 9: 63–84.

Rachlin, Benjamin. 2017. *Ghost of the Innocent Man: A True Story of Trial and Redemption*. New York: Little, Brown and Company.

Ralph, Anne E. 2018. "Narrative-Erasing Procedure." *Nevada Law Journal* 18: 573–627.

Redlich, Allison D., James R. Acker, Robert J. Norris, and Catherine L. Bonventre. 2014. *Examining Wrongful Convictions: Stepping Back, Moving Forward*. Durham: Carolina Academic Press.

Reichel, Philip L. 2013. *Comparative Criminal Justice Systems: A Topical Approach*. 6th ed. Boston: Pearson.

Renner, Kaspar. 2010. "Wie poetisch ist das Recht? Jacob Grimm zwischen Etymologie und Topik." In *Literatur und Recht im Vormärz*, edited by Claude D. Conter, 163–178. Jahrbuch (Forum Vormärz Forschung) 15. Jahrg., 2009. Bielefeld: Aisthesis.

Ricoeur, Paul. 2016. *Hermeneutics and the Human Sciences: Essays on Language, Action, and Interpretation*. New York: Cambridge University Press.

———. 1984. *Time and Narrative*. Chicago: University of Chicago Press.

Rideout, Chris. 2013. "A Twice-Told Tale: Plausibility and Narrative Coherence in Judicial Storytelling." *Legal Communication & Rhetoric: JALWD* 10: 67–88.

Roach, Kent. 2010. "Wrongful Convictions: Adversarial and Inquisitorial Themes." *North Carolina Journal of International Law and Commercial Regulation* 35: 387–446.

Rosenberg, Alexander. 2018. *How History Gets Things Wrong: The Neuroscience of Our Addiction to Stories*. Cambridge, MA: MIT Press.

Rossmo, D. Kim, and Jocelyn M. Pollock. 2019. "Confirmation Bias and Other Systemic Causes of Wrongful Convictions: A Sentinel Events Perspective." *Northeastern University Law Review* 11(2): 790–835.

Rückert, Sabine. 2007. *Unrecht im Namen des Volkes: Ein Justizirrtum und seine Folgen*. Hamburg: Hoffmann und Campe.

Schmidt-Langels, Daniela, and Otto Langels. 2011. "Unschuldig hinter Gittern: Verhängnisvolle Verhöre, falsche Geständnisse, Fehlurteile." Deutschlandfunk. With the assistance of U. Bajohr. February 4, 2011. Dossier.

Schönert, Jörg. 2015. *Kriminalität erzählen: Studien zu Kriminalität in der deutschsprachigen Literatur (1570–1920)*. Juristische Zeitgeschichte. Abt. 6, Recht in der Kunst Band 42. Berlin: De Gruyter.

Schönert, Jörg, Konstantin Imm, and Joachim Linder, eds. 1991. *Erzählte Kriminalität: Zur Typologie und Funktion von narrativen Darstellungen in Strafrechtspflege, Publizistik und Literatur zwischen 1770 und 1920: Vorträge zu einem interdisziplinären Kolloquium, Hamburg, 10.-12. April 1985*. Studien und Texte zur Sozialgeschichte der Literatur Bd. 27. Tübingen: Niemeyer.

Schünemann, Bernd. 2000. "Der Richter im Strafverfahren als manipulierter Dritter? Zur empirischen Bestätigung von Perseveranz- und Schulterschlußeffekt." *Strafverteidiger* 3: 159–65.

Schwartz, John. 2010. "Extreme Makeover: Criminal Court Edition." *New York Times*, December 5. www.nytimes.com.

Schwenn, Johann. 2010. "Fehlurteile und ihre Ursachen: Die Wiederaufnahme im Verfahren wegen sexuellen Missbrauchs." *Strafverteidiger*, 705–11.

———. 2013. "Merkmale eines Fehlurteils." *Forensische Psychiatrie, Psychologie, Kriminologie* 7(4): 258–63. doi:10.1007/s11757-013-0231-6.

Sebold, Alice. 1999. *Lucky*. First Back Bay paperback ed. Boston: Back Bay Books.

Sello, Erich. 2001. *Die Irrtümer der Strafjustiz und ihre Ursachen: Geschichte der Justizmorde von 1797–1910*. Leicht bearb. Nachdr. der Ausg. Berlin 1911. Schifferstadt: Hoffmann.

Sewell, William Hamilton. 2005. *Logics of History: Social Theory and Social Transformation*. Chicago Studies in Practices of Meaning. Chicago: University of Chicago Press.

Sherrod, Drury. 2019. "When It Comes to Jury Trials, Should You Tell a Story or Stick to the Facts?" www.abajournal.com.

Sherwin, Richard K. 1994. "Law Frames: Historical Truth and Narrative Necessity in a Criminal Case." *Stanford Law Review* 47: 39–83.

Simon-Kerr, Julia Ann. 2020. "Unmasking Demeanor." *George Washington Law Review Arguendo* 88: 158–74.

Simon-Shoshan, Moshe. 2013. *Stories of the Law: Narrative Discourse and the Construction of Authority in the Mishnah*. New York: Oxford University Press.

Slobogin, Christopher. 2015. "Plea Bargaining and the Substantive and Procedural Goals of Criminal Justice: From Retribution and Adversarialism to Preventive Justice and Hybrid-Inquisitorialism." *William & Mary Law Review* 15(4): 1–35.

Smith, Abbe. 2010. "In Praise of the Guilty Project: A Criminal Defense Lawyer's Grown Anxiety About Innocence Projects." *University of Pennsylvania Journal of Law and Social Change* 13: 316–329.

Smith, Andrew M., and Brian L. Cutler. 2013. "Introduction: Identification Procedures and Conviction of the Innocent." In *Reform of Eyewitness Identification Procedures*, edited by Brian L. Cutler, 3–21. Washington, DC: American Psychological Association.

Snyder, Leslie C., Peter J. McQuillan, William L. Murphy, and Richard Joselson. 2007. "Report on the Conviction of Jeffrey Deskovic: Prepared at the Request of Janet DiFiore, Westchester County District Attorney." www.westchesterda.net.

Sotomayor, Sonia. 2013. *My Beloved World*. New York: Knopf.

Spiegel, Der. 2012. "Rekonstruktion eines Justizskandals: Vier Mörder und ein Todesfall?" *Der Spiegel*, September 11. www.spiegel.de.

Stamm, Alex A. 2019. "The Conformity Rule and Relationship Evidence in Texas Domestic Assault Trials." *Texas Law Review Online* 97: 85–114.

Stamp, Frauke. 1998. *Die Wahrheit im Strafverfahren: Eine Untersuchung zur prozessualen Wahrheit unter besonderer Berücksichtigung der Perspektive des erkennenden Gerichts in der Hauptverhandlung*. Kieler rechtswissenschaftliche Abhandlungen. Neue Folge Bd. 16. Baden-Baden: Nomos.

Stern, Simon. 2018. "Narrative in the Legal Text: Judicial Opinions and Their Narratives." In *Narrative and Metaphor in the Law*, edited by Michael Hanne and Robert Weisberg, 121–39. Cambridge, UK: Cambridge University Press.

Sternberg, Meir. 2008. "If-Plots: Narrativity and the Law-Code." In *Theorizing Narrativity*, edited by John Pier and José Angel Garcia Landa, 29–107. Narratologia 12. Berlin and New York: Walter De Gruyter.

Stone Peters, Julie. 2005. "Law, Literature, and the Vanishing Real: On the Future of an Interdisciplinary Illusion." *PMLA* [Publications of the Modern Language Association of America] 102(2): 442–53.

Strassfeld, Robert N. 1992. "If . . . : Counterfactuals in the Law." *George Washington Law Review* 60(2): 339–416.

Syed, Matthew. 2015. "Why Don't We Learn from Our Mistakes—Even When It Matters Most?" *New Statesman*, November 13. www.newstatesman.com.

Thompson-Cannino, Jennifer, Ronald. Cotton, and Erin Torneo. 2009. *Picking Cotton: Our Memoir of Injustice and Redemption*. New York: St. Martin's Press.

Trüg, Gerson, and Hans-Jürgen Kerner. 2007. "Formalisierung der Wahrheitsfindung im (reformiert-) inquisitorischen Strafverfahren? Betrachtungen unter rechtsvergleichender Perspektive." In *Recht gestalten—dem Recht dienen: Festschrift für Reinhard Böttcher zum 70. Geburtstag am 29. Juli 2007*, edited by Dieter Dölling, Roland Helgerth, Peter König, and Heinz Schöch, 191–212. Berlin and Boston: De Gruyter.

Vaihinger, Hans. 1935. *The Philosophy of "As If": A System of the Theoretical, Practical and Religious Fictions of Mankind*. 2nd ed. Trans. C. K. Ogden. London: Routledge and Kegan Paul.

Van Hoecke, Mark. 2015. "Methodology of Comparative Legal Research." *Law and Method*. doi:10.5553/REM/.000010.

Van Kessel, Gordon. 1992. "Adversary Excesses in the American Criminal Trial." *Notre Dame Law Review* 67: 403–551.

Velten, Petra. 2015. "Fehlentscheidungen im Strafverfahren." *Golddammer's Archiv für Strafrecht*, 387–409.

Viehweg, Theodor. 1974. *Topik und Jurisprudenz: Ein Beitrag zur rechtswissenschaftlichen Grundlagenforschung*. 5., durchges. u. erw. Aufl. Beck'sche schwarze Reihe Bd. 110. München: Beck.

Vismann, Cornelia. 2000. *Akten: Medientechnik und Recht*. Fischer-Taschenbuch Forum Wissenschaft 14927. Frankfurt am Main: Fischer.

Vogler, Richard. 2008a. "Criminal Procedure in France." In *Criminal Procedure in Europe*, edited by Richard Vogler and Barbara Huber, 171–268. Schriftenreihe des Max-Planck-Instituts für ausländisches und internationales Strafrecht. Reihe S: Strafrechtliche Forschungsberichte 112. Berlin, Freiburg i. Br. Duncker & Humblot; Max-Planck-Institut.

———. 2008b. "Introduction." In *Criminal Procedure in Europe*, edited by Richard Vogler and Barbara Huber, 4–38. Schriftenreihe des Max-Planck-Instituts für ausländisches und internationales Strafrecht. Reihe S: Strafrechtliche Forschungsberichte 112. Berlin, Freiburg i. Br. Duncker & Humblot; Max-Planck-Institut.

Vogler, Richard, and Barbara Huber, eds. 2008. *Criminal Procedure in Europe*. Schrift-enreihe des Max-Planck-Instituts für ausländisches und internationales Strafrecht. Reihe S: Strafrechtliche Forschungsberichte 112. Berlin, Freiburg i. Br. Duncker & Humblot; Max-Planck-Institut.

Von Arnold, Andreas. 2008. "Was war, was ist—und was sein soll: Erzählen im juristischen Diskurs." In *Wirklichkeitserzählungen: Formen und Funktionen nicht-literarischen Erzählens*, edited by Christian Klein and Matías Martínez, 14–50. Stuttgart: J. B. Metzler.

———. 2017. "Norms and Narrative." *German Law Journal* 18(2): 309–30. doi:10.1017/S2071832200021970.

Von Arnauld, Andreas, and Stefan Martini. 2015. "Unreliable Narration in Law Courts." In *Unreliable Narration and Trustworthiness: Intermedial and Interdisciplinary Perspectives*, edited by Vera Nünning, 347–70. Narratologia 44. Berlin, Boston: De Gruyter.

Vonnegut, Kurt. 2005. "At the Blackboard: Kurt Vonnegut Diagrams the Shapes of Stories." www.laphamsquarterly.org/arts-letters/blackboard.

Warden, Rob. 2022a. "First Wrongful Conviction: Jesse Boorn and Stephen Boorn." www.law.northwestern.edu.

———. 2022b. "Juan Rivera: Juan Rivera Freed After More Than 19 Years Behind Bars for a Crime It Had Long Been Obvious He Could Not Have Committed." Bluhm Legal Clinic, Pritzker School of Law, Northwestern University. www.law.northwestern.edu.

Watson, Greig. 2017. "The Mother, the Medium and the Murder That Changed the Law." *BBC News*, January 4. www.bbc.com.

Weber, Max. 1949 [1904]. "Objectivity in Social Science and Social Policy." In *On the Methodology of the Social Sciences*, edited by Max Weber, 49–112. Illinois: The Free Press of Glencoe.

Weigend, Thomas. 2003. "Is the Criminal Process About Truth? A German Perspec-tive." *Harvard Journal of Law & Public Policy* 26: 157–74.

———. 2011. "Should We Search for the Truth, and Who Should Do It?" *North Carolina Journal of International Law and Commercial Regulation*.

Weigend, Thomas, and Jenia Iontcheva Turner. 2014. "The Constitutionality of Negoti-ated Criminal Judgments in Germany." *German Law Journal* 15(1): 81–105.

Weinberg, Steve. 2012. "The Literature of Wrongful Conviction." *Missouri Review* 35(2): 177–88. doi:10.1353/mis.2012.0034.

Weinreb, Lloyd L. 1999. "The Adversary Process Is Not an End in Itself." *Journal of the Institute for the Study of Legal Ethics* 2: 59–64.

Weisberg, Robert. 1996. "Proclaiming Trials as Narratives: Premises and Pretenses." In *Law's Stories: Narrative and Rhetoric in the Law*, edited by Peter Brooks and Paul D. Gewirtz, 61–83. New Haven: Yale University Press.

Wells, Michael. 1994. "French and American Judicial Opinions." *Yale Journal of Inter-national Law* 19: 81–133.

Wetlaufer, Gerald B. 1990. "Rhetoric and Its Denial in Legal Discourse." *Virginia Law Review* 76(8): 1545–97. www.jstor.org.

White, Hayden V. 1973. *Metahistory: The Historical Imagination in Nineteenth-Century Europe*. Baltimore: Johns Hopkins University Press.

———. 1978. *Tropics of Discourse: Essays in Cultural Criticism*. Baltimore and London: John Hopkins University Press.

———. 1980. "The Value of Narrativity in the Representation of Reality." *Critical Inquiry* 7(1): 5–27.

———. 1999. "Historical Emplotment and the Problem of Truth in Historical Representation." In *Figural Realism: Studies in the Mimesis Effect* (Johns Hopkins paperback ed.), edited by Hayden White, 27–42. Baltimore: Johns Hopkins University Press.

White, James Boyd. 1985a. *Heracles' Bow: Essays on the Rhetoric and Poetics of Law*. Rhetoric of the Human Sciences. Madison: University of Wisconsin Press.

———. 1985b. *The Legal Imagination*. Abridged ed. Chicago: University of Chicago Press.

———. 1995. "What's an Opinion for?" *University of Chicago Law Review* 62: 1363–69.

Whitman, James Q. 2003. *Harsh Justice: America's Solitary Place in the Liberal West*. New York and Oxford: Oxford University Press.

Williams, Melanie. 2009. *Empty Justice: One Hundred Years of Law Literature and Philosophy*. Abingdon and New York: Cavendish Pub. Ltd.

Wisconsin Innocence Project. 2022. "WIP Legal Assistance." https://law.wisc.edu.

Zak, Paul J. 2015. "Why Inspiring Stories Make Us React: The Neuroscience of Narrative." *Cerebrum*. www.ncbi.nlm.nih.gov.

Zalman, Marvin. 2008. "The Adversary System and Wrongful Conviction." In *Wrongful Conviction: International Perspectives on Miscarriages of Justice*, edited by C. R. Huff and Martin Killias, 71–91. Philadelphia: Temple University Press.

———. 2011. "An Integrated Justice Model of Wrongful Convictions." *Albany Law Review* 74(3): 101–60.

———. 2013. "Edwin Borchard and the Limits of Innocence Reform." In *Wrongful Convictions and Miscarriages of Justice: Causes and Remedies in North American and European Criminal Justice Systems*, edited by C. R. Huff and Martin Killias, 329–56. New York: Routledge.

Zalman, Marvin, and Ralph Grunewald. 2015–2016. "Reinventing the Trial: The Innocence Revolution and Proposals to Modify the American Criminal Trial." *Texas A&M Law Review* 3: 189–259. https://ssrn.com.

Zippelius, Reinhold. 2008. *Introduction to German Legal Methods*. Comparative Legal Thinking Series. Durham: Carolina Academic Press.

INDEX

Abbott, H. Porter, 20–21, 64–65, 71, 199, 203n33, 205n62
Abelson, Robert, 63
accusation, false, 23, 39, 46, 164–65, 241n28
accusatory sentence (*Anklagesatz*), 211n36
actual innocence, 5, 11, 26, 51, 67, 123, 162, 191, 227n197, 240n14
Actual Innocence (Scheck, Neufeld, and Dwyer), 11, 31, 42, 208n147, 209n153, 215n140, 227n202
actualization, by judge, 233n52
actus reus, 57, 65, 90
admissibility, of evidence (*Beweisverwertung*), 8, 152–53; prejudice influencing, 122–23, 229n235
adversarialism, 9, 132, 221n23, 230n249
adversarialness, justice achieved through, 66–67
adversarial systems, 94, 97, 228n204, 231n252; German civil procedure compared with, 232n16; innocence movement impacting, 89; inquisitorial systems contrasted with, 91–93, 129–30, 157, 194–95, 221n25, 229n237, 235n93; jury relied on by, 127; truth in, 9, 51, 222n43, 230n240. *See also* American system
agency, narrative, 43, 115, 151, 153
agents, narrating, 48–50, 95–100, 235n82
Aktenordnungen. See filing regulations
A la recherché du temps perdu (Proust), 19
American Bar Association, on opening statements, 53
American Prosecutors Research Institute, 72, 95

American system, 87, 92–94, 129–30; appeals disrupting, 5; Continental system contrasted with, 53; exceptionalism in, 194–98; factual truth in, 193; Germany contrasted with, 134, 161–62, 207n103, 231n4; inquisitorial systems contrasted with, 238n146
Amtsermittlungsgrundsatz. See official investigation
Amtsgericht. See municipal court
Anklagesatz. See accusatory sentence
Anklageschrift. See indictment
appeals, 27, 40, 56; American system disrupted by, 5; in German system, 154–56; on procedural errors, 187; procedures as base of, 187
Appellate Court, Illinois, 1–2
appellate courts, 1–2; evidence allowed by, 119–20; exoneration through, 5; facts in, 154; Morton, M., in, 120–23; narratives in, 119–20; storytelling in, 86
archetypes: of guilt, 95–96; masterplot relying on, 165; Morton, C., characterized by, 115
attorneys, 89; evidence lost by, 37; in Germany, 149–50, 231n3; narratives retold by, 157; public defense, 37; story relied on by, 67
authority, discourse free of (*herrschaftsfreier Diskurs*), 131
authorship, 87, 219n202; of confession, 79–80, 199–200; law simplifying, 86; witnesses and, 84
Avery, Steven, 44

ABOUT THE AUTHOR

RALPH GRUNEWALD is Associate Professor in the Department of English with a joint appointment in the Center for Law, Society, and Justice at the University of Wisconsin–Madison. He is Mellon-Morgridge Professor of the Humanities. He holds a law degree and PhD in Criminal Law and Criminology from the University of Mainz, Germany, and a Master of Laws Degree from the University of Wisconsin–Madison.